LEITH'S LATIN AMERICAN COOKERY

LEITH'S LATIN AMERICAN COOKERY

Valeria V. Sisti

Foreword by **Caroline Waldegrave**

Photographs by **Graham Kirk**

LATIN AMERICA

MEXICO

Gulf of Mexico

Mexico
City

Acapulco

Belize
BELIZE

Caribbean Sea

GUAT.
HOND.

Guatemala SAL. NICA.

COSTA
RICA

PANAMA

Panama
Canal

Caracas

VENEZUELA

Georgetown
Paramaribo
Cayenne

SURINAME

Bogota

COLOMBIA

Quito

ECUADOR

*Pacific
Ocean*

Belém

Manaus

Recife

BRAZIL

Salvador

Lima

Las Paz

BOLIVIA

Sucre

Rio de Janeiro

San Paulo

PARAGUAY

Anuncion

*South
Atlantic
Ocean*

Valparaiso

Santiago

Rosario

CHILE

ARGENTINA

Buenos Aires

Montevideo

URUGUAY

Mar del Plata

North

West

East

South

Scotia Sea

First published in Great Britain 1996
Bloomsbury Publishing Plc, 2 Soho Square, London W1V 6HB

Text copyright © 1996 Valeria V. Sisti
Design copyright © Bloomsbury Publishing Plc

The moral right of the author has been asserted

A CIP catalogue record for this book is available from the British
Library

ISBN 0 7475 2519 6
10 9 8 7 6 5 4 3 2 1

Printed in Italy

Book design by: David Palmer Design Practice, London
Photographer: Graham Kirk
Assisted by: David Barrett
Stylist: Helen Payne
Home economists: Valeria V. Sisti and Cherie Marshall
Line drawings by: Kate Simunek

PICTURE SOURCES – Robert Harding: pages 23, 27, 88, 139, 145 and 222; Impact
Photos: pages 8, 13, 73, 83 and 109; Lupe Cunha: pages 54, 101, 120, 127, 141
and 144; Panos Pictures: pages 36, 60, 80, 99, 103, 110, 130, 134, 147, 160, 164,
166, 172, 186, 202, 205, 213, 222, 230, 241, 246, 271 and 272; Pictor
International: pages 1, 2, 4, 190 and 269; Telegraph Colour Library: pages 41, 148
and 254.

CONTENTS

ACKNOWLEDGEMENTS

To write a cookery book has been a long-time dream of mine, but I was very naive to think that it would be a solitary task. A great many people helped me along the way, some in practical terms and others in supporting my ideas and plans. It is to thank them that I now write.

Caroline Waldegrave was the first to believe in the idea and her support, encouragement and help were invaluable. The staff of Leith's School were wonderfully keen to try all the recipes and their expert comments were a great help in adapting the recipes for a wider public. Special thanks go to Cherie Marshall, for all her hard work and good humour when helping with the photography, and to Puff Fairclough for all her kind and expert advice.

Also thanks to Dodie Miller from the Cool Chile Company for all her help with the dried chillies.

For this beautiful book I thank most heartily the photographer Graham Kirk who was assisted by David Barrett, the stylist Helen Payne and David Palmer the designer. At Bloomsbury the enthusiasm of David Reynolds, Monica Macdonald and everyone involved in the book made all my efforts worthwhile.

I would also like to thank Peter and Karin Thompson, Armand Sisti and Lilian Armfield for their support during the time I was working on the book. Finally, a special thanks to my mother for believing without seeing, and to Richard who put up with my changes of mood for months without ever failing to encourage me. To all of you my deepest gratitude and kindest thoughts.

FOREWORD

CAROLINE WALDEGRAVE

Working with Valeria has always been enjoyable and fascinating, and she has taught us all so much about Latin American food. Before the advent of Valeria we thought that there were two types of chilli: green and red. How wrong we were!

All the recipes have now been tried and tested at the school, and the staff have enjoyed using them so much that many of the recipes have been incorporated into the full-time and evening class curriculum, and we will be running an annual course in Latin American Cookery. This book is, in fact, quite a departure for us, because we have always had strict rules on the Leith's way of cooking. In this book we have returned to the rustic roots of Latin American methods. The recipes here are all based on classic recipes, but Valeria has adapted them so that they can be cooked and enjoyed by us in the West.

I do hope that you enjoy cooking from this book.

Caroline Waldegrave
Principal, Leith's School of Food and Wine

INTRODUCTION

All the nicest memories I have of my childhood are related to food. When I was about five years old, going to the baker to get the morning bread for my brothers and sisters for breakfast before they went to school was a real pleasure. Even though I did not go to school until I was seven, the errand made me take part in the morning eating ritual. Small, hot French bread was generously buttered and dipped into hot milky coffee or hot chocolate, making the bread soft and delicious.

From bread-buyer I was promoted to popcorn-maker, which was quite a feat considering my age and also that making popcorn for a family of 12 was no easy thing. I developed little sayings and dances to do around the popping pot, and firmly believed these voodoos were responsible for the perfect result every time, so I never dared not to do them. Even today, when it is difficult to find a corn that does not pop, I find myself going back to my routine to give it a better flavour, the sweet flavour of childhood.

I later progressed to making the much-loved crème caramel, always a favourite in any Latin American household, and was quick to learn that cooking has little to do with luck. All cooks know that crème caramel tastes better the next day, but try telling this to a house full of kids and their friends. I don't think a single one ever made it to the next day.

Almost without a sweet tooth myself, I always enjoyed making sweets, perhaps because of the popularity it won me with the family. I remember spending afternoons making coconut fondant sweets, milk pudding, chocolate fudge and my particular favourite, ambrosia, which in Brazil is made with milk, sugar and eggs and takes forever to do. I would persevere through intense heat, stirring the pan so the milk and sugar would not catch on the bottom. To make things even more difficult, I could not eat the finished dish until it was really cold because only then, when the sugar has lost its intensity, does it taste like the 'food of the gods'. My family was so large that we had an industrial four-door fridge in which it was easy to hide things, especially ambrosia, that I wanted to save for myself.

Another of my favourite occupations was to follow my mother to the market. She would buy fruit and vegetables for the whole week and we would go around the stalls looking, tasting, smelling and touching the foods on display. Fresh produce was and still is seasonal in most Latin countries and we would wait anxiously for the right time of the year for our favourite produce. The mango, sweetcorn and guava seasons were much longed for, although I cannot say as much for the avocado. It was so abundant that we were sick of it by the end of the first week. Neighbours with avocado trees in their gardens would become very generous and send us baskets of them. Unfortunately, that did not happen with mangoes. There could never be enough of them, and we would start eating them while they were still green, too anxious to wait for them to ripen. Later in the season one of my greatest pleasures was to sit with friends under a mango or guava tree and eat as many of the ripe fruits as possible.

During the season for wild fruits, the whole family, including grandmother, relatives and friends, would go out for the day armed with picnic foods, drinks, hammocks and ropes for making swings for the children. Once again, no fruit came back with us, as we ate everything we found on the spot. These idyllic days were before television arrived in our town: sadly, things are very different now. In my youth whole days were dedicated to cooking one single type of food, and usually one extra cook

would be hired for the occasion. Making compotes using fruits such as figs, green papaya and jackfruit, to name but a few, involves an extraordinary amount of work, so enough was made to last quite a while. Similarly, baking was usually done in large batches on Saturdays and kept in tins for use during the following week. My mother used to keep these tins of delicious biscuits, breads and brioches in her room, the only way she could make sure they lasted for more than one day.

Throughout my childhood and teenage years we always had a house cook, so it was difficult for me to use the kitchen while she was around. I used to wait until the middle of the afternoon, when everyone was resting, to do my cooking, and this is still my favourite time for it - when lunch has been taken care of and it is still too early to think about dinner.

In my late teens, parties were informal affairs. One of us would get a cook to make *galinhadas*, a dish of chicken, rice and turmeric served with chilli sauce and beans, and would invite all our friends to come around and eat it. Some cooks were famous locally for their *galinhadas* and could never keep up with the demand.

Years later, living in the United States, a whole new world of cooking possibilities opened up to me. For the first time I had Chinese and Mexican food, tasted frozen vegetables (I had been warned about them before I left home) and ate food out of cans. I can still remember my reaction when I was first offered an egg sandwich. I thought nothing could be less enticing and more bizarre than mashed-up boiled eggs between slices of soft white bread; fortunately, later in life I learned to be more tolerant about other people's taste in food.

While away from home at university, I virtually gave up cooking and didn't start again until I married a European and discovered that cooking could be a profession, not just a pastime. My professional training at Leith's School opened up a new world of possibilities for me and for many years I worked in the industry doing different jobs and learning about European cuisines. I have always been very interested in the history of food and finding out such things as where the different ingredients and techniques came from, who discovered them and how eating habits were formed. It is fascinating to learn how political and social history is determined by food.

Being a native of Brazil, it is only natural that I am also very interested in food from the Americas: it is a rich, complex and fascinating subject and it has taken over two years to compile this book about it. Within these pages you will find recipes from the classic Latin American repertoire, as well as new recipes inspired by the ingredients or techniques of particular countries. To make the traditional recipes suitable for modern needs, the heavier ones have been revised to reflect healthier eating habits and the time-consuming ones have been simplified.

The more we know about food, the more it helps us understand different people and their cultures.

The different cuisines of Latin America, so strongly rooted in the past, cannot be described using a single adjective. They are distinct, yet similar, just like the members of any family; studying the individuals throws light on the whole and vice versa.

Valeria Sisti September 1995

A BRIEF HISTORY OF LATIN AMERICA AND ITS FOOD

In the 15th century the wealthy classes of Europe depended on the East to supply luxury items such as spices, silks and porcelain. The trade was done through a chain of merchantmen, which started in Alexandria and Damascus and finished in Venice and Florence. By the time the goods reached their final destinations, their prices were so inflated by the profits of all the middlemen that finding new and less expensive ways of getting these goods was a constant preoccupation. As the main trade route to the East was dominated by the Ottoman Turks, a search also began for an alternative route.

The incentive was strong. During the Middle Ages, food – especially meat and game – was hardly palatable without strong seasoning. Meat was butchered in early November, salted to preserve it and consumed throughout the winter. Salting was the only way of preserving food and tolerance for saltiness was amazingly high, as food historians found when they recreated medieval dishes from recipes of that time; the results were impossible to eat. Spices were used in large quantities, to mask the salt as well as the rotting of the meat. Sugar did not then exist, so all sweet foodstuffs were made with honey and, again, generously spiced. Such practices, however, were confined to wealthy households as spices were very expensive.

Spain and Portugal, the most powerful maritime nations at the end of the 15th century, were also looking for a new route to the Orient. The discovery of such a route would lead to a monopoly in the very lucrative spice trade, and could also be used as a vehicle for spreading the Christian faith. Both nations were deeply

Catholic, a fact that would play a significant role in the fate of the countries they `discovered'.

Believing that the Earth was round, scholars thought that westward travel would eventually lead to the east. With that in mind, Christopher Columbus (1451–1506) set sail in August 1492 with the blessing and sponsorship of Queen Isabella of Spain. On 12 October he arrived in the Bahamas. Mistakenly believing that he had reached the Indies, he called the natives Indians. From this time forward Spain began its programme of colonizing in earnest: expeditions went north towards Mexico and south towards the Andes. The men who went into these places in search of wealth and fame were called *conquistadores* (conquerors). The Conquest of the Aztecs in Mexico and the Incas in Peru is deeply controversial, mainly because of the atrocities perpetuated by the *conquistadores* in the name of their king and the Catholic Church.

The continents of North and South America became known to Europeans as the `New World', a term first used by Amerigo Vespucci (1451–1512), an Italian explorer. Ironically, it is he, rather than Columbus, who gave his name to the new continent.

The Mayas: *Central America and the Caribbean*
The areas now known as Honduras and Guatemala were once home to the Mayas, creators of the most advanced and sophisticated culture in pre-Conquest America. The Mayas flourished between the 4th and 10th centuries AD, and declined, it is believed, because of civil war, epidemics and soil exhaustion. Temples and cities were abandoned to forest vegetation and people moved towards the Yucatan peninsula,

where descendants of the Mayas still live.

At its zenith the Mayan culture had amazingly rich and ornate religious architecture, and regular sacrifices were made to the gods in the hope of achieving a good harvest. When the Spaniards arrived, they found only vestiges of this ancient culture, but it endures none the less. Today, the people of the Yucatan peninsula still speak the Mayan language, have a cuisine distinct from the rest of Mexico and physically look very much like their ancestors.

The Caribbean and Central America were abundant in fruit, wild birds, seafood and vegetables, including sweet potatoes and cassava, which were unknown to the Spaniards. Maize was the main grain and more than 200 types were already developed by the time of the Conquest. It was eaten in a variety of forms, and its flour was made into a bread similar to the *tortilla* found in Mexico. Meat was very scarce in that tropical climate, but insects such as large spiders, worms and giant ants were abundant and used in the local cooking. In fact, some types of worm are still regarded as a delicacy in Mexico. Chillies and annatto seed were, and still are, the most common ingredients used for flavouring.

The Aztecs: *Mexico*

The Aztec empire was relatively new when the Spanish explorer Hernando Cortes (1485–1547) arrived in Mexico in 1519. Its creation was made possible by an alliance between three rival tribes about 70 years before the arrival of the Spaniards. The first Aztec emperor, Montezuma I, started his reign in 1440 and expanded his territory from the central plateau, where Mexico City is today, over 1,000 kilometres south to the border of modern Guatemala. When Montezuma II succeeded as the head of the empire in 1502, he started a campaign of conquering and absorbing new lands towards the south and the Pacific. Tenochtitlán, the Aztec capital, was the central point of the empire, receiving all the taxes collected from the conquered lands, and was also home to the major temples where human sacrifices were carried out.

The Aztec civilization was not as advanced and refined as that of the Mayas, but it was very organized none the less. Agriculture was all important and the land was owned by the community as a whole. On marriage, a young man would be granted a plot of land to provide for his family, and it would be given back to the community when he died.

Aztec society had a strict hierarchy, not unlike that found in European cultures. The emperor was at the top, followed by noble families, then priests, warriors and peasants. Prisoners of war were treated as serfs or used for human sacrifice, which was considered an honour. It was very important to have enough warriors to be sacrificed, so additional grants of land were given to those who could secure prisoners during a war; sometimes wars were fought with the sole purpose of acquiring prisoners for sacrifice.

Religion ruled the life of the Aztecs and was the glue that held the empire together. Apart from the ruling élite, people had no personal wealth and no freedom of thought since intellectual and religious life were one and the same thing, closely guided by the priests

towards war, human sacrifice and successful harvests. Ceremonial cannibalism was also practised by the Aztecs and it became the main excuse used by the Spaniards for the massacre of the Aztecs and the destruction of their cities.

The variety of ingredients and cooking techniques found in Mexico was a source of amazement to the Spaniards. Tomatoes, peppers, sweet potatoes, chillies, chocolate and turkey were among the many novelties the *conquistadores* introduced to Europe. The more bizarre parts of the Aztec diet, such as frogs, worms, spiders, lizards, small dogs and fungus-infested corn, were not exported.

The Incas: *Peru*

The Incas were the last in a series of great civilizations that existed in Peru. They arrived in the highlands of southern Peru in the 12th century AD and the city of Cuzco became their administrative and religious centre. The empire expanded north to Ecuador and south to Bolivia, spreading into parts of Chile and Argentina. It was ruled by the king of the Inca, who had unlimited powers and was considered the embodiment of God on earth.

Although writing and the wheel were unknown in the Inca empire, it was a highly efficient organization which managed to keep areas of difficult access together under a single ruler. Like the Aztecs, Incas had no private ownership of land, but they worked along more socialist principles. Crops were divided into three, one-third being kept by the farmers, one-third going to sustain the priests and the bureaucracy, and the final third going to the government, who distributed it to widows, the

aged, the infirm and non-productive people. The government also had a policy of storing grain in warehouses for distribution in the event of bad harvests.

The Incas are famous for their irrigation systems, which harnessed water from the Andes and made it possible for the lower valleys near the coast to be cultivated. They also excelled at road building, having the whole empire linked by a complex system of roads and bridges – no mean feat considering the difficulties posed by the Andean mountains. Another of their skills was masonry, but many of their stone buildings were dismantled by the Spaniards and used in the construction of colonial buildings.

The Incas and the cultures that preceded them, such as the Paracas, Chimu and Mochica, had highly skilled potters and weavers, and their surviving work testifies to their skill. Their highly crafted gold artefacts, however, were all melted down and sent to Spain.

With the conquest of Peru by the Spanish explorer Francisco Pizarro (1478–1541) and the breaking up of the Inca empire, the civilization fell apart. The complex irrigation systems were abandoned and the Incas who were not exterminated by European diseases or war retreated to the mountains.

The gold and emeralds which had attracted the Spanish to Peru were not the country's only wealth. It also had an abundance of fish and shellfish from the ocean and lakes, plus meat in the form of guinea-pigs and dogs, among other foodstuffs. While important, maize would grow only in the lowlands, so it had fewer uses than in Mexico. It was mainly fresh ground and made into a type of porridge. In the Peruvian

highlands, where corn did not grow, potatoes and quinoa were the main foods. Over a hundred different varieties of potatoes were grown, and the Incas even discovered a process of freeze-drying them. Potatoes would be left out at night in the freezing mountain air and in the morning they would be trodden on to extract all their moisture. The process was repeated for a few days until the potatoes were rock hard and free of liquid. The *chuño* or *papa gaca*, as they were known, were then stored and used in soups and casserole dishes, or grated to make flour. The very same technique is still used by the highland people of the Andes.

The Birth of Latin America

The term `Latin America' refers to the eighteen Spanish-speaking republics of the western hemisphere, together with Portuguese-speaking Brazil and French-speaking Haiti. The term `Meso-America' is sometimes used to denote the area covered by Central America and Mexico.

In the 400 years following the Conquest, the influence of the Portuguese in Brazil and the Spanish in the rest of Latin America led to a new race and a different cuisine being born. The introduction of cattle, pigs, wheat, sugar, citrus fruits, bananas, coconut and rice transformed the cuisines of Mexico and South America, but those new ingredients did not supersede existing ones. Old and new techniques also co-existed; for example, many foods continued to be boiled, or steamed in banana leaves or corn husks. With the arrival of the pig, however, fat became widely available and frying became popular. Indeed, a large percentage of modern Latin American food is fried.

Wheat did not make a huge impact in Mexico, where corn tortillas are still as popular as they were 500 years ago, but it did gain a foothold in the northern region. Wheat became widely used outside Mexico for bread-making, and Spanish- and Portuguese-style bread is very popular for breakfast.

Rice was immediately absorbed into the local cuisines and, together with potatoes and corn, quickly became a staple food. With cattle came dairy produce, then unknown to the natives, while beef became the major food crop for the southern regions of South America.

The Spanish, having lived under Arab occupation for over 700 years, already had a rich and varied cuisine, and were the major influence on the Spanish-speaking countries throughout the colonial years. In fact, traces of Arab cuisine can still be found in many recipes. The Portuguese influence on Brazilian cookery can be seen in their love of sweets, cakes and candies, a field in which Brazilian cooks excel. Brazil and the Caribbean share a unique Creole cuisine thanks to the African slaves who were brought into the New World to work on the sugar plantations. With them came a variety of ingredients and flavourings which distinguished their cooking from that found in the rest of Latin America.

The 19th century brought many other influences, not least the arrival of Italian, German, Japanese, Chinese, Arab and other immigrant groups. New foods were incorporated into the already rich local repertoire, creating a cuisine which is greater than the sum of its diverse parts.

CONVERSION TABLES

The tables below are approximate, and do not conform in all respects to the conventional conversions, but we have found them convenient for cooking.

Weight

Imperial	Metric	Imperial	Metric
$^1/_4$oz	7–8g	$^1/_2$oz	15g
$^3/_4$oz	20g	1oz	30g
2oz	55g	3oz	85g
4oz ($^1/_4$lb)	110g	5oz	140g
6oz	170g	7oz	200g
8oz ($^1/_2$lb)	225g	9oz	255g
10oz	285g	11oz	310g
12oz ($^3/_4$lb)	340g	13oz	370g
14oz	400g	15oz	425g
16oz (1lb)	450g	1lb	560g
1lb	675g	2lb	900g
3lb	1.35kg	4lb	1.8kg
5lb	2.3kg	6lb	2.7kg
7lb	3.2kg	8lb	3.6kg
9lb	4.0kg	10lb	4.5kg

Liquid measures

Imperial	ml	fl oz
1$^3/_4$ pints	1,000 (1 litre)	35
1 pint	570	20
$^1/_2$ pint	290	10
$^1/_3$ pint	190	6.6
$^1/_4$ pint (1 gill)	150	5
4 scant tablespoons	56	2
2 scant tablespoons	28	1
1 teaspoon	5	

Lengths

Imperial	Metric
$^1/_2$ in	1cm
1in	2.5cm

Lengths

Imperial	Metric
2in	5cm
6in	15cm
12in	30cm

Oven temperatures

°C	°F	Gas mark
70	150	$^1/_4$
80	175	$^1/_4$
100	200	$^1/_2$
110	225	$^1/_2$
130	250	1
140	275	1
150	300	2
170	325	3
180	350	4
190	375	5
200	400	6
220	425	7
230	450	8
240	475	8
250	500	9
270	525	9
290	550	9

Wine quantities

Imperial	ml	fl oz
Average wine bottle	750	25
1 glass wine	100	3
1 glass port or sherry	70	2
1 glass liqueur	45	1

Approximate American/European conversions

Commodity	USA	Metric	Imperial
Flour	1 cup	140g	5oz
Caster and granulated sugar	1 cup	225g	8oz
Caster and granulated sugar	2 level tablespoons	30g	1oz
Brown sugar	1 cup	170g	6oz
Butter/margarine/lard	1 cup	225g	8oz
Sultanas/raisins	1 cup	200g	7oz
Currants	1 cup	140g	5oz
Ground almonds	1 cup	110g	4oz
Golden syrup	1 cup	340g	12oz
Uncooked rice	1 cup	200g	7oz

NOTE: In American recipes, when quantities are stated as spoons, `level' spoons are meant. English recipes (and those in this book) call for rounded spoons except where stated otherwise. This means that 2 American tablespoons equal 1 English tablespoon.

Useful measurements

Measurement	Metric	Imperial
1 American cup	225ml	8fl oz
1 egg, size 3	56ml	2fl oz
1 egg white	28ml	1fl oz
1 rounded tablespoon flour	30g	1oz
1 rounded tablespoon cornflour	30g	1oz
1 rounded tablespoon caster sugar	30g	1oz
2 rounded tablespoons fresh breadcrumbs	30g	1oz
2 level teaspoons gelatine	8g	$1/4$oz

30g/1oz granular (packet) aspic sets 570ml (1 pint) liquid.

15g/oz powdered gelatine, or 3 leaves, will set 570ml (1 pint) liquid.

(However, in hot weather, or if the liquid is very acid, like lemon juice, or if the jelly contains solid pieces of food and is to be turned out of the dish or mould, $20g/^3/4oz$ should be used.)

CATERING QUANTITIES

Few people accurately weigh or measure quantities as a control-conscious chef must do, but when catering for large numbers it is useful to know how much food to allow per person. As a general rule, the more people you are catering for the less food per head you need to provide, e.g. 225g/8oz stewing beef per head is essential for 4 people, but 170g/6oz per head would feed 60 people.

SOUP
Allow 290ml/1/2 pint soup a head, depending on the size of the bowl.

POULTRY
Chicken and turkey Allow 450g/1lb per person, weighed when plucked and drawn. An average chicken serves 4 people on the bone and 6 people off the bone.
Duck A 3kg/6lb bird will feed 3–4 people; a 2kg/4lb bird will feed 2 people. 1 duck makes enough pâté for 6 people.

MEAT
LAMB OR MUTTON
Casseroled 285g/10oz per person (boneless, with fat trimmed away).
Roast leg 1.35kg/3lb for 3–4 people; 2kg/4lb for 4–5 people; 3kg/6lb for 7–8 people.
Roast shoulder 2kg/4lb shoulder for 5–6 people; 3kg/6lb shoulder for 7–9 people.
Roast breast 450g/1lb for 2 people.
Grilled best end cutlets 3–4 per person.
Grilled loin chops 2 per person.

BEEF
Stewed 225g/8oz boneless trimmed meat per person.
Roast (off the bone) If serving men only, 225g/8oz per person; if serving men and women, 200g/7oz per person.
Roast (on the bone) 340g/12oz per person.
Roast whole fillet 2kg/4lb piece for 10 people.
Grilled steaks 200–225g/7–8oz per person depending on appetite.

PORK
Casseroled 170g/6oz per person.
Roast leg or loin (off the bone) 200g/7oz per person.
Roast leg or loin (on the bone) 340g/12oz per person.
2 average fillets will feed 3–4 people.
Grilled 1 x 170g/6oz chop or cutlet per person.

MINCED MEAT
170g/6oz per person for shepherd's pie, hamburgers, etc.
110g/4oz per person for steak tartare.
85g/3oz per person for lasagne, cannelloni, etc.
110g/4oz per person for moussaka.
55g/2oz per person for spaghetti.

FISH
Whole large fish (e.g. sea bass, salmon, whole haddock), weighed uncleaned, with head on: 340–450g/12oz–1lb per person.
Cutlets and steaks 170g/6oz per person.
Fillets (e.g. sole, lemon sole, plaice), 3 small fillets per person (total weight about 170g/6oz).
Whole small fish (e.g. trout, slip soles, small plaice, small mackerel, herring), 225–340g/8–12oz weighed with heads for main course; 170g/6oz for first course.
Fish off the bone (in fish pie, with sauce, etc.) 170g/6oz per person.

SHELLFISH
Prawns 55–85g/2–3oz per person as a first course; 140g/5oz per person as a main course.
Mixed shellfish 55–85g/2–3oz per person as a first course; 140g/5oz per person as a main course.

VEGETABLES

Weighed before preparation and cooking, and assuming 3 vegetables, including potatoes, served with a main course: 110g/4oz per person, except (per person):

French beans 85g/3oz.
Peas 85g/3oz.
Spinach 340g/12oz.
Potatoes 3 small (roast); 170g/6oz (mashed); 10–15 (Parisienne); 5 (château); 1 large or 2 small (baked); 110g/4oz (new).
NOTE: As a general rule men eat more potatoes and fewer `greens' than women.

RICE

Plain, boiled or fried 55g/2oz (weighed before cooking) or 1 breakfast cup (measured after cooking).
In risotto or pilaf 30g/1oz per person (weighed before cooking) for first course; 55g/2oz per person for main course.

SALADS

Obviously, the more salads served, the less guests will eat of any one salad. Allow 1 large portion of salad, in total, per head – e.g. if only one salad is served make sure there is enough for 1 helping each. Conversely if 100 guests are to choose from five different salads, allow a total of 150 portions – i.e. 30 portions of each salad.

Soups

SOUPS

A wide range of ingredients, flavours and seasonings go into Latin America's favourite dishes, and soups are top of the list. They are widely eaten from Mexico to Argentina, and range from thin chicken or beef broth to creamy, stew-type potato and vegetable soups.

In Mexico, thinly sliced and fried tortillas are added to a simple tomato and chilli soup, then garnished with avocados and soured cream. The coastal areas, rich in seafood, provide a wide and exciting variety of soups flavoured with chillies, limes or coconut milk. The high Andean countries, namely Peru, Bolivia, Ecuador, Colombia and Chile, with their huge selection of potatoes (more than 100 varieties), make wonderful potato soups. In some recipes, which include different vegetables and meats, more than five different varieties of potatoes are used.

Colonial influences are still apparent in much Latin American cooking. Spanish gazpacho is common in Mexico, while the Portuguese soup *caldo verde* is very popular in Brazil. Native tropical ingredients, such as avocado and hearts of palm, have also played their part and are used to make delicious cold soups. The most common thickenings or enriching agents are potatoes, nuts, seeds and cornflour; cream is very seldom used in soups.

Some soups, like peanut soup, are common throughout Latin America, with slight variations. Starchy vegetables, such as sweetcorn, sweet potatoes and beans, are also widely used, and rice appears in many fish and chicken soups.

Unless stated otherwise, all recipes make 4 servings.

Peanut Soup

A popular soup throughout Latin America, this recipe uses dry chipotle chillies, which have a delicious smoky flavour and quite a bit of heat, so start with one chilli and add more to taste.

Ingredients

2 tablespoons sunflower oil
2 medium onions, finely chopped
2 chipotle chillies (see page 198)
2 red peppers, seeded and chopped
1 x 400g/14oz can chopped tomatoes in juice
1.14 litres/2 pints beef stock (see page 189)
340g/12oz smooth, unsweetened peanut butter
salt and freshly ground pepper
3 tablespoons chopped coriander

Method

1. Heat the oil in a large, heavy pan and cook the onions gently for 10 minutes.

2. Remove the seeds from the chillies and cut the flesh into small pieces. Add to the onions together with the peppers, tomatoes and beef stock. Bring to the boil, reduce the heat and simmer gently for 25 minutes.

3. Add the peanut butter and mix thoroughly into the soup. Process the soup in a blender or food processor and pour back into the rinsed-out pan. The soup should have the thickness of double cream; if too thick, add some more stock or water. Season to taste with salt and pepper. Just before serving mix in the chopped coriander and serve hot.

NOTE: The chipotle chilli can be substituted by 1 red jalapeño or Kenyan chilli.

WINE SUGGESTION: Verdelho madeira or dry amontillado sherry.

Avocado and Lime Soup with Cayenne Toasts

This is a delicious soup for a summer day, and the low-fat yoghurt balances the richness of the avocado. The Tabasco can be omitted or increased according to taste.

Ingredients

2 medium avocado pears, peeled and diced
juice of 4 limes
425ml/³/₄ pint low-fat yoghurt
salt and freshly ground white pepper
dash Tabasco sauce
3 tablespoons roughly chopped coriander
290ml/¹/₂ pint cold chicken stock (see page 188)

For the cayenne toasts:
1 French baguette
55g/2oz butter
1 teaspoon cayenne pepper

For the garnish:
1 red pepper, seeded and finely diced

Method

1. In a blender or food processor mix the avocado flesh and lime juice until smooth. Add the yoghurt, salt and pepper, Tabasco and chopped coriander and blend well until completely smooth.

2. With the motor still running, add the chicken stock and process until the soup is smooth and not too thick. Season to taste with salt and pepper. Chill well.

3. Preheat the oven to 200°C/400°F/gas mark 6.

4. To prepare the toasts, slice the bread into 2.5cm/1 inch rounds. Melt the butter and add the cayenne pepper. Brush both sides of the bread generously with the butter and place on a baking tray.

5. Bake for 10 minutes or until lightly browned, turning once to brown both sides.

6. Serve the soup garnished with the diced red pepper and hand the cayenne toasts separately.

WINE SUGGESTION: Crisp, dry white.

Sweet Potato, Corn and Green Chilli Soup

This soup includes the two most-loved starchy foods in the Americas – potatoes and corn. White or yellow-fleshed sweet potatoes can be used as both produce equally creamy results.

Ingredients

1 medium onion, finely chopped
55g/2oz butter
675g/1³/₄ lb sweet potatoes, peeled and
    chopped
1.14 litres/2 pints chicken stock (see page 188)
200g/7oz fresh or defrosted corn kernels
1 green Fresno or Jalepeño chilli, seeded and
    finely diced (see page 194)
salt and freshly ground pepper

To serve: Cuban white bread (see page 241)

Method

1. Sweat the onion in the butter for 5 minutes. Add the sweet potatoes and stock and bring to the boil. Cover and simmer until the potatoes are tender, about 20 minutes.

2. Strain, reserving the liquid. Purée the potatoes until smooth. Return the stock to the rinsed-out pan and mix in the potato purée. Add the corn, chilli, salt and pepper to taste and simmer for a further 10 minutes. If the soup is too thick, add more chicken stock.

3. Just before serving, heat the soup thoroughly. Serve with the Cuban white bread.

WINE SUGGESTION: Full-bodied white.

Sweetcorn Velouté

An easy and quick soup to make, and sure to please children because of the sweet taste of corn.

Ingredients

30g/1oz butter
1 onion, chopped
2 tablespoons flour
¹/₂ teaspoon cayenne pepper
¹/₂ teaspoon mild chilli powder
kernels from 3 corn cobs, or 450g/1lb frozen
    corn kernels
570ml/1 pint chicken stock (see page 188)
freshly ground pepper
425ml/³/₄ pint milk
3 tablespoons finely chopped flat-leaf parsley

To serve: Cuban white bread (see page 241)

Method

1. Melt the butter in a large pan and sweat the onion until soft, about 20 minutes. Add the flour, cayenne and chilli powder and cook for a further 3 minutes, stirring constantly.

2. Add the corn kernels, stock and milk and bring to the boil. Season to taste with salt, reduce the heat and simmer for 20 minutes or until the corn is very soft.

3. Remove the soup from the heat and process or blend it. Strain into the rinsed-out saucepan. Reheat for 5 minutes, then add the chopped parsley. Season to taste. Serve hot with Cuban white bread.

WINE SUGGESTION: Chilled fino or manzanilla sherry.

Roast Pepper and Tomato Soup with Spicy Corn Muffins

Peppers, tomatoes and potatoes – all ingredients native to Latin America – make up this delicious soup.

Ingredients

3 red peppers, quartered and deseeded
15g/^{1}/2 oz butter
1 tablespoon olive oil
1 medium onion, chopped
^{1}/2 teaspoon cayenne pepper
^{1}/2 teaspoon ground cumin
pinch cinnamon
2.5ml/^{1}/2 teaspoon fresh thyme
1 teaspoon tomato purée
2 medium potatoes, peeled and roughly
  chopped
1 x 400g/14oz can chopped tomatoes
570ml/1 pint hot chicken stock (see page 188)
salt and freshly ground pepper

For the garnish:
1 spring onion, finely chopped

To serve: spicy corn muffins (see page 240)

Method

1. Preheat the grill to its highest setting. Grill the peppers, skin-side up, until they are blistered and blackened all over. Place them inside a plastic bag until they are cool enough to handle. Remove and discard the skins and chop the peppers into strips.

2. Melt the butter and oil in a large, heavy saucepan. Add the onion and cook gently until soft but not coloured, about 15 minutes. Add the cayenne, cumin, cinnamon, thyme and tomato purée and fry for 2 minutes. Add the potatoes, chopped tomatoes and grilled pepper strips and mix well with the onions and spices. Add the stock and cook over gentle heat until the potatoes are soft, about 25 minutes.

3. Liquidize the soup until smooth and return to the rinsed-out pan. Season to taste with salt and pepper. Garnish with the finely chopped spring onion. Serve at once with the spicy corn muffins.

WINE SUGGESTION: Dry rosé.

Green Soup with Hazelnuts

As in many dishes from Latin America, this recipe uses nuts as a thickening agent rather than cream or butter. This is a substantial soup which can be served as a meal on its own.

Ingredients

2 tablespoons sunflower oil
2 medium onions, peeled and chopped
2 green Fresno or Kenyan chillies, seeded and
   finely chopped (see page 194)
2 slices white bread, crusts off and cut into
   cubes
110g/4oz hazelnuts, roasted and peeled
1/2 teaspoon cayenne pepper
1.14 litres/2 pints chicken stock (see page 188)
salt and freshly ground pepper
450g/1lb fresh spinach, or 170g/6oz frozen
   leaf spinach
225g/8oz watercress, trimmed

Method

1. Heat the oil in a large pan, add the onions and chillies and cook for 5 minutes, until they are nearly soft but not coloured.

2. Add the bread and hazelnuts and cook over medium heat until the nuts have some colour. Add the cayenne, chicken stock and salt and pepper, cover and simmer for 10 minutes.

3. Meanwhile, prepare the fresh spinach by removing the stalks and any thick veins. Wash thoroughly in several changes of water and chop roughly. If using frozen spinach, defrost before using. Prepare the watercress by picking over the leaves carefully and wash thoroughly.

4. Add all the spinach and the watercress stalks to the hot soup and cook for 5 minutes. Mix well and process or blend until smooth. Pour the soup back into the rinsed-out pan. Season to taste and if too thick, add a little extra chicken stock.

NOTE: To keep the bright green colour, do not reheat the soup more than once.

WINE SUGGESTION: Dry sherry.

Crab and Fish Soup

Found in abundance in the coastal areas of South America, crab is used in many recipes with delicious results.

Ingredients

2 pasilla dried chillies (see page 199)
55g/2oz butter
2 medium onions, thinly sliced
55g/2oz flour
860ml/1^1/$_2$ pints fish stock (see page 189)
1 bay leaf
225g/8oz crab meat
225g/8oz haddock fillet, skinned and cut
　into 5cm/2 inch strips
150ml/^{1}/$_4$ pint single cream
150ml/^{1}/$_4$ pint milk
salt and freshly ground pepper

For the garnish:
1 bunch of chives, finely chopped

Method

1. Remove the stalks and cut the chillies in half. Brush out their seeds and cut away large ribs. Tear into small pieces, put them into a bowl and pour over enough hot water to cover. Leave to soak for 20 minutes. Drain and discard the soaking liquid.

2. In a large pan, melt the butter, add the onions and cook slowly for 8 minutes or until the onions begin to soften. Add the flour and cook for 1 minute.

3. Add the soaked chillies, fish stock, bay leaf, half the crab meat and all the fish. Simmer for 20 minutes.

4. Remove the soup from the heat, liquidize it very well and pour it through a sieve back into the rinsed-out pan. Add the remaining crab meat, the cream and milk. Season to taste with salt and pepper, then reheat over gentle heat without boiling. If the soup is too thick, add a few tablespoons of fish stock.

5. Sprinkle with chives just before serving.

WINE SUGGESTION: Dry white.

Chilled Hearts of Palm and Avocado Soup

Although chilled soups are not very common in Latin America, the combination of rich avocado and delicately acid hearts of palm makes this soup a success.

Ingredients

425ml/^{3}/$_4$ pint good-quality chicken stock (see page 188)
290ml/^{1}/$_2$ pint single cream
290ml/^{1}/$_2$ pint milk
1 x 400g/14oz can hearts of palm, drained and cut into chunks
1 avocado, skinned, stoned and cut into cubes
juice of 2 limes
pinch cayenne pepper
dash Tabasco sauce
salt and freshly ground white pepper

For the garnish:
1 tablespoon chopped coriander

Method

1. In a blender or food processor process all the ingredients together until smooth. Season to taste with salt and pepper, then cover and refrigerate until chilled. The mixture should have the consistency of double cream. If the soup is too thick, add a few more tablespoons of chicken stock or water.

2. Serve well chilled, sprinkled with the chopped coriander.

WINE SUGGESTION: Light summery white.

Tropical-style Rice Soup

The basis for this soup is a strong-flavoured stock made from chicken, beef or fish to which rice and coconut are added. Finely chopped vegetables can also be included for extra flavour and texture.

Ingredients

1.14 litres/2 pints chicken stock (see page 188)
1 bouquet garni
1 green Thai chilli, seeded and finely chopped (see page 194)
170g/6oz long-grain rice
55g/2oz butter
30g/1oz desiccated coconut
salt and freshly ground black pepper
2 tablespoons finely chopped flat-leaf parsley

Method

1. In a large pan bring the stock, bouquet garni and green chilli to a boil. Add the rice and cook for 10 minutes. Remove the bouquet garni. Stir in the butter and coconut and cook for another 5 to 10 minutes. Season to taste with salt and pepper.

2. Just before serving add the chopped parsley and serve hot.

NOTE: Leftover chicken, fish or turkey can be added to this soup with delicious results.

WINE SUGGESTION: New World chardonnay.

Prawn and Fish Soup

Fish and shellfish soups are found in all the coastal areas of Latin America, with prawns being the favourite shellfish. Places with a more profound African influence, such as the Caribbean and north east Brazil, add coconut and a larger amount of chillies to their fish soups, but either way they are always delicious and easy to make.

Ingredients

2 tablespoons sunflower oil
4 garlic cloves, crushed
4 small onions, finely chopped
$1/2$ teaspoon mild chilli powder
1 teaspoon chopped marjoram
1 x 230g/8oz can chopped tomatoes
1 green pepper, seeded and diced
1 red pepper, seeded and diced
1.14 litres/2 pints fish stock (see page 189)
salt and freshly ground pepper
400g/14oz cod or haddock fillet, skinned and
    cut into 5cm/2 inch chunks
340g/12oz raw, medium prawns, without shells,
    deveined (see page 277)

For the garnish:
2 tablespoons finely chopped flat-leaf parsley
1 bunch of chives, finely chopped

To serve: crusty white bread

Method

1. In a large saucepan, heat the oil and sweat the onions for 10 minutes.

2. Stir in the garlic, chilli powder, marjoram, tomatoes with their juice and the peppers and cook for a further 5 minutes. Pour in the fish stock and season with salt and pepper. Bring to the boil, reduce the heat and add the fish and prawns. Cover and simmer gently for about 4–5 minutes or until the fish is cooked.

3. Season again to taste with salt and pepper, then mix in the parsley and chives. Serve at once with the white crusty bread.

NOTE: For a richer soup add 200g/7oz creamed coconut together with the uncooked fish. Other types of shellfish can be used with equally good results.

WINE SUGGESTION: Crisp, dry white.

First Courses
and Salads

FIRST COURSES AND SALADS

A first course served as an individual separate dish is not usually found in Latin America. It is more common to serve a variety of appetizers, normally arranged on one plate and shared by all. The appetizers can vary from very light nibbles, such as grilled prawns and chicken-heart kebabs, to more substantial *empanadas* or *tamales*, small baked or steamed pies filled with chicken, fish or cheese.

Throughout Latin America there is a tradition of selling snack-type foods in the streets, markets and cafés. They are basically finger foods eaten at odd hours and they vary from country to country. In Peru *antichudos* (spicy ox-heart brochettes) are very popular, and there are seafood equivalents along the coast. In central Brazil one finds vendors with huge vats of salted boiling water filled with corn on the cob, while street vendors of ceviche are common in Lima and Quito.

The Portuguese and Spanish, who were themselves influenced by invading nations, introduced their love of fried food to South America when they arrived in 1492. Frying was then unknown in local cuisines, but has since become a favourite method of food preparation. A variety of fried food, from small potato dumplings with different fillings to light pastry snacks such as *pastelzitos*, filled with the same fillings as *empanadas*, are found in many Latin countries.

Chile, Argentina, Brazil and Uruguay all have shops where these savoury snack foods, as well as sweets and cakes, coffee, tea and soft drinks, are sold throughout the day to the delight of the locals and foreigners. These shops have different names in different countries but they can be easily spotted by the crowds that throng there around 11 in the morning and 4 in the afternoon.

Salads are usually simple and served with a meal. The most popular include a variety of steamed or boiled vegetables tossed in a light dressing. Pickled vegetables are also very popular, and glass jars containing beautifully arranged carrots, cauliflowers, onions, French beans and baby corn can be found in many South American supermarkets. Again, what would be thought of as a salad or first course in Europe is an appetizer for Latin Americans.

One of the most unusual salads is found in Mexico, where *nopales*, the young and tender `paddles' of the prickly pear cactus, are eaten as a vegetable. When the spines are removed, the pads are thinly sliced and eaten raw in salads, or cooked until very tender and eaten as a vegetable. Canned *nopales* are called *nopalitos*.

Ceviches almost deserve a chapter on their own, being among the most widely known dishes from South America. Their birthplace is disputed between Peru and Ecuador, and as both countries have an amazing variety of fish and shellfish, they could easily have come from either. There are innumerable recipes and variations of ceviche, all with delicious results. It can be eaten as a first course or main dish, depending on the accompaniments served with it.

Unless stated otherwise, all recipes make 4 servings.

Hearts of Palm Flan with Herb Pastry

Hearts of palm have a delicate flavour and texture and are used very much like asparagus – in dressing on their own, in salads, or in pies and quiches. Fresh hearts of palm are very hard to come by, even in South America, so canned ones are widely used.

Ingredients

170g/6oz herb pastry (see page 251)
30g/1oz butter
2 x 400g/14oz cans palm hearts, drained and
    cut into 2.5cm/1 inch chunks
2 tablespoons finely chopped flat-leaf
    parsley
1 teaspoon chopped oregano
2 eggs
2 yolks
150ml/$\frac{1}{4}$ pint single cream
150ml/$\frac{1}{4}$ pint milk
salt and freshly ground black pepper
3 tablespoons grated Parmesan cheese

To serve: spicy tomato sauce (see page 181)

Method

1. Preheat the oven to 200°C/400°F/gas mark 6.

2. Roll out the pastry, use to line a 28cm/ 11inch flan ring and chill well.

3. Melt the butter, add the hearts of palm, parsley and oregano and cook over a medium heat for 5 minutes. Set aside to cool slightly.

4. Bake the pastry blind: prick the bottom of the flan case to prevent bubbling up while baking. Line with greaseproof paper and fill with blind beans. Bake in the centre of the oven for 15 minutes, then remove the beans and paper and bake for a further 5 minutes. Cool slightly. Lower the oven temperature to 180°C/350°F/gas mark 4.

5. Mix together the eggs, the yolks, the single cream and the milk and season with salt and pepper.

6. Spoon the hearts of palm mixture into the bottom of the flan, sprinkle with the cheese and carefully pour the liquid on top. Bake in the centre of the oven until golden and just set, about 25 minutes.

7. Remove from the oven and allow to cool in the flan ring for 10 minutes before transferring to a serving dish. Serve warm with the spicy tomato sauce.

NOTE: *Apart from being easier to use, flan rings or loose-bottomed metal tins conduct the heat better, preventing the pastry from becoming soggy.*

WINE SUGGESTION: Dry white.

Flaky Prawn and Coconut Torte

Latin Americans are very fond of any sort of pie, torte or turnover, and the filling will vary according to the region and the occasion. Seafood is usually reserved for special days, while chicken, beef or cheese fillings are eaten more frequently.

Ingredients

340g/12oz flour quantity puff pastry (see page 252), or 450g/1lb frozen puff pastry
1 egg, beaten, for glazing

For the filling:
2 tablespoons butter
1 onion, finely chopped
1 garlic clove, crushed
1 green Thai chilli, seeded and chopped (see page 194)
$1/2$ red pepper, seeded and diced
$1/2$ green pepper, seeded and diced
$1/2$ teaspoon cayenne pepper
3 large tomatoes, peeled, seeded and chopped
3 spring onions, roughly chopped
3 tablespoons chopped parsley
450g/1lb large uncooked prawns, shelled and deveined (see page 277)
110g/$3^1/2$oz creamed coconut, chopped
salt and freshly ground pepper

For the salad:
2 tablespoons sunflower oil
1 tablespoon lemon juice
salt and freshly ground pepper
2 bunches of watercress, trimmed and washed

For the garnish:
2 tablespoons sesame seeds, lightly toasted

Method

1. Preheat the oven to 220°C/425°F/gas mark 7.

2. Make the filling: melt the butter in a large pan. Add the onion, garlic, chilli and peppers and cook over medium heat until nearly soft but not coloured.

3. Add the cayenne, chopped tomatoes, spring onion and parsley. Bring to the boil and cook uncovered for 20 minutes.

4. Add the prawns and creamed coconut and cook for 5 minutes, or until the prawns are cooked. Season, transfer to a bowl to cool.

5. On a floured surface, roll half of the pastry into a rectangle the size of an A4 sheet of paper. Transfer to a baking sheet and prick well all over. Chill for 10 minutes. Bake in the oven for 15 minutes or until light brown. Reduce the oven temperature to 200°C/400°F/gas mark 6.

6. Roll the remaining pastry until it is a little larger than the baked base. Mound the filling in the centre of the cooked base and gently tuck the uncooked pastry under. Brush the torte with the beaten egg and chill for 15–20 minutes. Glaze again and score the top in a criss-cross pattern.

7. Bake in the oven for 30–35 minutes, or until the pastry is golden brown. Remove from the oven, transfer to a serving plate and keep warm while making the salad.

8. In a large bowl mix the oil, lemon juice and salt and pepper. Just before serving toss the watercress leaves in the dressing and sprinkle with the sesame seeds. Serve the torte warm with the watercress salad.

WINE SUGGESTION: Medium-dry white.

Potato and Cheese Cakes with Peanut Sauce

Ecuador has many wonderful recipes using potatoes and this is one of them. Although cheese is not used very often, it makes a delicious combination with the spicy peanut sauce.

Ingredients

900g/2lb potatoes
30g/1oz butter
2 medium onions, finely chopped
200g/7oz sweetcorn
3 spring onions, finely chopped
1 egg, beaten
1/2 teaspoon cayenne pepper
225g/8oz Cheddar cheese, grated
salt and freshly ground pepper
seasoned flour
2 eggs, beaten
dry white breadcrumbs
oil for frying

For the peanut sauce:
3 tablespoons sunflower oil
2 onions, finely chopped
2 garlic cloves, crushed
1 green Fresno or Kenyan chilli, seeded and
  chopped (see page 194)
2 medium tomatoes, peeled, seeded and
  chopped
2 tablespoons crunchy, unsweetened peanut
  butter
salt and freshly ground pepper

For the garnish:
1 small bunch of watercress

Method

1. Peel, boil, drain and mash the potatoes while still warm.

2. Melt the butter, add the onions and cook gently until nearly soft, about 10 minutes. Mix in the sweetcorn and spring onions and cook for a further 2 minutes.

3. In a large bowl, mix the potatoes, the beaten egg, onion mixture, cayenne and cheese. Season with salt and pepper.

4. With hands dipped in seasoned flour, shape the mixture into 12 balls, then flatten into patties. Dip each patty into the beaten egg, then the breadcrumbs. Refrigerate for at least 15 minutes.

5. Make the sauce: heat the oil and sweat the onions and chilli for about 10 minutes. Add the garlic, tomatoes and peanut butter and cook over a low heat for 10 minutes. Season to taste with salt and pepper and set aside to cool.

6. Heat enough oil in a frying pan to reach halfway up the patties until a crumb will sizzle vigorously in it. Fry the patties a few at a time, turning only once, until golden brown. Drain well on absorbent paper and keep warm until they are all fried.

7. To serve: put 3 cakes on each plate and garnish with the watercress. Hand the sauce separately or put into small ramekins on each plate.

WINE SUGGESTION: New World chardonnay.

Chick Pea Soufflé Cakes with Red Pepper Mayonnaise

Chick peas arrived in the Americas with the Spanish, who were introduced to them by the Arabs. They are especially popular in Mexico. These soufflé cakes are quick and easy to make, and look and taste wonderful.

Ingredients

1 x 400g/14oz can chick peas
2 tablespoons sunflower oil
1 small onion, chopped
1 garlic clove, crushed
pinch sugar
1/2 teaspoon paprika
1/2 teaspoon cayenne pepper
1/2 teaspoon ground cumin
1 teaspoon plain flour
4 tablespoons double cream
2 eggs, separated
2 tablespoons sunflower oil
salt and freshly ground pepper

For the garnish:
coriander leaves

To serve: spicy red pepper mayonnaise (see page 187)

Method

1. Drain the chick peas and rinse well. Place in a blender or food processor and purée. Transfer to a large bowl and set aside.

2. Heat the oil and gently sweat the onion until nearly soft, about 10 minutes. Add the garlic, sugar, paprika, cayenne and cumin and cook, stirring for a further minute.

3. Add the flour and cook for 1 minute. Mix in the cream and simmer for 1 minute. Add the sauce to the chick pea purée together with the egg yolks. Season to taste with salt and pepper.

4. Whisk the egg whites until stiff but not dry and fold in batches into the chick pea mixture.

5. Heat the oil in a large frying pan, and fry spoonfuls of the mixture, turning only once when they are golden brown, about 2 minutes on each side. Drain on absorbent paper and keep warm until all the cakes are fried.

6. Garnish with the coriander leaves and serve warm with the mayonnaise.

WINE SUGGESTION: Light-acidity white.

Crab Gratin

Crab is found in abundance along the coasts of Latin America. Chile, Peru and Ecuador have a great variety and quantity of shellfish, with prawns, crab and lobster being among the favourites.

Ingredients

340g/12oz cooked crab meat, well picked over
juice of 1 lime
salt and freshly ground pepper
2 tablespoons sunflower oil
1 medium onion, finely chopped
2 garlic cloves, crushed
2 spring onions, white and green parts, chopped
3 tomatoes, peeled, seeded and diced
4 tablespoons chopped coriander
55g/2oz fresh white breadcrumbs
100ml/3 fl oz double cream
3 tablespoons grated Parmesan cheese

To serve: lemon and lime wedges

Method

1. Season the crab meat with the lime juice, salt and pepper.

2. Preheat the oven to 220°C/430°F/gas mark 7.

3. Heat the oil in a sauté pan, add the onion and gently cook for 8 minutes. Add the garlic, spring onions, tomatoes and half the coriander and cook for a further 5 minutes over medium heat.

4. Put the mixture into a bowl and add the crab meat, the remaining coriander, half the breadcrumbs, the double cream, salt and pepper and mix thoroughly. The mixture should have the consistency of soft potato purée. If the mixture is too wet, add some more breadcrumbs. If too dry, add some more cream or milk.

5. Brush a medium crab shell or scallop shells with oil, pile the mixture into it and sprinkle the top with some breadcrumbs and Parmesan. Place on a baking sheet and bake on the top shelf of the oven until bubbly and golden brown, about 15 minutes. Serve hot with the lemon and lime wedges.

NOTE: This recipe can also be baked in a well-buttered shallow gratin dish.

WINE SUGGESTION: Dry white.

Spicy Shrimp and Crab Cake

Of all the shellfish found in Latin America, prawns and shrimps are the favourites, followed closely by crabs and lobsters.

Ingredients

For the batter:
170g/6oz flour
$^1/_2$ teaspoon turmeric
100ml/3 fl oz sunflower oil
190ml/$^1/_3$ pint milk
2 teaspoons baking powder
3 eggs
salt and freshly ground pepper

For the filling:
2 tablespoons sunflower oil
1 onion, finely chopped
1 red pepper, seeded and diced
1 red jalapeño or Kenyan chilli, seeded and
    diced (see page 194)
3 spring onions, finely chopped
2 tomatoes, peeled, seeded and diced
225g/8oz uncooked prawns, shelled and
    deveined (see page 277), or 170g/6oz
    cooked prawns
170g/6oz crab meat, well picked over
3 tablespoons chopped coriander

To serve: mixed green salad

Method

1. Preheat the oven to 200°C/400°F/gas mark 6.

2. Mix all the batter ingredients together in a food processor or blender until smooth. Season well and set aside while making the filling.

3. Heat the oil, add the onion, red pepper and chilli and cook until soft but not coloured, about 10 minutes. Add the spring onions and tomatoes and cook, uncovered, over medium heat for about 10 minutes, or until there is very little liquid left. Add the prawns and crab meat, season well and cook for a further 5 minutes. Transfer to a plate to cool.

4. Lightly oil a 25cm/10 inch square ovenproof dish and pour in half the batter mix. Spread the prawn mixture gently over the top, sprinkle with the coriander and pour the remaining batter on top.

5. Bake for 25 minutes, then reduce the oven to 180°C/350°F/gas mark 4 and bake until a sharp knife or skewer inserted into the centre comes out clean. Serve warm, cut into diamonds, with a mixed green salad.

NOTE: *The shrimp and crab filling can be substituted by picadillo (see page 92), shredded chicken or leftover chilli con carne (see page 85).*

WINE SUGGESTION: Full dry white.

Marinated Quail's Eggs

Quails' eggs are very popular, especially in Brazil, where they are hard-boiled, peeled and left overnight to marinate in an oil and vinegar dressing, then served with French bread as an appetizer.

Ingredients

24 quails' eggs

For the dressing:
100ml/3 fl oz olive oil
2 garlic cloves, crushed
4 tablespoons white wine vinegar
1 Thai red chilli, seeded and diced (see
   page 194)
1 x 5cm/2 inch cinnamon stick
salt and freshly ground black pepper
good pinch cayenne pepper
2 tablespoons finely chopped parsley

Method

1. Boil the quails' eggs for 4 minutes in boiling
    salted water. Remove and put into a bowl of
    cold water to prevent further cooking. When
    cold, peel carefully and set aside.

2. Put all the dressing ingredients into a small
    saucepan and bring to the boil. Remove
    from the heat, add the eggs and set aside
    until cold. When cold, remove the crushed
    garlic and cinnamon stick. This can be done
    a day in advance and the marinated eggs
    kept in refrigerated.

WINE SUGGESTION: Crisp, dry white.

Avocado and Red Pimiento Salad with Lime Chilli Dressing

Avocado dishes in many different forms are served with almost any meal in Mexico. In this recipe the chilli dressing balances a little of the avocado richness and the pimientos add a touch of sweetness.

Ingredients

1 x 400g/14oz can whole red pimientos in water
3 tablespoons olive oil
2 tablespoons sunflower oil
1 garlic clove, crushed
1/2 teaspoon crushed chillies
1 tablespoon white wine vinegar
salt and freshly ground black pepper
2 ripe avocados
juice of 1 lemon
juice of 3 limes
2 tablespoons roughly chopped coriander

For the garnish:
2 tablespoons chopped flat-leaf parsley

To serve: tortilla chips

Method

1. Drain the pimientos well and cut into 1cm/ inch strips.

2. In a small saucepan mix the olive oil, sunflower oil, garlic, crushed chillies and vinegar and bring to the boil. Transfer to a bowl and season with salt and pepper. Add the pimiento strips to the hot dressing and set aside to marinate until cold.

3. Cut the avocado flesh into large cubes. Toss the avocado in the lemon juice, then pile into the centre of a serving plate. Remove the pimientos strips from the dressing and arrange them around the avocado.

4. Remove the crushed garlic from the dressing and discard. Add the lime juice and chopped coriander and whisk with a fork until emulsified. Season to taste with salt and pepper and spoon over the avocados and pimientos. Sprinkle with the chopped parsley and serve with the tortilla chips.

WINE SUGGESTION: Rosé.

Tortilla Salad with Watercress and Chilli Dressing

This is a good recipe for using up leftover tortillas and is a complete meal in itself.

Ingredients

1 red pepper, seeded and cut into 1cm/ inch
  strips
1 yellow pepper, seeded and cut into 1cm/ inch
  strips
$1/2$ large cucumber, seeded and cut into julienne
  strips
2 medium courgettes, cut into julienne strips
3 large tomatoes, peeled, seeded and cut into
  thin strips
1 iceberg lettuce
2 x 15cm/6 inch wheat-flour tortillas (see
  page 166)

For the dressing:
100ml/3 fl oz sunflower oil
100ml/3 fl oz olive oil
100ml/3 fl oz lemon juice
1 red chilli, seeded and finely chopped (see
  page 194)
1 small bunch of watercress, leaves only
2 tablespoons chopped flat-leaf parsley
juice of 1 lime
dash chilli sauce (optional)
salt and freshly ground pepper

For the garnish:
30g/1oz double Gloucester cheese, coarsely
  grated

Method

1. Blanch the peppers, cucumber and courgettes for a few seconds in boiling salted water. Refresh them under cold running water, drain and pat dry with absorbent paper.

2. Put all the dressing ingredients together into a blender or food processor and blend until smooth. Season to taste with salt and pepper.

3. Transfer the dressing to a bowl, add the peppers, cucumber, courgettes and tomatoes and leave to marinate for 30 minutes.

4. Cut the iceberg lettuce into 1cm/$1/2$ inch strips and keep refrigerated until ready to assemble the salad.

5. Put one tortilla on top of the other and roll them up like a cigar. Cut into 1cm/$1/2$ inch strips.

6. When ready to serve, mix the lettuce and tortilla strips with the vegetables and toss well. Pile on to a serving plate and scatter the grated cheese on top. Serve at once.

WINE SUGGESTION: Rosé.

Courgette and French Bean Salad

This delicious Mexican recipe has been adapted from *The Mexican Cookbook* by Sue Style.

Ingredients

340g/12oz French beans, trimmed and halved
340g/12oz courgettes, trimmed and cut
   lengthwise into 5cm/2 inch strips
1 avocado, peeled, stoned and cubed
2 green apples, cored and chopped

For the dressing:
1 egg
120ml/4 fl oz plain yoghurt
salt and pepper
150ml/¼ pint sunflower oil
juice of 2 lemons
1 teaspoon clear honey
½ garlic clove, peeled and crushed

For the garnish:
seeds from 1 pomegranate (optional)

Method

1. Cook the beans and courgettes in lightly salted boiling water until just tender. Drain and refresh under cold running water.

2. Place all the dressing ingredients in a blender or food processor and mix well. Pour half the dressing over the beans and courgettes and toss to coat.

3. Mix the avocado and apples gently into the salad. Garnish with the pomegranate seeds. Serve well chilled.

NOTE: The raw egg in the dressing can be substituted by 2 hardboiled yolks.

WINE SUGGESTION: Crisp, dry white.

Warm Okra Salad with Couscous Timbales

Okra arrived in the Caribbean and Brazil with the African slaves and has been a favourite vegetable ever since. In this recipe the couscous, also from Africa, is coloured with turmeric, a very popular food colouring in many Latin American countries.

Ingredients

225g/8oz okra
3 tablespoons sunflower oil
2 garlic cloves, crushed
1 medium onion, thinly sliced
juice of 1 lemon
pinch caster sugar
$^1/_2$ teaspoon cayenne pepper
3 tablespoons cider vinegar
2 tablespoons olive oil
3 tomatoes, peeled, seeded and cut into strips
salt and freshly ground pepper

For the couscous:
150ml/$^1/_4$ pint chicken stock (see page 188)
$^1/_2$ teaspoon ground turmeric
140g/5oz couscous
1 tablespoon wine vinegar
1 tablespoon olive oil
salt and freshly ground black pepper

For the garnish:
55g/2oz salted peanuts, coarsely chopped

Method

1. Rinse the whole okra, drain well and pat dry with kitchen paper. Top and tail the pods and set aside.

2. Place the chicken stock and turmeric in a small saucepan and bring to a boil.

3. Put the couscous into a medium bowl, add the vinegar, olive oil, salt and pepper and mix well. Pour in enough boiling stock just to cover the mixture. Cover the bowl with cling film. After 10 minutes, fluff up the couscous with a fork, then cover with a plate or clean kitchen towel until ready to use.

4. In a large frying pan or wok, heat the oil and garlic together. When the garlic begins to brown, remove and discard it. Add the onion and stir fry for 2 minutes, taking care not to burn them.

5. Turn the heat high, add the okra and quickly stir-fry them for 2 minutes. Add the lemon juice, sugar and cayenne and toss the okra until bright green. Add the vinegar, olive oil and tomatoes and season with salt and pepper. Cook for a further 2 minutes.

6. To serve, pile the couscous into small, oiled ramekins and press down with the back of a spoon. Turn the couscous out on to warm plates, spoon the okra on the side and pour the remaining dressing around. Scatter the peanuts on top and serve at once.

WINE SUGGESTION: Medium-dry white.

Ceviche

Ceviche is eaten in great quantities in Peru and Ecuador, and the fish mostly used is corvina, which is found only on the Pacific coast of South America.

Ingredients

450g/1lb halibut fillets or other firm white fish
juice of 3 limes
juice of 2 lemons
2 red Thai chillies, seeded and finely diced (see page 194)
salt
4 tablespoons unsweetened orange juice
3 tomatoes, peeled, seeded and finely diced
3 tablespoons sunflower oil
3 tablespoons coarsely chopped coriander
2 spring onions, white and green parts, finely chopped
pinch cayenne pepper
1 ripe avocado, peeled, stoned and diced small
freshly ground black pepper

For the garnish:
cured or pink onions (see page 144)

To serve: corn on the cob or boiled potatoes

Method

1. Cut the fish into 3cm/1½ inch chunks. In a glass bowl mix the fish, lime and lemon juice, the chillies and salt and toss well. Cover and refrigerate for 2 hours, stirring occasionally.

2. Add the rest of the ingredients and toss gently to blend all the flavours.

3. Garnish with the onions and serve with boiled potatoes or hot corn on the cob.

VARIATION: Mixed ceviche can be made using fresh salmon, mackerel, prawns and scallops.

NOTE: If the fish is freshly caught, the marinating time can be reduced to 1 hour.

WINE SUGGESTION: Spicy white.

Avocado, Papaya and Grapefruit Salad

This is a very simple, summery salad using native tropical American ingredients in a light and refreshing way.

Ingredients

2 pink grapefruit, peeled and segmented
1 ripe avocado, peeled, stoned and thinly sliced
1 ripe papaya, quartered, seeded, peeled and
   thinly sliced
5 tablespoons sunflower oil
3 tablespoons white wine vinegar
1 teaspoon crushed chillies
salt and freshly ground pepper

To serve: Cuban white bread (see page 241)

Method

1. Pile the grapefruit segments in the centre of
    a plate. Arrange the avocado slices around
    them. Finally, arrange the papaya slices
    around the avocados. Chill 10 minutes.

2. Whisk the oil, vinegar and crushed chillies
    together. Season to taste with salt and
    pepper. Pour the dressing over the salad and
    serve at once with thinly sliced Cuban white
    bread.

VARIATION: Segment the grapefruit over a plate
to collect the juices and substitute for the
vinegar in the dressing.

WINE SUGGESTION: Friuty, dry white.

Seafood, Avocado and Hearts of Palm Salad

A delicious summer dish which can be prepared in advance and mixed together just before serving.

Ingredients

For the dressing:
150ml/¼ pint soured cream
150ml/¼ pint crème fraîche
juice of 2 limes
3 red Fresno or jalapeño chillies, seeded and
  finely chopped (see page 194)
1 tablespoon chopped chives
salt and freshly ground pepper

For the salad:
1 x 400g/14oz can of hearts of palm, drained
  and cut into 2.5cm/1 inch rounds
3 large tomatoes, peeled, seeded and cut into
  dice
2 large avocados, peeled and cut into 3.5cm/
  1inch cubes
450g/1lb mixed seafood (ready cooked)

For the garnish:
1 small bunch of watercress

Method

1. Mix all the dressing ingredients together in
    a bowl, season to taste with salt and pepper
    and refrigerate.

2. In a medium bowl combine the hearts of
    palm, the tomatoes, avocados and seafood
    and mix with enough dressing to coat
    lightly.

3. Arrange the salad on a plate, garnish with
    watercress and hand the remaining dressing
    separately.

NOTE: If using frozen seafood, put into a colander, add the juice of 1 lemon and a sprinkle of salt and let it thaw for 1 hours, or until thoroughly defrosted.

WINE SUGGESTION: Dry white.

Mixed Kidney Bean Salad

Beans are hugely popular in all Latin American countries, but, strangely enough, there are very few salad recipes that include them.

Ingredients

1 x 340g/12oz can black kidney beans
1 x 340g/12oz can red kidney beans
$1/2$ quantity cured or pink onions (see page 144)
4 tablespoons sunflower oil
1 garlic clove, crushed
3 tablespoons white wine vinegar
$1/2$ teaspoon mild chilli powder
$1/2$ teaspoon ground cumin
$1/2$ teaspoon ground coriander
salt and freshly ground pepper
4 tablespoons finely chopped flat-leaf parsley
1 teaspoon chopped oregano

Method

1. Drain and rinse the black and red kidney beans. Transfer to a bowl and add the cured onions.

2. In a small saucepan mix the oil, garlic, vinegar, spices and salt. Bring to a boil and pour the hot dressing on top of the beans. Mix well to coat them, add the parsley and oregano and season to taste with salt and pepper. Cover and allow the mixture to marinate at room temperature for at least 3 hours, or refrigerate overnight, tossing once or twice.

3. Serve cold or at room temperature.

NOTE: Any selection of beans can be used for this recipe (black-eyed, borlotti, pinto, black, etc.). It is also delicious made with chick peas or lentils.

WINE SUGGESTION: Fruity red.

Marinated Vegetable Salad

A hugely popular salad in Brazil and other South American countries, delicious as an accompaniment to barbecued meats, or on its own.

Ingredients

200g/7oz French beans, topped and tailed
200g/7oz broccoli, cut into small florets
200g/7oz cauliflower, cut into small florets
200g/7oz baby new potatoes, scrubbed and halved
2 courgettes, cut into 2.5cm/1 inch rounds
1 bunch of radishes, trimmed
1 red pepper, grilled, peeled and cut into 1cm/ 1/2 inch strips
1 yellow pepper, grilled, peeled and cut into 1cm/1/2 inch strips
1 x 200g/7oz can sweetcorn, drained and rinsed

For the dressing:
150ml/1/4 pint sunflower oil
1 large onion, finely chopped
1 red Dutch chilli, seeded and chopped (see page 194)
2 garlic cloves, crushed (optional)
1 teaspoon ground cumin
4 tablespoons white wine vinegar
juice of 2 limes
2 tablespoons chopped oregano
4 tablespoons chopped flat-leaf parsley
salt and freshly ground pepper

Method

1. Boil the beans, broccoli, cauliflower, potatoes, courgettes and radishes separately until just tender. Drain and refresh under cold water until cold. Drain thoroughly.

2. Make the dressing: heat the oil in a frying pan and sweat the onions and chillies until nearly soft, about 10 minutes. Add the garlic and cumin and cook for a further 2 minutes.

3. Transfer the onions and oil to a bowl, add the vinegar, lime juice, herbs and seasoning to taste.

4. Combine all the vegetables in a large bowl, pour the dressing over and mix gently but thoroughly. Cover and refrigerate for at least 1 hour, tossing the vegetables in the dressing once.

5. Remove the salad from the refrigerator 20 minutes before serving,

NOTE: Almost any vegetables can be used for this salad – mangetout, baby corn, etc. It is particularly good served with barbecued meat. To make it into a main dish, add a few hardboiled quails' eggs.

WINE SUGGESTION: Dry rosé.

Peruvian Quinoa Salad

Quinoa is a grain which has been popular in Peru since Inca times, when it was considered a holy grain and more highly regarded than the potato. It has a high nutritional value, is easy to prepare and digest, and is normally used in Peruvian soups, stews and casseroles.

Ingredients

450g/1lb raw quinoa
1.75 litres/3 pints cold chicken or vegetable
   stock (see page 188)
1 red pepper, grilled, peeled and finely diced
1 green pepper, grilled, peeled and finely diced
2 green Anaheim chillies, grilled, peeled and
   finely diced (see page 194)
2 tomatoes, peeled, seeded and diced
110g/4oz roasted peanuts, roughly chopped

For the dressing:
55ml/2 fl oz groundnut oil
juice of 1 lime
1 tablespoon white rum
5 tablespoons roughly chopped coriander
pinch ground turmeric
1 garlic clove, crushed (optional)
3 tablespoons roughly chopped flat-leaf parsley
salt and freshly ground black pepper

Method

1. Rinse the quinoa thoroughly under cold water until the water runs clear. In a large saucepan mix the quinoa with the stock, bring to the boil and simmer for about 8–10 minutes, or until the grains are translucent. Drain well and spread on a flat dish to cool.

2. In a large bowl mix the peppers, chillies, tomatoes and half the peanuts.

3. In a liquidizer or food processor mix all the dressing ingredients together until thoroughly combined.

4. Add the cooled quinoa and dressing to the peppers and mix well. Season to taste with salt and pepper, cover and chill. Before serving, sprinkle with the remaining peanuts. Serve with barbecued meat, cold cuts or on its own as a light meal.

NOTE: Quinoa is available from healthfood shops.

WINE SUGGESTION: Medium-dry white.

Poultry

POULTRY

One of the most popular foods brought to Europe from Mexico was the turkey. It reached England around 1524 through Turkish merchants, so it became known as the `turkie cock', later just `turkey'. In fact, the turkey has many different names, all wrongly attributing its origins to places like India and Peru. It slowly replaced the traditional festive birds used until then in England and France, such as swans and peacocks, and by the mid-17th century the turkey was already the established meat for Christmas lunch. Around the world it became the bird to use at large gatherings, especially in Latin America where families are usually large, and the relatively low price of turkey meat made it accessible to everyone.

Migrating ducks, geese and other wildfowl passing through Mexico and Central America were a source of game before 1500, and the Aztecs had already domesticated some types of duck, quail and dove, as well as the turkey. To this day there are many duck, pigeon and even grouse recipes in Latin America.

Another bird quickly adopted by Latin Americans soon after the Conquest was the chicken. Together with the pig, the chicken is easily and cheaply raised on scraps, even by the poorest household, and it became the most popular of the poultry throughout the continent. Recipes using turkey or game were easily adapted to chicken, and new methods of cooking introduced by the Spaniards made it a complete and almost instant success. In the countryside free-range chickens are bought alive in markets and killed at home, just before being cooked, but in city supermarkets the `battery' chicken is now all too common.

The following recipes have exotic and ancient influences: from the Mayan and Aztec cuisines comes the practice of using oily seeds to thicken and enrich sauces, while African slave cookery uses dried shrimp and okra. Chillies are often included and serve to unite all the ingredients and techniques of several very different cultures.

Unless stated otherwise, all recipes make 4 servings.

Roasting Tables

If using a fan (convection) oven, reduce the cooking times by 15 per cent or lower the oven temperature by 20° C/40° F.

Meat		Temperature			Cooking time	
		°C	°F	Gas	per kg	per lb
Beef	Brown	220	425	7	20 mins +	20 mins +
	Rare roast	160	325	3	35 mins	15 mins
	Medium roast				45 mins	20 mins
Pork	Roast	200	400	6	65 mins	25 mins
Lamb	Brown	220	425	7	20 mins	20 mins
	Roast	190	375	5	55 mins	20 mins
Chicken		200	400	6	35–45 mins	15–20 mins

Note: Few chickens, however small, will be cooked in much under an hour.

Meat		Temperature			Cooking time	
Turkey	Small *(under 6kg/13lb)*	200	400	6	25 mins	12 mins
	Large	180	350	4	35 mins	15 mins

Note: For more detailed timings see chart over. (Few turkeys, however small, will be cooked in under 2 hours.)

Meat		Temperature			Cooking time	
Duck/goose	Small *(under 2.5kg/5lb)*	190	375	5	45 mins	20 mins
	Large	180	350	4	55 mins	25 mins

Jointing a Chicken

Stages 1 and 2 *Stages 3 and 4*

Stages 6,7 and 8 *Stages 9 and 11*

Garlic-roasted Chicken with Sweet Potatoes

Although this recipe uses a lot of garlic, the final result is quite mild in flavour. The slow and enclosed cooking process results in a deliciously tender and full-flavoured chicken. When cooking in an enclosed pot do not preheat the oven. This makes for a better flavour as the aromas develop more slowly.

Ingredients

1.8kg/4lb roasting chicken
4 tablespoons chicken stock (see page 188)
6 garlic cloves, crushed
juice of 2 lemons
30g/1oz butter, melted
1 green apple, cored and quartered
salt and freshly ground pepper
2 tablespoons chopped parsley
1 teaspoon chopped thyme
675g/1$\frac{1}{2}$lb sweet potatoes, peeled and cut into
   rounds 2.5cm/1 inch thick
2 medium onions, thinly sliced
2 tablespoons olive oil

To serve: Mexican rice (see page 158)

Method

1. Wipe the chicken with a damp paper towel inside and out.

2. Mix together the stock, half the garlic, the lemon juice and melted butter and brush all over the chicken.

3. Place the apple quarters inside the breast cavity, season the chicken with salt and pepper, then place in an ovenproof casserole dish with a well-fitting lid.

4. Mix the parsley and thyme together. Arrange layers of sweet potatoes, onions and the remaining garlic around the chicken, scattering the herbs and seasoning each layer with salt and pepper. Pour the olive oil over the sweet potatoes.

5. Cover tightly and put the chicken into a cold oven. Set the oven to 200°C/400°F/gas mark 6 and bake for 1 hour. Check that the potatoes are not getting too dry; if they are, add a few tablespoons of chicken stock. Cook covered for a further 30 minutes.

6. Remove the lid from the casserole dish and cook for a further 15 minutes or until the chicken and sweet potatoes are slightly browned. Serve in the baking dish for a rustic appearance, or transfer to a warm serving dish. Serve hot with the Mexican rice.

WINE SUGGESTION: Zesty white.

Creamy Chicken Gratin

This is a very simple, homey dish which can be made using turkey as well as chicken.

Ingredients

1 x 1.8kg/4lb chicken
1 carrot, roughly sliced
1 small onion, quartered
1 celery stalk, roughly chopped
6 peppercorns
1 bay leaf

For the sauce:
2 tablespoons sunflower oil
1 large onion, finely chopped
2 garlic cloves, crushed
5 tomatoes, peeled, seeded and chopped
1 tablespoon tomato purée
2 tablespoons chopped spring onions
2 tablespoons finely chopped parsley
$1/2$ teaspoon cayenne pepper
salt and freshly ground pepper
150ml/$1/4$ pint double cream
225g/8oz Mascarpone cheese
2 tablespoons fresh white breadcrumbs

Method

1. Place the chicken in a large saucepan, add the carrot, onion, celery, peppercorns and bay leaf and cover with water. Bring to the boil, reduce the heat and simmer for 1 hour or until the chicken is cooked. Remove the chicken from the cooking liquid, let it cool, then remove the meat from the bones. Save the stock for later use.

2. In a large frying pan heat the oil, add the onion and cook over gentle heat for 10 minutes or until the onion is nearly soft. Add the garlic, tomatoes, tomato purée, spring onion, parsley, cayenne and salt and pepper and cook over medium heat for 10 minutes.

3. Heat the oven to 200°C/400°F/gas mark 6. Lightly oil a medium-sized gratin dish.

4. Mix half the double cream into the tomato sauce and gently fold in the chicken pieces; it should have a little sauce but not too much. Pile the chicken mixture into the gratin dish.

5. Put the Mascarpore cheese and remaining cream into a bowl and season with salt and pepper. Beat with a wooden spoon until soft. Spread the cheese over the chicken. Scatter the breadcrumbs over the cheese and bake on the top shelf of the oven for about 20 minutes or until lightly browned and bubbly.

WINE SUGGESTION: White vinho verde.

Chicken, Pepper and Chilli Sausages

Sausages are very popular throughout Latin America, from the Spanish *chorizo* and many variations of it, to the milder Portuguese *linquica*. Pork sausages are the most common, but this chicken recipe is a favourite with children and delicious for barbecues.

Ingredients

55g/2oz butter
3 tablespoons sunflower oil
1 large onion, very finely chopped
2 large garlic cloves, crushed
1 red pepper, seeded and finely diced
1 green pepper, seeded and finely diced
1 teaspoon ground cumin
1 tablespoon chopped oregano
1 teaspoon crushed chillies
6 chicken thighs, skinned and boned
2 chicken breasts, skinned and boned
2 spring onions, chopped
2 tablespoons finely chopped parsley
salt and freshly ground black pepper
about 1.8m/6ft sausage casing
oil for frying

To serve: sweet potato purée (see page 146)
salsa cruda (see page 176)

Method

1. Melt the butter and oil together. Add the onion in a pan and cook over medium heat for 10 minutes or until the onion is nearly soft. Add the garlic, peppers, cumin, oregano and crushed chillies and cook for a further 2 minutes.

2. Using a food processor, pound the chicken meat to a coarse purée. Transfer to a bowl and add the onions and peppers with all the fat. Add the spring onions and parsley and season to taste with salt and pepper.

3. Make the sausages: put a 1cm/^{1}/$_2$ inch plain nozzle into a piping bag and fill with the chicken mixture. Insert the nozzle into the sausage casing and hold it there with one hand while squeezing the mixture through the piping bag with the other. Do not fill the skins too tightly or they will burst during cooking. Tie into 10cm/4 inch sausages. Refrigerate, covered, for 1–2 hours.

4. Poach the sausages: bring a deep medium-sized saucepan of water to the boil. Drop in the sausages, reduce the heat abd simmer gently for 10 minutes. Remove the sausages and pat dry with absorbent paper.

5. Heat 1 tablespoon oil in a shallow frying pan over moderate heat and fry the sausages gently for 10 minutes or until browned. Drain on absorbent paper. Serve with sweet potato purée and salsa cruda.

NOTE: This recipe makes 20 x 10cm/4 inch sausages. They can be barbecued or grilled and make a delicious sandwich filling.

WINE SUGGESTION: Light, fruity red.

Chicken and Okra Casserole

This is a typical Brazilian dish, having distinct influences from Portugal (casserole dishes), Africa (use of okra) and native Indian cuisine (colouring).

Ingredients

3 tablespoons sunflower oil
1 x 1.8kg/4lb chicken, jointed into 8 pieces (see page 63)
290ml/^{1}/$_2$ pint hot chicken stock (see page 188)
2 medium onions, chopped
1 red Fresno or jalapeño chilli, seeded and chopped (see page 194)
2 garlic cloves, crushed
1 teaspoon ground turmeric
^{1}/$_2$ teaspoon ground coriander
^{1}/$_2$ teaspoon ground cumin
1 x 400g/14oz can chopped tomatoes
3 tablespoons finely chopped parsley
bunch spring onions, white and green parts, chopped
salt and freshly ground pepper
450g/1lb okra
juice of 1 lemon
2 tablespoons roughly chopped coriander

To serve: polenta (see page 245)
salsa cruda (see page 176)

Method

1. Heat half the oil in a large saucepan and brown the chicken pieces, skin side first. Transfer the browned pieces to a bowl. Add 150ml/5 fl oz of stock to the pan. Bring to the boil, stir well with a wooden spoon and scrape off any sediment. Pour the liquid over the chicken.

2. Add the remaining oil to the deglazed pan and sweat the onions and chilli until nearly soft, about 10 minutes. Add the garlic, turmeric, ground coriander and cumin and cook stirring for a further minute.

3. Add the tomatoes, parsley, half the spring onions, the remaining chicken stock and season with salt and pepper. Return the chicken pieces to the pan, cover and cook over gentle heat until the chicken is tender, about 35 minutes.

4. Wash and dry the okra well. Top and tail them when completely dry.

5. Just before serving, transfer the chicken pieces to a warm dish. Bring the sauce to the boil and add the okra. Stir gently and add the lemon juice and fresh coriander. Cook for 5 minutes, add the remaining spring onions and season to taste with salt and pepper. Pour the sauce and okra over the chicken pieces and scatter the remaining spring onions on top. Serve with polenta and hand the salsa cruda separately.

NOTE: If the okra is cooked for too long, it will become sticky, slimy and lose its bright green colour. If you prefer, the okra can be quickly stir-fried and served as a separate dish.

WINE SUGGESTION: Medium-bodied red.

Chicken Thighs in Pumpkin Seed Sauce

Nuts and seeds are used for thickening and enriching many classic Mexican sauces. Dairy products, such as cream, butter and cheese, were introduced in the 16th century by the Spaniards, but the traditional recipes using nuts have survived almost unchanged to the present day.

Ingredients

8 chicken thighs
salt and freshly ground pepper
2 tablespoons groundnut oil

For the sauce:
110g/4oz pumpkin seeds
2 teaspoons ground cumin
$1/2$ teaspoon paprika
2 green jalapeño or Fresno chillies, seeded
   and finely chopped (see page 194)
290ml/$1/2$ pint chicken stock (see page 188)
4 tablespoons chopped parsley
4 tablespoons chopped coriander
salt and freshly ground pepper

For the garnish:
2 tomatoes, peeled, seeded and finely diced
1 tablespoon chopped parsley

Method

1. Season the chicken thighs with salt and pepper. Heat the oil in a large frying pan and brown the thighs on both sides. Remove from the pan with a draining spoon and set aside.

2. Make the sauce: drain off any excess fat from the pan, and toast the pumpkin seeds over medium heat until lightly browned, about 2 minutes. Add the cumin, paprika and chillies and cook, stirring, for a further minute.

3. Add half the stock to the pan and mix thoroughly, scraping any sediment from the base of the pan. Tip the sauce into a blender, process until smooth, then pour back into the pan. Add the remaining stock, parsley and coriander and season with salt and pepper. Bring to the boil and add the browned thighs, coating well with the sauce. Reduce the heat, then cover and simmer gently for 25 minutes or until the chicken is tender.

4. Transfer to a serving plate and scatter the tomatoes on top. Sprinkle with the parsley and serve warm.

WINE SUGGESTION: Alsace white.

Chicken in Tomatillo and Nut Sauce

Pollo en mole verde, as this traditional Mexican dish is called, is made using tomatillos – small, ripe green tomatoes also known as husks or Mexican green tomatoes. *Moles* are thick sauces made with a combination of nuts, dried or fresh chillies, and other ingredients such as onions, tomatoes and coriander. They play an important part in Mexican cuisine and are the basis of many famous dishes, such as the festive turkey with chocolate and chilli sauce (see page 75).

Ingredients

2 tablespoons sunflower oil
1 x 1.8kg/4lb chicken, jointed into 8 pieces (see page 63)

For the sauce:
2 tablespoons sunflower oil
55g/2oz pumpkin seeds
30g/1oz walnuts
55g/2oz blanched almonds
1 green pepper, skinned, seeded and chopped
2 green Thai chillies, skinned, seeded and chopped (see page 194)
290ml/$\frac{1}{2}$ pint chicken stock (see page 188)
1 x 450g/1lb can tomatillos, drained (see note)
1 large onion, chopped
3 tablespoons chopped coriander
1 garlic clove, crushed
salt and freshly ground black pepper

To serve: baked red rice (see page 159)
jalapeño and lime salsa (see page 177)

Method

1. Heat the oil in a saucepan and brown the chicken pieces, skin side first. Transfer the browned pieces to a bowl and rinse the pan.

2. Make the sauce: heat the oil in a frying pan, add the pumpkin seeds, walnuts and almonds and cook, stirring, over medium heat until they are lightly browned, about 2 minutes.

3. Put the browned nuts, the green pepper and chillies into a blender or food processor and process until smooth. Add the chicken stock, tomatillos, onion, coriander and garlic to the nuts and process to a thick, smooth purée. If the sauce is very thick, add a few more tablespoons of chicken stock.

4. Preheat the oven to 200°C/400°F/gas mark 6.

5. Pour the chilli–nut purée back into the rinsed-out frying pan and cook over moderate heat for about 5 minutes, stirring frequently until all the flavours are well blended. Season to taste with salt and pepper.

6. Toss the chicken pieces in the sauce and arrange them in a shallow gratin dish. Pour over any remaining sauce. Cover and bake in the oven for 35 minutes or until the chicken is cooked through. Serve with the baked red rice and hand the jalapeño and lime salsa separately.

NOTE: Tomatillos can be substituted by green gooseberries with good results. In the classic recipe the chicken is poached gently in chicken stock and then added to the sauce: both versions give delicious results.

WINE SUGGESTION: Full-bodied white.

Spicy Chicken Wings

This is finger food, usually served with cold beer on a summer day. It can also be made with chicken hearts marinated in the same way and grilled on wet bamboo skewers for 5 minutes on each side.

Ingredients

20 chicken wings
oil for frying

For the marinade:
2 garlic cloves, crushed
2 tablespoons sunflower oil
juice of 2 limes
1 teaspoon chilli powder
2 teaspoons sugar
$^1/_2$ teaspoon salt
$^1/_2$ teaspoon paprika

For the garnish:
lemon wedges

Method

1. Wipe the chicken wings with absorbent paper.

2. Mix all the marinade ingredients together. Add the chicken wings and toss them well. Cover and set aside for at least 30 minutes, turning the wings in the marinade once.

3. Heat the oil in a frying pan until a crumb will sizzle vigorously in it. Add the chicken wings in batches of 5 and fry, turning once, until golden brown and cooked. Drain well on absorbent paper.

4. Transfer the wings to a plate lined with absorbent paper, sprinkle with salt and serve at once with the lemon wedges.

NOTE: Alternatively, the wings can be skewered and barbecued.

WINE SUGGESTION: Crisp, dry white.

Chunky Chicken Mousse

This is a very light and lemony chicken mousse – ideal for a buffet or summer lunch.

Ingredients

3 chicken breasts on the bone
1.14 litres/2 pints chicken stock (see page 188)
juice of 1 lemon
8g/$^1/_4$ oz or 2 level teaspoons gelatine
2 tablespoons olive oil
1 medium onion, finely chopped
2 spring onions, finely chopped
1 red pepper, seeded and finely diced
170g/6oz fromage frais
150ml/$^1/_4$ pint double cream
2 tomatoes, peeled, seeded and finely diced
3 tablespoons finely chopped parsley
1 teaspoon Dijon mustard
salt and freshly ground black pepper

For the garnish:
1 small bunch of watercress
lemon wedges

Method

1. Poach the chicken breasts in the stock for 15 minutes or until cooked. Remove from the stock and allow to cool. Remove the meat from the bones, shred and set aside.

2. Put the lemon juice into a small, heavy saucepan. Sprinkle over the gelatine and leave to soak for 10 minutes.

3. Heat the olive oil in a frying pan and sweat the onion, spring onions and red pepper until nearly soft, about 10 minutes.

4. In a large bowl mix the fromage frais, cream, tomatoes, parsley and mustard with the onion mixture. Season to taste with salt and pepper and mix in the chicken shreds.

5. Dissolve the gelatine over gentle heat. When warm, stir into the chicken mixture.

6. Brush a 1.14 litre/2 pint ring mould with a little oil and spoon the mixture into it. Cover and refrigerate for at least 4 hours.

7. Remove the mousse ring from the refrigerator 30 minutes before serving. Unmould on to a serving dish and garnish with the watercress and lemon wedges.

NOTE: The mousse can be made into individual portions using small ramekins.

WINE SUGGESTION: Light white.

Chicken with Shrimp and Peanut Sauce

This unusual dish is called *xinxim de galinha* in Brazil and is a good example of African slave cuisine incorporating native ingredients such as peanuts. The result is as unique and exciting as the cuisine of Bahia, where it comes from.

Ingredients

juice of 3 limes
2 garlic cloves, crushed
salt and freshly ground pepper
1 x 1.8kg/4lb chicken, jointed into 8 pieces (see page 63)
4 tablespoons sunflower oil
1 large onion, finely chopped
2 teaspoons paprika
110g/4oz dried shrimps, ground (see page 277)
55g/2oz roasted peanuts, ground
2 red Thai or Indian chillies, seeded and finely chopped (see page 194)
150ml/$^1/_4$ pint chicken stock (see page 188)
3 tablespoons chopped flat-leaf parsley
3 tablespoons chopped coriander

Method

1. Mix the lime juice, garlic, salt and pepper in a large bowl, then toss the chicken pieces in the mixture. Set aside for 30 minutes to marinate.

2. In a heavy pan heat 2 tablespoons of the oil and sweat the onion until nearly soft, about 10 minutes. Add the paprika, shrimps, peanuts and chillies and cook, stirring, for a further 2 minutes.

3. Heat the remaining oil in a frying pan and brown the chicken pieces. Remove from the pan with a slotted spoon.

4. Add the chicken stock to the onion mixture and bring to the boil. Add the chicken pieces and season with salt and pepper. Reduce the heat, cover and simmer gently until the chicken is tender, about 30 minutes. Turn the chicken pieces once during cooking and add a few tablespoons of stock if necessary.

5. Just before serving, mix in the parsley and coriander and season to taste. The sauce should be quite thick.

VARIATION: This dish can also be made with duck which has been jointed into 6 portions and from which the excess fat has been removed.

WINE SUGGESTION: New World white.

Lime-and-lemon-glazed Poussins

Lime is used extensively as an initial seasoning for poultry, pork and fish in many Latin American countries. In this recipe the lemon juice is mixed with lime and lemon sugar syrup, giving a delicate yet tangy flavour.

Ingredients

4 small poussins
4 tablespoons olive oil
salt and freshly ground black pepper
1 tablespoon roughly chopped thyme
1 tablespoon roughly chopped rosemary
juice of 2 lemons
425g/15oz granulated sugar
1 litre/1 pints water
2 limes
4 lemons

For the garnish:
1 small bunch of watercress

To serve: yellow coconut rice (see page 157)

Method

1. Preheat the oven to 200°C/400°F/gas mark 6.

2. Put the poussins, breast side up, into a roasting tin. Brush with the olive oil and season with salt and pepper. Mix the herbs with the juice of 2 lemons and pour over the poussins. Set aside to marinate for 20 minutes.

3. Put the sugar and water into a large saucepan and cook over gentle heat until the sugar has dissolved completely. Increase the heat and boil for 10 minutes.

4. Pierce the limes and 4 lemons all over with a skewer, place them in the syrup and continue boiling until the syrup has thickened slightly and the fruits are soft with a glassy appearance, about 15 minutes.

5. Remove the fruits from the syrup with a slotted spoon and add to the roasting tin with the poussins. Baste each poussin with 2 tablespoons of the syrup and bake in the oven for 30–35 minutes, basting once, or until the poussins are golden brown and cooked through.

6. Serve each poussin with one whole lemon and half a lime, and garnish with watercress. Spoon a good portion of the juices over the top and serve with the yellow rice. The inside of the lemon and lime can be scooped out and eaten.

NOTE: The remaining lemon and lime syrup can be saved and used to make ice-creams, served warm with cakes or used to sweeten fresh fruit.

WINE SUGGESTION: White Graves.

Turkey in Chocolate and Chilli Sauce

This is the national dish of Mexico and, like most national dishes, it is a little costly and requires extra time in the kitchen, so it is reserved for special occasions and large gatherings. Its Mexican name, *mole poblano de Guajelote*, indicates its origins. *Poblano* means `from Puebla', the capital of the state with the same name, which was founded in 1531 by the Spaniards and is one of the two cities with the most churches in Mexico. In colonial times, when illustrious visitors came to town, all the local convents tried to outdo each other in preparing unusual dishes. Legend has it that Sister Andrea de la Asunción, cook for the Santa Rosa convent, was walking in despair within the walls of the convent not knowing what to cook for the visiting viceroy, when an angel appeared and gave her this recipe. Neither the nun nor the angel can claim the recipe as their own, however, since a dish very similar was served to Hernando Cortes at the court of the Emperor Montezuma I and recorded in the chronicles around 1519.

Ingredients

1 x 3.6kg/8lb turkey, jointed into 8–10 pieces (see page 63)
1 small bunch of parsley, stalks and leaves
4 dried pasilla chillies (see page 199)
4 dried mulato chillies (see page 199)
6 dried ancho chillies (see page 199)
5 tablespoons sunflower oil
3 onions, finely chopped
3 garlic cloves, crushed
85g/3oz raisins
55g/2oz sesame seeds, lightly roasted (see note)
110g/4oz blanched almonds, lightly roasted (see note)
1 teaspoon ground cinnamon
1/2 teaspoon aniseed
1/2 teaspoon cumin seeds
1/2 teaspoon coriander seeds
1/4 teaspoon ground cloves
4 tomatoes, peeled, seeded and chopped
110g/4oz cornmeal
425ml/3/4 pint chicken stock (see page 188)
55g/2oz bitter chocolate, finely chopped or grated

For the garnish:
2 tablespoons toasted sesame seeds

To serve: Mexican rice (see page 158)

Method

1. Put the turkey pieces into a large saucepan. Add the parsley and enough water to cover and bring to the boil. Reduce the heat and simmer for about 2 hours, until the turkey is just cooked. Drain the pieces well and reserve the poaching liquid.

2. Prepare the chillies: cut them in half, remove all the veins and seeds and discard. Tear the chillies into small pieces and put into a small bowl. Pour on enough of the hot poaching liquid to cover and set aside to soak for 40 minutes.

3. In a sauté or frying pan heat 3 tablespoons oil and brown the turkey pieces, a few at a time, on all sides. Set aside while making the sauce.

4. Rinse out the large saucepan, add 2 tablespoons oil and gently cook the onions for 10 minutes. Add the garlic, raisins, toasted sesame seeds, almonds, cinnamon, aniseed, cumin, coriander and cloves and mix thoroughly over medium heat for 10 minutes. Add the tomatoes.

Recipe continued on next page

5. Process the sauce with the chillies and their soaking liquid to a smooth purée. Return to the pan, add the cornmeal and stock and simmer for 20 minutes or until all the ingredients are well blended.

6. Add the chocolate and mix thoroughly. Add the turkey pieces to the sauce and simmer gently for another 30 minutes.

7. To serve, transfer the turkey and sauce to a serving dish and sprinkle with the toasted sesame seeds. Serve with the rice.

NOTE: The nuts can be roasted in a medium hot oven (190°C/375°F/gas mark 5) – about 12 minutes for the almonds and 4 minutes for the sesame seeds. Alternatively, dry-toast them in a frying pan over a medium heat: start with the almonds and when they are almost done (about 8 minutes), add the sesame seeds and stir continuously until they start popping and turn light brown. Remove the toasted nuts from the hot pan or baking sheet and leave to cool.

VARIATION: This dish can also be made with chicken.

WINE SUGGESTION: Full-bodied white.

Turkey Blanquette with Coconut Milk and Chillies

The mixing of chillies and coconut is always a happy one: the coconut milk counteracts the heat of the chillies and also adds lots of flavour to the turkey.

Ingredients

3 garlic cloves, peeled
4 shallots, peeled
570ml/1 pint coconut milk
juice of 2 limes
1$\frac{1}{2}$ teaspoons ground ginger
790g/1 lb 12oz turkey breast meat, cut into
   4cm/1 inch pieces
salt and freshly ground white pepper
4 small red serrano chillies or 2 small Thai
   chillies (see page 197)
1 teaspoon crushed coriander seeds

For the garnish:
2 tablespoons chopped coriander

To serve: green rice (see page 156)

Method

1. In a blender or food processor, purée the garlic and shallots together. Add 150ml/$\frac{1}{4}$ pint of the coconut milk, the lime juice and ground ginger and blend until smooth and creamy.

2. Pour the sauce into a large, shallow pan and arrange the pieces of turkey side by side on the sauce, taking care not to pile them up. Season with salt and pepper. Bring to the boil, reduce the heat, cover and simmer for 5 minutes.

3. Add the remaining coconut milk, the whole chillies and the crushed coriander seeds. Cover and cook over very gentle heat for a further 20 minutes.

4. When ready to serve, remove the turkey pieces with a slotted spoon and keep warm. Reduce the sauce to half its original quantity by boiling rapidly. Season to taste with salt, then pour over the turkey pieces, sprinkle with the fresh coriander and serve with green rice.

WINE SUGGESTION: New World white.

Turkey Escalopes with Chilli Cream Sauce

Although not native to Latin America, coriander is hugely popular throughout the continent and used generously by every cook. To ensure a strong flavour of coriander, add some freshly chopped leaves to any dish just before serving.

Ingredients

900g/2lb turkey breast meat
3 tablespoons plain flour
2 tablespoons sunflower oil

For the sauce:
3 green Fresno or jalapeño chillies, seeded and
    chopped (see page 194)
290ml/^{1}/$_2$ pint double cream
2 shallots, finely chopped
8 tablespoons coarsely chopped
    coriander
1 garlic clove, crushed
salt and freshly ground pepper

For the garnish:
2 tomatoes, peeled, seeded and finely diced

Method

1. Trim the turkey breast and discard any fat. Cut into 8 portions and place the meat between sheets of wet greaseproof paper or cling film. Flatten with a rolling pin or a meat mallet to 1cm/^{1}/$_2$ inch thickness.

2. Coat the turkey lightly in flour, shaking off any excess. Cover and refrigerate while making the sauce.

3. Combine the chillies, cream, shallots, coriander and garlic in a heavy, medium saucepan. Bring to the boil and simmer for about 5 minutes or until the sauce has thickened slightly. Stir the sauce every so often to prevent the cream from catching at the bottom of the pan. Process the sauce in a blender until smooth. Return to the rinsed-out pan. Season to taste with salt and pepper and keep warm.

4. Heat the oil in a large frying pan and brown the turkey quickly on both sides. Reduce the heat and cook for a further 4 minutes or until the meat is just cooked.

5. Place 2 escalopes on each plate, pour the sauce over and garnish with the tomatoes.

NOTE: The chilli sauce can be made up to a day in advance, refrigerated and heated thoroughly just before serving. It is also a very good sauce to serve with grilled fish or chicken.

WINE SUGGESTION: Crisp, dry white.

Duck with Rice and Mint

The Spanish tradition of cooking poultry or meat with rice is also very strong in many Latin American countries. In Spain itself various types of meat, fish and shellfish are cooked with rice and flavoured with saffron. Latin American recipes, on the other hand, tend to use only one type of meat, usually poultry, and the most common flavouring is turmeric, which imparts a bright yellow colour and very subtle flavour to any dish.

Ingredients

1 duck, jointed into 8 pieces
1 tablespoon sunflower oil
2 onions, finely chopped
2 garlic cloves, crushed
285g/10oz long-grain rice, washed and
   drained well
1 teaspoon crushed cumin seeds
1 teaspoon ground turmeric
2 tablespoons finely chopped mint
salt and freshly ground black pepper
4 tablespoons brandy
570ml/1 pint chicken stock (see page188)

To serve: salsa cruda (see page 176)

Method

1. Render (melt) some of the duck fat in a large saucepan and brown the duck pieces, skin side first. Transfer the browned pieces to a bowl and drain all the excess fat from the pan. If necessary, deglaze the pan with a few tablespoons of water and pour the liquid over the duck.

2. Add a dessertspoon of oil to the deglazed pan, then add the onions and cook until the onions are nearly soft. Add the garlic and dry rice and cook, stirring, over medium heat for about 5 minutes. Mix in the cumin and turmeric and cook for a further minute.

3. Add the chopped mint and duck pieces to the pan and mix thoroughly with the rice. Season with salt and pepper and add the brandy and enough stock just to cover. Cover with a tight-fitting lid and cook over medium heat for 20 minutes.

4. Remove the lid and check if the rice and duck are both cooked. If not, add a few tablespoons of hot stock and simmer, covered, for another 5 minutes or until the rice is cooked and all the liquid is absorbed.

5. Serve in the cooking dish or transfer to a warm serving dish and hand the salsa cruda separately.

WINE SUGGESTION: Medium-bodied red.

Meat

MEAT

When the Spanish reached Mexico in 1519, they were amazed to see the variety of wild birds, game and other sources of meat available to the Aztecs. The turkey was already domesticated and much appreciated, together with a species of small dog that was specially bred for cooking. Insects, lizards, young ducks, rabbits, hare and deer were all relatively common parts of the diet, and a taste for the exotic continues to this day, with such things as snakes, armadillos, giant ants and monkeys being eaten with great gusto by many people.

In Peru, the Incas raised llamas, vicuñas and a type of guinea-pig called *cuy* which, even today, still provides more than 50 per cent of the animal protein eaten in Peru. The basis of the Inca and Aztec diet at the time of the Conquest was grains and potatoes; meat was reserved for the aristocracy and royalty.

The Spanish introduced chickens, pigs, cattle, sheep and goats. The pig and chicken became very popular and slowly replaced animals like dogs and lizards on native tables. As with all the other ingredients brought by the *conquistadores*, the new meats were mixed into the local cuisine, adapted into old recipes and became an intrinsic part of the cuisine of Latin America.

Today, with the exception of Argentina and parts of Brazil and Uruguay which are large producers of beef cattle, beef is still reserved for special occasions. Poultry and pork are the most commonly eaten meats in Latin American countries, and in Peru and Ecuador *cuy* is still the most popular.

The average Argentinian eats one pound of beef a day, and in the southern part of Brazil beef is consumed regularly in great quantities. Uruguay produces and eats large quantities of lamb and beef, and Uruguayans enjoy their meat as much as their Argentinian neighbours.

With the introduction of pork, Latin American cooking underwent something of a transformation. Until then, no fat or oil had been used and food was mostly steamed in corn husks or banana leaves. With the pig came fat, and thus began the love of fried food. Today, in almost all Latin American countries, a large percentage of the food is fried, and oil is used generously in most dishes.

The influences in meat recipes range far and wide. From the Arabs, via the Spaniards, came recipes for meat cooked with fruit, raisins, nuts and spices like cinnamon. From the Portuguese in Brazil comes a tradition of rich, slow-cooked stews, as well as a love of fried food. Added to this pot of influences were the culinary traditions of African slaves.

Chillies were the major form of seasoning before the Conquest and remain so today, although in countries where there was a greater European influence, such as Argentina, Costa Rica, Chile and Uruguay, the food tends to be milder.

Unless stated otherwise, all recipes make 4 servings.

Beef and Dried Fruit Stew

The Argentinian pampas (grasslands) produce wonderful beef, and although most of the time it is simply grilled or roasted, some unusual recipes do exist. Certainly brought to Argentina by the Spaniards, this recipe has Middle Eastern influence in the use of dried fruit.

Ingredients

255g/9oz mixed dried fruit, such as prunes and
  apricots
290ml/$^1/_2$ pint beef stock, warmed (see
  page 189)
3 tablespoons sunflower oil
900g/2lb chuck steak, trimmed and cut into
  2.5cm/1 inch cubes
290ml/$^1/_2$ pint dry red wine
15g/$^1/_2$oz butter
1 medium onion, finely chopped
1 garlic clove, crushed
1 carrot, peeled and roughly chopped
salt and freshly ground pepper

To serve: fried rice (see page 155)

Method

1. Put the mixed dried fruit into a bowl with the stock and set aside to soak for 1 hour. Drain, reserving the soaking liquid, and set the fruit aside.

2. In a heavy casserole, heat the oil and brown the meat, a few pieces at a time. Transfer the meat to a bowl. Deglaze the pan with some of the wine and add to the meat.

3. Melt the butter in the deglazed pan, sweat the onion until nearly soft, about 10 minutes. Add the garlic and carrot, the remaining wine and reserved liquid from the dried fruit and bring to the boil. Lower the heat, add the browned meat pieces and simmer, covered, for 2 hours or until the beef is tender.

4. Add the dried fruit and simmer for a further 20 minutes. If the sauce is too thick, add a little more water. Season to taste with salt and pepper and serve with the fried rice.

WINE SUGGESTION: Fruity red.

Two-bean Chilli with Vegetables

Chilli con carne was created in Texas during the 1870s as an interpretation of Mexican cuisine. Mexicans, however, deny any part in the creation of the dish, and anyone who has travelled in Mexico will testify to its non-existence on restaurant menus. Nevertheless, this delicious culinary mistake is worth perpetuating.

Ingredients

2 tablespoons sunflower oil
2 large onions, chopped
4 garlic cloves, crushed
675g/1¹/₂lb minced beef
2 teaspoons mild chilli powder
2 teaspoons ground cumin
¹/₂ teaspoon cayenne pepper
1 x 800g/1lb 13oz can chopped tomatoes with juice
570ml/1 pint beef stock (see page 189)
2 medium potatoes, peeled and cut into 2.5cm/1inch cubes
1 large carrot, peeled and cut into 2.5cm/1inch cubes
2 celery stalks, diced
1 red pepper, seeded and diced
1 x 4 25g/15oz can red kidney beans, drained and rinsed
1 x 425g/15oz can pinto beans, drained and rinsed
salt and freshly ground pepper
¹/₂ teaspoon chilli sauce (optional)

To serve: fried rice (see page 155)

Method

1. Heat the oil in a large pan. Add the onion and cook until the onions are nearly soft, about 10 minutes. Add the garlic and minced beef in batches and cook, stirring constantly with a fork to break up any lumps.

2. Stir in the chilli powder, cumin and cayenne and cook for 3 minutes.

3. Mix in the tomatoes, stock, potatoes, carrot, celery and pepper and bring to the boil. Reduce the heat, cover and simmer for 40 minutes.

4. Stir in the beans, season to taste with salt, pepper and chilli sauce and simmer for a further 15 minutes, or until all the flavours are well blended. Serve with fried rice.

NOTE: This recipe is best made a day in advance and then reheated. Any leftovers can be used in pies, empanadas, pancake stack pie (see page 91), tamales or tacos.

WINE SUGGESTION: Full-bodied red.

Grilled Steak with Spiced Parsley Sauce

Parsley sauce is a traditional Argentinian accompaniment to grilled or roasted meat. With 97 per cent of the population claiming European descent, and a large percentage of that from the UK, it is no surprise to find Worcestershire sauce as an ingredient in this recipe.

Ingredients

4 x 170g/6oz rump or sirloin steaks

For the marinade:
4 tablespoons white wine
2 garlic cloves, crushed
1 tablespoon white rum
2 tablespoons Worcestershire sauce
6 peppercorns
1 teaspoon chopped marjoram
1 bay leaf

For the parsley sauce:
8 tablespoons sunflower oil
4 tablespoons white wine vinegar
1 red onion, chopped
1/2 garlic clove, crushed
4 tablespoons chopped flat-leaf parsley
1 teaspoon finely chopped oregano
1/2 teaspoon cayenne pepper
dash chilli sauce
salt and freshly ground pepper

Method

1. Trim the steaks of all excess fat.

2. Combine all the marinade ingredients together. Put the steaks in a shallow dish, pour the marinade over them and refrigerate for 2 hours, turning once.

3. Mix all the sauce ingredients together in a blender. Season to taste with salt and pepper and transfer to a bowl. Leave the sauce at room temperature to develop its flavour for up to 2 hours before serving.

4. Heat the grill to its highest setting. Drain and pat dry the meat. Discard the marinade.

5. Grill the steaks to your preferred rareness, turning once. Season with salt and pepper. Transfer the meat to a hot serving plate and serve at once with the parsley sauce.

NOTE: The steaks can also be cooked on a very hot griddle or in a frying pan.

WINE SUGGESTION: Full-bodied, dry red.

Beef Casserole in Dried Chilli Sauce

The much-loved dried ancho chilli from Mexico is the chief seasoning in the sauce for this rich and aromatic casserole.

Ingredients

675g/1¹/₂lb chuck steak, trimmed
1 tablespoon sunflower oil

For the sauce:
3 dried ancho chillies (see page 199)
190ml/¹/₃ pint beef stock (see page 189)
good pinch crushed chillies or mild chilli powder
1 x 800g/1lb 13oz can chopped tomatoes
2 large onions, chopped
2 garlic cloves, crushed
1 tablespoon tomato purée
2 tablespoons sunflower oil
¹/₂ teaspoon ground cumin
1 tablespoon flour
1 teaspoon chopped oregano
¹/₂ teaspoon sugar
salt and freshly ground pepper

For the garnish:
2 tablespoons chopped parsley

To serve: sweet potato purée (see page 146)

Method

1. Preheat the oven to 150°C/300°F/gas mark 2.

2. Cut the beef into 3cm/1¹/₂ inch cubes, discarding any fat.

3. Heat the oil in a thick-bottomed casserole and brown the beef pieces very well, a few at a time. Put them into a bowl as they are done. If the bottom of the pan becomes very dark or too dry, deglaze it by pouring in a little stock and scraping off any sediment stuck to the bottom; bring it to the boil and pour over the meat. Heat up a little more oil and continue to brown the meat. When it is all browned, repeat the deglazing process.

4. Remove the stalks and cut the dried chillies in half. Brush out their seeds and cut away any large ribs. Tear into small pieces, put them into a bowl and pour over the remaining hot stock. Leave to soak for 20 minutes, then drain, reserving the liquid.

5. In a blender or food processor mix the crushed chillies, soaked chillies, tomatoes, onions, garlic and tomato purée and process until smooth.

6. Heat 2 tablespoons of oil in the rinsed-out pan and cook the cumin for 1 minute. Add the flour and oregano and cook for a further minute. Add the tomato mixture and the reserved soaking liquid from the chillies. Cook for 10 minutes over medium heat, stirring from time to time. Stir in the sugar and season with salt and pepper.

7. Put the meat and sauce together in an ovenproof casserole dish. Cover and cook in the oven for 2¹/₂ hours or until the meat is very tender. Mix in 1 tablespoon of the parsley and transfer to a serving dish. Sprinkle with the remaining parsley. Serve with the sweet potato purée.

WINE SUGGESTION: Full-bodied, fruity red.

Minced Beef with Apples, Olives and Almonds

This is a festive version of picadillo (see page 92) and has an exquisite flavour resulting from the sweetness of the raisins and apples and the heat of the chillies.

Ingredients

2 tablespoons sunflower oil
1 large onion, finely chopped
675g/1¹/₂lb minced beef
2 red chillies, seeded and coarsely chopped (see page 194)
1 garlic clove, crushed
3 tomatoes, peeled, seeded and chopped
2 green apples, peeled, cored and coarsely chopped
55g/2oz raisins
10 green olives, pitted and halved
¹/₂ teaspoon ground cinnamon
pinch ground cloves
salt and freshly ground black pepper
55g/2oz flaked almonds

To serve: refried beans (see page 151)
yellow coconut rice (see page 157)

Method

1. Heat the oil in a large saucepan, add the onion and cook until soft, about 10 minutes. Add the minced beef in batches and cook, stirring constantly with a fork to break up any lumps.

2. Add the chillies and garlic and cook for 5 minutes.

3. Reduce the heat and add the tomatoes, apples, raisins, olives, cinnamon and cloves and season with salt and pepper to taste. Simmer, covered, for 40 minutes, stirring occasionally.

4. Dry-roast the almonds in a frying pan over medium heat, stirring continuously until they are light brown.

5. Stir half the almonds into the meat mixture and transfer to a warmed serving dish. Scatter the remaining almonds on top and serve with refried beans and yellow coconut rice.

NOTE: Like picadillo, this recipe can be used as a stuffing for tamales, pies, turnovers and suchlike.

WINE SUGGESTION: Fruity, full-bodied red.

Spicy Shredded Beef

The beef produced on the plains around the Orinoco River in Venezuela and Colombia can be quite tough, so the cooks from both countries have developed numerous recipes for tenderizing the meat without losing any of the flavour. This recipe comes from Venezuela and is mildly hot.

Ingredients

675g/1^1/$_2$lb piece flank steak
425ml/^{3}/$_4$ pint beef stock (see page 189)

For the sauce:
3 tablespoons sunflower oil
2 onions, finely chopped
2 garlic cloves, crushed
^{1}/$_2$ teaspoon ground cumin
^{1}/$_2$ teaspoon ground coriander
4 red Indian chillies, seeded and finely chopped
  (see page 194)
1 x 800g/1lb 13oz can chopped tomatoes
1 teaspoon tomato purée
^{1}/$_2$ teaspoon sugar
2 bay leaves
salt and freshly ground black pepper
2 tablespoons chopped coriander

For the garnish:
2 tablespoons chopped parsley

Method

1. Put the meat into a heavy saucepan and cover with the stock. Bring to the boil, reduce the heat, cover and simmer until the meat is very tender, about 2 hours. Remove the meat from the pan and allow to cool. Reserve the cooking stock.

2. Heat the oil and sweat the onions until soft. Add the garlic, cumin, coriander, chillies, tomatoes, tomato purée, sugar, bay leaves and salt and pepper and cook for 5 minutes. Add 150ml/^{1}/$_4$ pint of the reserved stock and simmer, uncovered, for 35 minutes or until the sauce is slightly thickened.

3. Discard the bay leaves and keep the sauce warm.

4. Transfer the cooled meat to a carving board and shred, using a fork. Mix the shredded meat and coriander into the sauce and cook over medium heat for 5 minutes or until the meat is heated through.

5. Transfer to a serving plate and sprinkle with the chopped parsley.

NOTE: The meat can be finely sliced rather than shredded, if you prefer. It can also be cooked the day before and assembled just before serving.

WINE SUGGESTION: Full-bodied red.

Brazilian Meat and Black Bean Stew

Originally an African slave concoction, *feijoada* is now the national dish of Brazil. Where pig's ears, trotters, tail and other minor cuts were once slowly cooked together in a pot with black beans, today better cuts of smoked and salted pork, dried meat and sausages are used, making a deliciously rich and unique dish. Traditionally, it is eaten for lunch on Saturdays and followed by a long siesta. It is a costly and time-consuming dish to prepare, so is reserved for special occasions and large parties. This recipe will feed up to 12 people if all the accompaniments are served with it.

Ingredients

900g/2lb black beans, soaked overnight
450g/1lb smoked chorizo sausages
450g/1lb sirloin beef, in one piece
170g/6oz bacon (prime hock), in one piece
450g/1lb smoked loin of pork, in one piece
1 fresh pig's trotter (optional)
4 garlic cloves, crushed
1 bouquet garni
2 bay leaves, crumbled
1 bunch of spring onions, white and green
   parts, chopped
4 tablespoons chopped parsley
salt and freshly ground pepper

To serve: shredded kale (see page 145)
fried rice (see page 155)
creoja salsa (see page 179)
6 oranges, peeled and sliced
toasted cassava meal (see page 247)

Method

1. Preheat the oven to 200°C/400°F/gas mark 6.

2. Drain and rinse the beans under running water. Put into a large, ovenproof saucepan and cover with water (do not add salt as this toughens the skins). Bring to the boil and continue boiling for 10 minutes before reducing the heat to a simmer. Cook gently for 30–35 minutes or until the bean are just cooked. Drain the beans and discard the cooking liquid.

3. Put all the meat cuts and the trotter (if using) into a roasting tin and roast until well done. After 20 minutes remove the sausages and bacon and continue cooking the remaining cuts for a further 20 minutes.

4. Once all the meat is cooked, cut it into large chunks and cut the trotter in half. Reserve the roasting oil and reduce the oven to 150°C/300°F/gas mark 2.

5. Place all the meat, the garlic, bouquet garni, bay leaves, half the spring onions and parsley, the beans, salt and pepper in a large ovenproof casserole dish, stir thoroughly and add enough water to cover the beans and meat completely. Cover and cook in the oven for 1 1/2 hours. After 45 minutes check and add more water if the stew is getting dry. The meat and beans should be covered with liquid. Just before serving, remove the bouquet garni and mix the remaining parsley and spring onions. Season to taste with salt and pepper. The meat and beans should be very tender and the liquid syrupy.

6. Add 3 tablespoons of liquid from the beans to the creoja salsa.

7. To serve: A buffet table is the best way to serve a faijoada. Place the bean and meat stew in the centre and arrange the other dishes around it. Serve with pickled chillies and beer.

WINE SUGGESTION: Spicy, oak-aged red.

Pancake Stack Pie

This is a delicious dish where all the ingredients can be prepared in advance and assembled just before cooking.

Ingredients

1 quantity crêpes/pancakes (see page 219)
$^{1}/_{2}$ quantity two-bean chilli (see page 85)
1 quantity spicy tomato sauce (see page 181)
30g/1oz grated Cheddar cheese
oil for greasing

To serve: mixed green salad

Method

1. Preheat the oven to 200°C/400°F/gas mark 6. Lightly grease a 30cm/12 inch round, ovenproof dish.

2. Make 10 pancakes 25cm/10 inches in diameter, according to the recipe.

3. Start layering the pancakes, spreading 4–5 tablespoons bean chilli and 1 tablespoon sauce between each layer. Finish with a pancake and pour the remaining sauce around the stack. Sprinkle the top pancake with the cheese and bake in the oven for about 25 minutes or until the cheese is golden brown and the sauce is bubbly and very hot. Serve at once with a mixed green salad.

VARIATION: To make a vegetarian dish use drunken beans (see page 152) for the filling, omitting the bacon in the recipe and increasing the cheese to 85g/3oz. Sprinkle some cheese on top of the beans in each layer.

WINE SUGGESTION: Fruity red.

Picadillo

This dish, sometimes known as *picadinho*, is found throughout Latin America, where it is also called `hangover hash' because it is believed to cure the after-effects of alcohol. There are many variations: pork, sausages, potatoes, eggs and carrots can be added according to taste and budget. Picadillo is used in empanadas, tacos, burritos, turnovers and pies, or eaten with beans and rice.

Ingredients

1 tablespoon sunflower oil
1 large onion, finely chopped
2 garlic cloves, crushed
675g/1^1/2lb minced beef
2 tablespoons tomato purée
1 green Kenyan or Fresno chilli, seeded and
    finely chopped (see page 194)
1 x 400g/14oz can chopped tomatoes
^{1}/2 teaspoon ground cumin
1 teaspoon chopped oregano
2 tablespoons chopped parsley
3 spring onions, finely chopped
pinch of sugar
salt and freshly ground black pepper
150ml/^{1}/4 pint beef stock (see page 189)
1 large potato, peeled and cut into small cubes

Method

1. Heat the oil in a large pan and add the onions and garlic. Cook until the onions are nearly soft, about 10 minutes.

2. Add the minced beef in batches and cook it, stirring constantly with a fork to break up any lumps.

3. Stir in the tomato purée, chilli, chopped tomatoes, cumin, oregano, half the parsley and spring onions, the sugar and mix well. Season to taste with salt and pepper, bring to the boil, reduce the heat and cook, covered, for 20 minutes.

4. Add the beef stock and potato and cook, uncovered, for another 20 minutes, or until the potato is tender and there is very little liquid left. Mix in the remaining parsley and spring onions and season to taste with salt and pepper. Serve hot or use to fill empanadas, pies and suchlike.

WINE SUGGESTION: Full-bodied New World red.

Veal Chops in Chilli Paste

There are not many recipes for veal in Latin America and Argentina with its Italian ancestry is the country where it is mostly eaten.

Ingredients

4 x 200–225g/7–8oz veal chops
juice of 2 limes
2 teaspoons chilli powder
2 teaspoons paprika
1 teaspoon ground cumin
5 garlic cloves, crushed
4 tablespoons olive oil
salt
150ml/¼ pint chicken stock (see page 188)
2 tablespoons chopped coriander

To serve: root vegetable gratin (see page 134)

Method

1. Trim the veal chops of any excess fat. Season with 4 tablespoons of the lime juice, then cover and refrigerate for 1 hour.

2. Combine the chilli powder, paprika, cumin, garlic and half the oil. Brush over both sides of the chops and season with salt.

3. Heat the remaining oil in a frying pan, add the veal and cook for about 5 minutes on each side, turning only once. The meat should be tender and browned all over.

4. Remove the meat from the pan and add the chicken stock. Scrape any sediment from the bottom of the pan. Add the remaining lime juice and the coriander. Season, then pour over the meat and serve at once with the root vegetable gratin.

WINE SUGGESTION: Fruity red with good acidity.

Roast Breast of Veal Stuffed with Jalapeño Purée

This recipe combines the delicate flavour of veal with the popular jalapeño chilli. It also works well with pork.

Ingredients

1 x 1.35kg/3lb boned breast of veal
30g/1oz butter
2 tablespoons sunflower oil
250ml/¹/₂ pint orange juice

For the purée:
8 jalapeño or Fresno green chillies (see
  page 196)
6 tablespoons olive oil
juice of 1 lime
2 garlic cloves, crushed
1 big bunch of flat-leaf parsley
4 tablespoons fresh breadcrumbs
salt and freshly ground pepper

To serve: sweet potato purée (see page 146)

Method

1. Heat the grill to its highest setting. Preheat the oven to 180°C/350°F/gas mark 4.

2. Make the purée: put the whole chillies on to a baking tray and grill, turning them until the skin is blistered and charred. Put the chillies into a plastic bag and set aside until cool enough to handle.

3. Using rubber gloves, remove the skins and seeds from the chillies and discard. Put the chillies, olive oil, lime juice, garlic, parsley leaves and breadcrumbs in a blender or food processor and process to a purée. Season with salt and pepper.

4. Place the veal on a work surface, open it up and spread the purée inside. Roll up the meat and tie it into a suitable shape for roasting.

5. Heat the butter and oil together in a roasting tin, add the meat and cook in the oven for 30 minutes. Add the orange juice and roast for about 50 minutes more or until the meat is done, basting frequently with the pan juices.

6. Remove the veal from the roasting pan and keep warm. Season the sauce with salt and pepper and strain into a small pan. Slice the meat and arrange on a serving plate, reheat the sauce and spoon over the meat. Serve with sweet potato purée and a green vegetable.

WINE SUGGESTION: Full-bodied red.

Hot Pork Roast

Pork is the favourite meat in many Latin American countries, and country cooks still tend to use pig fat for cooking. In this recipe a mixture of orange juice and honey gives the pork a golden crust and sweet sauce, while the chillies impart a gentle heat.

Ingredients

1.35kg/3lb boned and rolled foreloin of pork

For the marinade:
grated zest and juice of 2 lemons
juice of 1 orange
1 teaspoon tomato purée
2 tablespoons clear honey
2 green Dutch chillies, finely chopped (see page 194)
1 tablespoon ground ginger
1 teaspoon freshly chopped thyme
2 garlic cloves, crushed
salt and freshly ground pepper
8 tablespoons water
2 tablespoons sunflower oil

To serve: potato, cheese and cayenne puffs (see page 136)

Method

1. In a small saucepan mix together the lemon zest and juice, orange juice, tomato purée, honey, chillies, ginger, thyme, garlic and salt and pepper. Bring to the boil, remove from the heat and set aside to cool.

2. Put the pork into a glass bowl or dish and pour the marinade over it. Cover and refrigerate for 8–12 hours, turning the meat occasionally.

3. Preheat the oven to 200°C/400°F/gas mark 6.

4. Remove the meat from the marinade and pat dry with absorbent paper. Put the marinade and water into a roasting tin.

5. Heat the oil in a frying pan, brown the meat evenly, then put into the roasting tin with the marinade. Cook for 1 1/4 hours (see page 63), basting the meat frequently with the marinade. Serve with the potato puffs and hand the marinade as a sauce separately.

WINE SUGGESTION: Dry white.

Spicy Pork with Root Vegetable Gratin

The use of citrus juice to tenderize and flavour meat dishes is common in many Latin American recipes. Orange and lime juice are the most commonly used citrus fruits, but in more tropical parts, pineapple juice and papaya extract are used as well.

Ingredients

2 x 340g/12oz pork fillets
5 garlic cloves, crushed
1 teaspoon ground annatto or achiote (see note and page 274)
2 teaspoons ground cumin
$^{1}/_{2}$ teaspoon cayenne pepper
290ml/$^{1}/_{2}$ pint white wine vinegar
150ml/$^{1}/_{4}$ pint unsweetened orange juice
2 tablespoons sunflower oil
salt and freshly ground pepper
2 tablespoons chopped coriander

To serve: root vegetable gratin (see page 134)

Method

1. Trim the fillets and put into a glass bowl.

2. Mix the garlic, annatto or achiote, cumin, cayenne, vinegar and orange juice together. Add to the fillets and mix thoroughly to coat. Cover and place in the refrigerator for 8 hours or overnight.

3. Strain and reserve the marinade. Heat the oil in a large pan with a well-fitting lid. Fry the pork fillets until golden brown all over. Add the reserved marinade, cover and cook over very gentle heat until the meat is tender, about 35 minutes.

4. Transfer the fillets from the pan to a carving board and slice. Season the sauce with salt and pepper and mix in the chopped coriander. Serve the pork with the sauce and root vegetable gratin.

NOTE: If neither annatto nor achiote is available, ground turmeric may be substituted.

WINE SUGGESTION: Full-bodied white.

Sweet Roast Pork

The combination of milk and vinegar (or sometimes lemon juice) in this recipe is unusual but easily explained. The acid in the vinegar curdles the milk and tenderizes the meat. In this Peruvian recipe the addition of raisins, cinnamon and butter adds sweetness and richness to the exotic character of the dish.

Ingredients

900g/2lb boned and rolled shoulder of pork, skin left on
salt and freshly ground pepper

For the marinade:
190ml/^{1}/$_3$ pint dry white wine
4 whole cloves
55g/2oz soft light brown sugar
55g/2oz unsalted butter, melted
190ml/^{1}/$_3$ pint full-fat milk
^{1}/$_2$ teaspoon ground cinnamon
^{1}/$_2$ teaspoon ground nutmeg
110g/4oz raisins

Method

1. Season the meat with salt and pepper and score the skin with a sharp knife.

2. In a large, non-metallic bowl combine the wine, cloves and sugar. Add the meat and turn it well to coat with the marinade. Cover and refrigerate overnight.

3. Preheat the oven to 180°C/350°F/gas mark 4.

4. Remove the meat from the marinade, pat dry with absorbent paper and put into a roasting tin.

5. Add the melted butter, milk, cinnamon, nutmeg and raisins to the marinade, mix thoroughly and pour over the meat. Bake for 1^3/$_4$ hours (see page 63), basting every so often until the pork is tender.

6. Transfer the meat to a carving board and cut into slices. Season the sauce to taste with salt and pepper and serve with the pork.

NOTE: This recipe works equally well with rolled breast of veal.

WINE SUGGESTION: Dry white.

Pork Chops with Pineapple and Lime Salsa

Pork chops are not particularly common in Latin American cuisine as the loin joint, from which they are cut, is usually cooked whole. If you prefer, this dish can be made using small pork tenderloins.

Ingredients

4 x 170g/6oz pork loin chops
30g/1oz butter
1 tablespoon sunflower oil

For the marinade:
2 tablespoons sunflower oil
4 tablespoons white wine vinegar
1 garlic clove, crushed
$1/2$ teaspoon mild chilli powder
1 teaspoon freshly chopped oregano
pinch caster sugar

For the salsa:
5 tablespoons sunflower oil
juice of 2 limes
3 tablespoons chopped flat-leaf parsley
2 celery stalks, finely diced
1 red pepper, seeded and finely diced
1 fresh pineapple, cut into small cubes
$1/2$ teaspoon cayenne pepper
1 red Fresno or Kenyan chilli, seeded and finely diced (see page 194)
salt and freshly ground pepper

Method

1. Prepare the chops by nicking through the fat at regular intervals with a sharp knife.

2. Mix all the marinade ingredients together in a bowl. Turn the chops in the marinade and set aside at room temperature for 1 hour, or refrigerate overnight.

3. Combine all the salsa ingredients and season to taste with salt and pepper. Keep at room temperature until needed.

4. Remove the pork chops from the marinade, pat dry with absorbent paper and discard the marinade.

5. Heat the butter and oil together in a heavy frying pan until very hot. Add the pork chops. Brown well on both sides, reduce the heat and cook for a further 5 minutes or until the meat is cooked. Season well with salt and pepper. Serve hot with the pineapple salsa.

NOTE: The salsa should not be made more than 3 hours in advance as it loses its crunch if allowed to stand.

VARIATION: Veal chops can also be used in this recipe.

WINE SUGGESTION: Full-bodied white.

Pork, Allspice and Onion Casserole with Haricot Beans

Beans and pork are two of the best-loved foods in South America; in fact, a meal without beans is considered hardly worth eating. Allspice is widely used in Central America in savoury as well as sweet dishes.

Ingredients

3 tablespoons sunflower oil
675g/1$\frac{1}{2}$lb stewing pork, cut into 3cm/1$\frac{1}{2}$ inch cubes
450g/1lb Spanish onions, thinly sliced
2 teaspoons ground allspice
1 teaspoon ground cumin
$\frac{1}{2}$ teaspoon paprika
150ml/$\frac{1}{4}$ pint white wine
150ml/$\frac{1}{4}$ pint chicken stock (see page 188)
2 x 5cm/2 inch cinnamon sticks
salt and freshly ground pepper
1 x 400g/14oz can haricot beans, rinsed and drained

For the garnish:
2 tablespoons chopped parsley

Method

1. Preheat the oven to 170°C/325°F/gas mark 3.

2. Heat half the oil in a frying pan and brown the pork pieces evenly. Transfer the meat to an ovenproof casserole dish.

3. In the same frying pan, cook the onions until golden brown, but not burnt, adding a little more oil if necessary. Add the allspice, cumin and paprika and fry for a further 30 seconds. Spoon the browned onions and spices over the meat.

4. Add the wine and stock to the frying pan, bring to the boil and using a wooden spoon scrape any sediment from the bottom of the pan and add to the casserole dish. Add the cinnamon sticks and season with salt and pepper. Cover tightly and cook in the oven for about 1$\frac{1}{2}$ hours, or until the meat is very tender.

5. Remove the cinnamon sticks and discard. Add the haricot beans to the meat, mix well and cook, covered, for a further 15 minutes. Season to taste with salt and pepper. Sprinkle with the parsley and serve.

NOTE: This is a `dryish' casserole dish.

WINE SUGGESTION: Dry, light white.

Shredded Pork

This recipe is used for stuffing tamales, tacos and empanadas, or eaten with beans and rice.

Ingredients

15g/½oz butter
1 tablespoon sunflower oil
3 x 225g/8oz pork fillets
1 onion, thinly sliced
½ teaspoon ground cumin
1 x 225g/8oz can chopped tomatoes
1 garlic clove, crushed
1 teaspoon chopped oregano
2 tablespoons chopped spring onions
2 tablespoons chopped parsley
salt and freshly ground black pepper

Method

1. Preheat the oven to 180°C/375°F/gas mark 4.

2. Heat the butter and oil in a frying pan until hot. Add the pork and brown quickly all over. Transfer to a roasting tin and cook in the oven for 25–30 minutes, or until the fillets are tender.

3. Place the onion and cumin in the same pan used for frying the pork and cook slowly until the onion is nearly soft, about 10 minutes. Add the tomatoes, garlic, oregano, spring onions, parsley and seasoning. Bring the sauce to the boil, reduce the heat and cook, uncovered, for 20 minutes.

4. Remove the pork from the oven and set aside to cool. When cold, shred the meat or slice it thinly with a carving knife. Add to the sauce and reheat thoroughly before serving.

WINE SUGGESTION: Dry white.

Lamb Stew with Red Peppers

In many Ecuadorean recipes mashed bananas are added at the last minute to thicken sauces. They give a rich, sweet texture and flavour to any dish.

Ingredients

675g/1½lb lean boneless lamb, cut into
   3cm/1½ inch cubes
3 large garlic cloves, crushed
salt and freshly ground black pepper
4 tablespoons sunflower oil
4 large red peppers, seeded and cut into
   2.5cm/1 inch strips
2 red jalapeño or Fresno chillies, seeded and
   finely chopped (see page 194)
1 teaspoon ground cumin
2 limes, washed and cut into quarters
290ml/½ pint dry white wine
150ml/¼ pint chicken stock (see page 188)
3 tablespoons roughly chopped coriander
2 large ripe bananas, mashed

To serve: green rice (see page 156)

Method

1. Season the lamb with the garlic, salt, pepper and 1 tablespoon of the oil. Set aside at room temperature to marinate for 30 minutes.

2. In a large frying pan, heat the remaining oil and fry the lamb in batches until brown. Remove to a large saucepan.

3. Add the peppers, chillies and cumin to the frying pan and fry for 3 minutes. Add to the lamb.

4. Add the wine and stock to the frying pan, bring to the boil and stir well with a wooden spoon, scraping the sediment from the bottom of the pan; pour the liquid over the lamb. Add the limes and peppers and simmer, covered, for about 1 hour, or until the lamb is very tender.

5. Just before serving, take out the lime quarters, add the coriander and mashed bananas and mix well. Cook for a further 5 minutes, stirring constantly. Season to taste with salt and pepper and serve with the green rice.

NOTE: *If you prefer, the meat can be put into an ovenproof casserole and cooked at 170°C/325°F/ gas mark 3 for 1½ hours.*

WINE SUGGESTION: Full-bodied red.

Lamb Roast with Mint and Fried Pinto Beans

Lamb is eaten most frequently in Chile, Uruguay and Argentina, where a large number of European immigrants settled in the 19th and early 20th centuries. Uruguay produces very good quality lamb and beef. The use of mint comes from Spain, to which it was introduced from the Middle East.

Ingredients

1 x 1.8kg/4lb leg of lamb, boned
85g/3oz butter, softened
8 garlic cloves, crushed
salt and freshly ground pepper
4 tablespoons finely chopped fresh mint
290ml/^{1}/$_2$ pint white wine

For the beans:
2 tablespoons sunflower oil
1 small onion, finely chopped
1 garlic clove, crushed
255g/9oz pinto beans, cooked
dash chilli sauce
salt and freshly ground pepper
2 tablespoons finely chopped parsley
3 spring onions, white and green parts,
   chopped

To serve: raisin and walnut rice (see page 155)

Method

1. Preheat the oven to 170ºC/325ºF/gas mark 3.

2. Trim the lamb well. Mix the butter, garlic, salt and pepper and chopped mint to a paste. Cut the leg to open flat and spread the paste on the inside. Roll it up and tie at 5cm/2 inch intervals with string.

3. Put the meat into a roasting tin, add the white wine and roast in the preheated oven for 1 hour (15 minutes per 450g/1lb) for rare lamb. Baste every 20 minutes with the pan juices.

4. To prepare the beans: heat the oil in a large frying pan, add the onion and cook until nearly soft, about 15 minutes. Add the garlic, cooked beans, chilli sauce and season to taste with salt and pepper. Cook over medium heat until the beans begin to catch at the bottom of the pan. Add the parsley and spring onions, and keep warm until the lamb is cooked.

5. When the lamb is done, transfer to a warm serving dish. Sieve the juices from the roasting tin into the frying pan with the beans and mix thoroughly. Serve the meat with the beans and raisin and walnut rice.

WINE SUGGESTION: Full-bodied red.

MEAT

SERVES 6-8

Braised Shoulder of Lamb in Dried Chilli Sauce

Chipotle chillies are smoked red jalapeños, which impart a delicious tannic and earthy flavour to this sauce. They can be quite hot, so start with two chillies and if the result is not hot enough, add some more.

Ingredients

1 shoulder of lamb, boned
2 garlic cloves, crushed
30g/1oz butter, softened
2 tablespoons chopped parsley
1 teaspoon chopped oregano
salt and freshly ground pepper
2 tablespoons sunflower oil

For the sauce:
2 dried chipotle chillies (see page 198)
50ml/1pint chicken stock (see page 188)
2 tablespoons sunflower oil
3 onions, chopped
1 tablespoon ground cumin
2 teaspoons tomato purée
1 x 800g/1lb 13oz can chopped tomatoes
1 teaspoon ground rice or polenta flour
3 tablespoons chopped parsley

Method

1. Trim the lamb of any excess fat, leaving a thin layer on the outside. Mix the garlic, butter, parsley and oregano to a paste. Open out the lamb, season the inside and spread the garlic paste on one half. Using thin string, sew up the lamb, but not too tightly. Set aside while making the sauce.

2. Break the chillies into pieces, discarding the stems and seeds. Place in a small pan with the stock, cover and simmer for about 15 minutes or until the chillies are soft. Blend or process the chillies with the liquid.

3. Heat the oil in a large heavy pan and brown the lamb on all sides. Remove the lamb from the pan, pour in a few tablespoons of chicken stock and chilli liquid and scrape up any brown particles. Reserve the liquid.

4. Make the sauce: in a saucepan large enough to fit the lamb, heat the oil and add the onions. Fry quickly until the onions are lightly browned but not burnt. Add the cumin, tomato purée, reserved chilli sauce, the liquid from deglazing the pan, the chopped tomatoes and salt and pepper.

5. Bring to the boil, add to the lamb and baste well with the sauce. Reduce the heat, cover and cook over gentle heat for 1–2 hours or until the lamb is really tender, turning once or twice during cooking.

6. Remove the lamb from the sauce and carefully remove the string. Lift the lamb on to a warm serving dish.

7. Blend the ground rice or polenta flour with 2 tablespoons of the sauce. Pour it back into the roasting pan, add the parsley and stir until the mixture boils and thickens slightly. Season to taste with salt and pepper and serve with the lamb.

WINE SUGGESTION: Full-bodied red.

Lamb Brochettes with Mango and Avocado Salsa

Brochettes are hugely popular in many Latin American countries and sometimes involve unusual ingredients – spicy ox hearts in Peru and chicken hearts in Brazil. Fish, prawns, beef, chicken and pork brioches are found in markets and on street corners throughout the continent and they are delicious.

Ingredients

900g/2lb lamb, trimmed and cut into 3cm/1^1/$_2$
   inch cubes
4 wooden skewers, soaked in water for at least
   20 minutes
1 teaspoon paprika

For the marinade:
juice of 4 limes
same quantity of olive oil
^{1}/$_2$ teaspoon coarse sea salt
1 teaspoon freshly chopped marjoram
salt and freshly ground pepper

To serve: mango and avocado salsa (see
   page 176)

Method

1. Mix the marinade ingredients in a bowl. Add the lamb cubes and stir to coat well. Cover and leave to marinate for 3 hours in a cool place, turning occasionally.

2. Heat the grill to its highest setting.

3. Thread the lamb on to 4 large skewers. Baste with the marinade and sprinkle with the paprika. Grill for 10 minutes for pink lamb or 15 minutes for well done. Turn the skewers and baste the meat once or twice during grilling. Serve at once with the mango and avocado salsa.

WINE SUGGESTION: Light, fruity red.

Rabbit Stew in Coconut Milk

This recipe comes from Venezuela, where coconut is used extensively in cooking savoury dishes. Venezuela is very rich in different food produce because of its geographical position: it has the Andes on its border with Colombia, the rain forest on its border with Brazil and the Caribbean Sea along its coastline.

Ingredients

1 rabbit, skinned, cleaned and jointed into
   8 pieces
salt and freshly ground pepper
2 tablespoons olive oil
30g/1oz butter
2 garlic cloves, crushed
1 large onion, finely chopped
1 red Kenyan or jalapeno chilli, seeded and
   diced (see page 194)
1 x 800g/1lb 13oz can chopped tomatoes
$1/2$ teaspoon paprika
290ml/$1/2$ pint chicken stock (see page 188)
110g/4oz creamed coconut
2 tablespoons finely chopped parsley

To serve: fried rice (see page 155)

Method

1. Season the rabbit pieces with salt and pepper.

2. Heat the oil and brown the rabbit pieces all over. Set aside while making the sauce.

3. In a large saucepan melt the butter, add the garlic and onion and sweat over medium heat until the onion is nearly soft, about 10 minutes.

4. Add the chilli, tomatoes, paprika and stock and bring slowly to the boil. Season with salt and pepper and add the rabbit pieces to the sauce. Cook, covered, over medium low heat until the rabbit is tender, about 1 hour.

5. Lift the rabbit pieces on to a warm serving dish. Add the creamed coconut, spring onions and parsley to the sauce and cook for 5 minutes. If the sauce is very thin, reduce it by boiling rapidly until shiny and rich in appearance. Season to taste with salt and pepper and pour over the rabbit pieces. Serve with fried rice.

WINE SUGGESTION: Rioja.

Rabbit with Peanut Sauce

This recipe comes from Chile and has been adapted from *Latin American Cooking*, by Elisabeth Lambert Ortiz.

Ingredients

1 rabbit, jointed into 8 serving pieces
salt and freshly ground pepper
3 tablespoons sunflower oil
2 large onions, finely chopped
1 garlic clove, crushed
2 teaspoons paprika
1 green Fresno or jalapeño chilli, seeded and
 finely chopped (see page 194)
110g/4oz unsweetened, crunchy peanut butter
^{1}/$_2$ teaspoon ground cumin
1 tablespoon white wine vinegar
425ml/^{3}/$_4$ pint chicken stock (see page 188)
290ml/^{1}/$_2$ pint dry white wine

To serve: yellow coconut rice (see page 157)

Method

1. Season the rabbit pieces with salt and pepper.

2. Heat half the oil in a large, heavy pan and brown the rabbit pieces evenly. Lift the pieces into a bowl and set aside. Add half the stock to the pan and stir well with a wooden spoon, scraping up any sediment. Pour the liquid over the rabbit pieces.

3. Add the remaining oil and cook the onions until nearly soft, about 10 minutes. Add the paprika, garlic and chilli and mix well.

4. Add the peanut butter, cumin, vinegar, the remaining stock and wine to the onions. Bring to the boil and season to taste with salt and pepper.

5. Return the rabbit pieces to the pan and mix well into the sauce. Cover and simmer until the rabbit is tender, about 1^1/$_2$ hours. Serve with yellow coconut rice.

WINE SUGGESTION: Full-bodied white.

Seafood

SEAFOOD

With thousands of miles of coastline on the Atlantic and Pacific oceans and the Caribbean Sea, the seafood in Latin America is varied, exciting and abundant. Apart from Paraguay and Bolivia, which are inland, all the other countries are rich in fish and shellfish. Paraguay makes up for its lack of seafood with very good freshwater fish, like the much-praised dorado fish from the Paraguay River.

The countries richest in seafood are Chile, Peru and Ecuador. The Humboldt or Peru current from the Antarctic washes the coasts of these countries and provides a variety of fish and shellfish unequalled anywhere else in Latin America. Chile alone has 2,600 miles of coastline and is the country with the largest variety of seafood. In fact, seafood constitutes the main source of protein in the Chilean diet. Many varieties of fish and shellfish are found only in Latin America, and others are common to the tropical or subtropical waters of the world. Chile boasts the famous *pibre*, a type of large sea urchin, and the *congrio*, a conger eel-type of fish; from Peru comes a pink and white scallop called *conchita*, and *corvina*, a relative of sea bass, also found in Ecuador, which is widely used for making ceviches.

With the exception of the Caribbean and Bahia in Brazil, fish cookery throughout Latin America is kept simple and easy. The slaves brought from West Africa to work on sugar plantations in the Caribbean and Brazil transformed their local cuisines into something unique and different from the rest of Latin America. They brought with them spices, vegetables and flavourings, and the similar climatic conditions made it possible to produce their native foodstuffs, such as okra, dried shrimp, yams, coconuts, plaintains, dendê or palm oil, in their new homeland.

White male slaves worked in planting and processing sugar cane, the women did housework and cooked. The African cook, with an almost inbred capacity for making something tasty from very little, was, and still is, a major influence in the cooking of Brazil and the Caribbean. Tropical fish like grouper, douphinfish or mahi mahi, scad, surgeon or doctor fish, snapper or vara vara are now found in good fishmongers and speciality shops in the UK. More commonly known fishes such as tuna, sardines and salt cod are widely used in Latin American cuisine and available in most supermarkets. Of all the shellfish, prawn are the most popular, being a main ingredient in many classic dishes. Crab and lobsters are also very popular, and usually cooked in a very simple way.

Flavourings vary from country to country, annatto oil being used extensively in Caribbean and Ecuadorean cuisines. Dendê or palm oil is the main flavouring for seafood in Brazil and, together with coconut milk, chillies and peanuts, makes fish cookery an exciting experience. Citrus juices and salt are also standard ingredients.

All the olive oil consumed in Latin American countries is imported, mostly from Spain and Portugal, and is therefore rather expensive. It tends to be used only when the budget allows and in special recipes.

Unless stated otherwise, all recipes make 4 servings.

Cod with Spicy Nut Sauce

This rich, smooth and delicious sauce from Mexico's exquisite cuisine can be served with any firm, white-fleshed fish.

Ingredients

juice of 1 lemon
4 x 170g/6oz cod fillets, skinned and pinboned
salt and freshly ground white pepper
2 tablespoons chopped coriander

For the sauce:
8 slices white bread, crusts off and quartered
425ml/$\frac{3}{4}$ pint hot milk
4 tablespoons sunflower oil
2 medium onions, finely chopped
1 garlic clove, crushed
1 tablespoon red chilli paste (see page 180)
  or $\frac{1}{2}$ teaspoon cayenne pepper
110g/4oz ground walnuts
salt and freshly ground pepper
$\frac{1}{2}$ teaspoon ground annatto or achiote (see note and page 274)

For the garnish:
1 teaspoon paprika
2 tablespoons finely chopped parsley

Method

1. Preheat the oven to 200°C/400°F/gas mark 6.

2. Season the fish with the lemon juice, salt and white pepper. Place the fillets in a large roasting dish in a single layer. Cook in the oven for 25 minutes.

3. Meanwhile, make the sauce. In a large bowl mix the bread and half the hot milk and leave to soak for 5 minutes. Process until smooth in a blender or food processor, or push through a sieve.

4. Heat the oil in a large frying pan. Add the onions and garlic and cook until the onions are soft, but not coloured, about 15 minutes. Add the garlic, chilli paste, walnuts and salt and pepper and cook over gentle heat, stirring, for about 5 minutes.

5. Stir in the ground annatto or achiote and bread purée and gradually add the rest of the milk. Cook, stirring constantly, until the sauce thickens. The sauce should be the consistency of double cream; if too thick, add more milk or water.

6. Gently lift the cooked fish from the dish on to a serving plate and sprinkle with a pinch of paprika. Pour the hot sauce around, sprinkle with the parsley and serve at once.

NOTE: If neither annatto nor achiote is available, it can be substituted by adding a good pinch of paprika and $\frac{1}{2}$ teaspoon of ground turmeric to the sweated onions.

WINE SUGGESTION: Full-bodied white.

Salmon Tacos

Tacos are tortillas which have been stuffed and rolled up like cigars. These `soft tacos' are eaten in the hand. They can also be stuffed and fried, and make an exciting meal since each person `composes' his or her own taco. A variety of dips, salsas, beans or salads accompanies a traditional taco (see page 165). This recipe is for a more sophisticated taco, using salmon.

Ingredients

4 x 170g/6oz salmon fillets, skinned
1 x 400g/14oz can black beans, drained and
 rinsed
2 tablespoons chopped coriander
2 tablespoons sunflower oil
juice of 1 lime

For the marinade:
85g/3oz clear honey
2 tablespoons coarse-grained mustard
juice of 1 lemon
2 teaspoons ground cumin
1 teaspoon ground coriander
1 teaspoon chilli powder
salt and freshly ground black pepper

To serve: 8 x 20cm/8 inch wheat-flour tortillas
 (see page 166)
1 iceberg lettuce, shredded
lime wedges
salsa cruda (see page 176)
guacamole (optional, see page 185)

Method

1. Combine all the marinade ingredients, then add the salmon and turn to coat. Cover and chill for up to 1 hour.

2. Heat the grill to its highest setting. Arrange the salmon on a baking sheet and grill without turning until cooked. Keep warm.

3. Preheat the oven to 180°C/350°F/gas mark 4. Wrap the tortillas in tin foil and heat until warm, about 10 minutes.

4. In a bowl, mix together the black beans, coriander, oil and lime juice. Season to taste with salt and pepper.

5. Arrange the grilled salmon, lettuce, black beans and lime wedges on a large platter, serve with the warmed tortillas and hand the salsa and guacamole separately. Allow the guests to assemble their own tacos.

WINE SUGGESTION: Full-bodied, dry white.

Fish and Prawns in Ginger-flavoured Peanut Sauce

Another classic dish from Brazil, where the African and native cuisines meet so interestingly. Rich and exciting, *vatapa*, as this dish is called locally, can be made really hot or very mild.

Ingredients

450g/1lb sea bass, halibut or swordfish fillet, skinned and cut into large pieces
2 tablespoons sunflower oil
225g/8oz raw, medium prawns, weighed shelled and deveined (see page 277)
1 large onion, finely chopped
1 x 800g/1lb 13oz can chopped tomatoes with juice
1 dried red chilli, seeded and crumbled
110g/4oz creamed coconut, chopped
2 tablespoons crunchy, unsweetened peanut butter
3 tablespoons dried shrimps (see page 277)
2.5cm/1 inch ginger root, peeled and grated
$1/2$ teaspoon ground ginger
570ml/1 pint coconut milk
salt and freshly ground pepper
1 tablespoon rice flour
5 teaspoons dendê or palm oil (see page 277)
3 tablespoons coarsely chopped coriander

For the garnish:
30g/1oz coarsely chopped toasted peanuts
2 tablespoons coarsely chopped coriander

To serve: steamed long-grain rice or potatoes

Method

1. Cut the fish into 5cm/2 inch pieces.

2. Heat the oil in a large saucepan, add the onion and cook until nearly soft, about 10 minutes.

3. Add the tomatoes, chilli, creamed coconut, peanut butter, dried shrimps, fresh and ground ginger and the coconut milk and season with salt and pepper. Bring to the boil, reduce the heat and simmer, covered, for 25 minutes.

4. Remove the sauce from the heat, liquidize or process it well and pour it through a sieve back into the rinsed-out pan.

5. In a small bowl mix the rice flour with 5 tablespoons of the sauce and add to the sauce, stirring constantly over medium heat until it is thick enough to coat the back of a wooden spoon. Taste and adjust seasoning.

6. Add the dendê oil, the fresh coriander and the browned fish and prawns and simmer for the 5-8 minutes, or until the fish is cooked.

7. To serve, transfer the fish and sauce to a warm, deep plate, scatter the toasted peanuts on top and sprinkle with chopped coriander. Serve with rice or boiled potatoes.

WINE SUGGESTION: Medium-dry white.

Salt Cod Cakes with Three Pepper Salsa

Salt cod travels a long way before it reaches Latin America, where it is extremely popular. Most of it comes from Norway, where the fresh cod is soaked in brine and exported mainly to Portugal, Spain and other Mediterranean countries. Brazil inherited its love of salt cod from the Portuguese, and most of its salt cod dishes are direct copies of traditional Portuguese recipes. Among them is *bolinho de bacalhau*, a cocktail version of this fish cake recipe. Served as an appetizer or just before serving the main salt cod dish, this recipe is really worth the trouble of making.

Ingredients

450g/1lb salt cod
15g/^{1}/$_2$oz butter
1 tablespoon flour
pinch cayenne pepper
^{1}/$_2$ teaspoon chilli powder
150ml/^{1}/$_4$ pint milk
450g/1lb mashed potatoes
3 tablespoons finely chopped flat-leaf parsley
freshly ground pepper
flour
2 eggs, beaten
dry white breadcrumbs
oil for frying

To serve: three pepper salsa (see page 177)

Method

1. Soak the salt cod in water for a minimum of 16 hours, changing the water 4 or 5 times.

2. Put the fish in a shallow pan, skin side up, and add enough water to cover. Cook over gentle heat for about 20 minutes or until the skin peels off easily. Drain and discard the cooking liquid. Skin and flake the fish roughly and set aside.

3. In a small saucepan melt the butter, add the flour, cayenne and chilli and cook for 1 minute. Mix in the milk and gradually bring to the boil, stirring continuously. Simmer for about 1 minute.

4. In a large bowl mix the flaked fish with the mashed potatoes, white sauce and parsley. Season to taste with pepper.

5. With floured hands, shape the mixture into 8 rounds 5cm/2 inches wide and 2cm/1inch deep. Dip them into the beaten egg and breadcrumbs and refrigerate for 1 hour.

6. Heat the oil in a frying pan until a crumb will sizzle vigorously in it and fry the fish cakes, turning only once, until golden brown. Drain on absorbent paper. Serve immediately with the red pepper salsa and/or lime wedges.

NOTE: These cakes are delicious as appetizers. Shape them into golf-ball size spheres and fry until golden brown. Serve with the lime wedges.

WINE SUGGESTION: Medium-dry white.

Prawns with Okra and Peanuts

A typical dish from Bahia in Brazil, *caruru*, as it is known locally, includes African ingredients such as dried shrimp, okra, dendê or palm oil and peanuts (see page 280). It makes a rich, thick sort of stew with an unusually delicious mixture of flavours. It can be made without the prawns and served as a vegetable dish. This dish was a great favourite with the teachers at Leith's when the recipe was tested.

Ingredients

900g/2lb large, raw prawns in their shells, weighed without heads
30g/1oz butter
1 teaspoon paprika
1 small onion, finely chopped
$^1/_2$ green pepper, finely diced
1 x 400g/14oz can chopped tomatoes with juice
225g/8oz fresh okra, washed, topped and tailed
15g/$^1/_2$oz dried shrimps, finely chopped or pounded in a mortar (see page 277)
425ml/$^3/_4$ pint coconut milk
2 tablespoons crunchy, unsweetened peanut butter
5 tablespoons coarsely chopped coriander
salt and freshly ground pepper

To serve: fried rice (see page 155)
jalapeño and lime salsa (see page 177)

Method

1. Shell and devein the prawns (see page 277), leaving 3 unshelled for garnish.

2. Melt the butter in a large, heavy frying pan, add the paprika and cook the prawns for 3 minutes, or until they are firm and pink. Transfer to a plate, cover and place in the refrigerator while making the sauce.

3. Place the onion and green pepper in the same frying pan and cook over medium heat until soft but not brown, about 10 minutes.

4. Add the tomatoes with their juice, the prepared okra and dried shrimps. Stir in the coconut milk and mix well. Cover, reduce the heat and simmer for 25 minutes or until the okra is very tender.

5. Add the cooked prawns, peanut butter, coriander, salt and pepper to taste and cook, stirring, for about 5 minutes, or until the prawns are heated through. Serve with fried rice and hand the jalapeño and lime salsa separately.

VARIATION: Although not traditional, the okra can be cooked separately (sauté with 1 tablespoon of oil and the juice of $^1/_2$ lemon for 8 minutes) and added at the last minute, so that it will keep its bright green colour and crisp texture.

WINE SUGGESTION: Dry white with good acidity.

Fresh Tuna Steamed with Fruit Juice

Fresh tuna is now relatively easy to find in Europe. In this recipe the firm pink flesh marinates in a combination of citrus juice and spices, and when the cooked parcels are unwrapped, a delicious sweet aroma is released. The annatto imparts a bright yellow colour to the sauce but is not essential to the taste.

Ingredients

4 x 170g/6oz fresh tuna fillets or steaks
4 x 25cm/10 inch circles of tin foil
salt and freshly ground black pepper

For the marinade:
150ml/^{1}/$_4$ pint fresh orange juice
juice of 1 lime
1^1/$_2$ teaspoons ground annatto (see page 274)
1 garlic clove, crushed
1 teaspoon finely chopped oregano
^{1}/$_2$ teaspoon ground cumin
^{1}/$_4$ teaspoon ground cloves
^{1}/$_2$ teaspoon ground cinnamon

To serve: 8 x 20cm/8 inch wheat-flour tortillas
   (see page 166)

Method

1. Skin the fish if using fillets, or bone and skin if using steaks; cut into 3.5cm/1^1/$_2$ inch cubes.

2. Mix all the marinade ingredients together in a bowl and put the tuna chunks into it. Mix thoroughly, cover and marinate for at least 6 hours, or overnight, in the refrigerator.

3. Preheat the oven to 190°C/375°F/gas mark 5.

4. Brush the tin foil circles with oil. Divide the tuna chunks and the marinade between them. Season to taste with salt and pepper. Bring the edges together and give a firm twist to the top, sealing the parcel well. Put the parcels on a baking sheet and bake in the oven for 15 minutes.

5. To warm the tortillas, wrap them in tin foil and place in the oven with the fish; they will be ready at the same time.

6. To serve, put one parcel on each plate and let the guests unwrap them. Serve with the warmed tortillas.

VARIATION: Chicken can be used in this recipe with very good results. Chop 4 skinned and boned breasts of chicken into 3.5cm/1^1/$_2$ inch cubes and follow the recipe as above.

WINE SUGGESTION: Fruity red.

Salt Cod Bahian Style

Salt cod is a legacy from the Portuguese in Brazil. Although it is imported from Norway and therefore quite costly, Brazilians always find a way of eating it. This recipe is authentically Brazilian, using ingredients such as coconut milk and chillies.

Ingredients

560g/1¼lb salt cod
3 tablespoons sunflower oil
2 onions, thinly sliced
450g/1lb tomatoes, peeled, seeded and chopped
2 green peppers, seeded and thinly sliced
5 spring onions, roughly chopped
5 tablespoons roughly chopped coriander
110g/4oz coconut cream, roughly chopped
1 x 400g/14oz can thick coconut milk
juice of 1 lime
2 green chillies, Kenyan or serrano, seeded and finely chopped (see page 194)
freshly ground pepper
450g/1lb potatoes, peeled and sliced into 1cm/ ½ inch thickness

To serve: green rice (see page 156)

Method

1. Soak the salt cod in water for a minimum of 16 hours, changing the water 4 or 5 times.

2. Preheat the oven to 190°C/375°F/gas mark 5.

3. Put the fish into a shallow pan, skin side up, and add enough water to cover. Cook over gentle heat for about 20 minutes, or until the skin peels off easily. Drain and discard the cooking liquid. Skin and flake the fish into quite large pieces and set aside.

4. Heat the oil in a large saucepan and cook the onions until nearly soft, about 10 minutes. Add the tomatoes, peppers, spring onions, coriander, coconut cream, coconut milk, lime juice and chillies and cook gently for about 10 minutes, or until all the flavours are well blended. Season to taste with pepper (the cod is quite salty, so it might not need any more salt).

5. In a large ovenproof serving dish, start layering with potatoes, then fish and a few tablespoons of the sauce, finishing with the sauce.

6. Bake in the oven for 30–35 minutes, or until bubbly and the potatoes are cooked. Serve hot with the rice.

WINE SUGGESTION: Medium-dry white.

Prawns in Pimiento, Pumpkin Seed and Coriander Sauce

Apart from their beautiful red colour, pimientos have a delicate and delicious sweet flavour. In this recipe they are blended with dried chillies and pumpkin seeds to make a rich and unique sauce.

Ingredients

900g/2lb raw large prawns, in their shells, weighed with heads on
2 dried cayenne or tabasco chillies, crumbled (see page 194)
4 tablespoons sunflower oil
55g/2oz roasted, salted pumpkin seeds
1 medium onion, chopped
1 x 400g/14oz can whole red pimientos, drained and roughly chopped
1 1/2 teaspoons ground coriander
1 garlic clove, crushed
1/2 teaspoon sugar
5 tablespoons coarsely chopped coriander
salt and freshly ground black pepper
juice of 1 lime

To serve: yellow coconut rice (see page 157)

Method

1. Shell and devein the prawns (see page 277). Put the shells with the dried chillies in a medium pan and add enough cold water to cover. Bring to the boil, reduce the heat and simmer, uncovered, for about 15 minutes or until the stock is reduced by one third.

2. Put the prawn shells, the chillies and liquid into a food processor or blender and process for a few seconds. Pass the liquid through a sieve, pressing the shells well to extract all the liquid. Discard the pulp.

3. Heat half the oil in a frying pan and add the pumpkin seeds, onion, pimientos, ground coriander, garlic, sugar and half the fresh coriander. Season with salt and pepper. Cook, stirring occasionally, for 5 minutes. Add the reduced shell stock and cook for a further 15 minutes. Process the sauce to a smooth consistency in a blender or food processor.

4. In a large frying pan heat the remaining oil, add the prawns and cook for 3 minutes or until they are firm and opaque. Add the sauce to the prawns.

5. Stir in the remaining coriander, and cook for a further 2 minutes or until the flavours are well blended. Season to taste with salt and add the lime juice. Serve at once with the yellow coconut rice.

WINE SUGGESTION: Still or sparkling rosé.

Grilled Snapper with Mango Chilli Sauce

A simple and delicious way of serving snapper. The sauce can be made up to a day in advance and reheated just before serving.

Ingredients

4 x 70g/6oz snapper fillets, skin on

For the marinade:
juice of 2 lemons
3 tablespoons groundnut oil
2 tablespoons chopped coriander
salt and freshly ground pepper

For the garnish:
few sprigs of coriander

To serve: thick mango and chilli sauce (see page 181)

Method

1. Wash and thoroughly dry the snapper fillets.

2. Mix the marinade ingredients together. Season with salt and pepper. Add the fish fillets, turn well and set aside to marinate for at least 30 minutes.

3. Heat the grill to its highest setting. Remove the fish from the bowl and discard the marinade. Oil a baking sheet and arrange the fillets, skin side down. Grill until the flesh is firm to the touch and completely opaque, about 5–8 minutes. Gently transfer to a warm serving plate and add a generous spoonful of mango sauce. Garnish with a coriander sprig and serve.

NOTE: The fish can also be cooked on an oiled hot griddle or in a frying pan.

WINE SUGGESTION: Full-bodied white.

Baked Stuffed Trout

This simple recipe reveals its Spanish influences in the use of olives, pimientos and olive oil.

Ingredients

4 x 340g/12oz whole trout, cleaned, head and
   tail on
85g/3oz green olives, pitted and halved
1 medium onion, finely chopped
3 canned red pimientos, diced
55g/2oz flaked almonds
1/2 teaspoon cayenne pepper
55g/2oz button mushrooms, sliced
salt and freshly ground black pepper
4 tablespoons olive oil
juice of 1 lemon

To serve: lemon and lime wedges

Method

1. Preheat the oven to 200°C/400°F/gas mark 6.

2. Wash the trout well and pat dry with absorbent paper.

3. In a large bowl mix the olives, onions, pimientos, flaked almonds, cayenne and mushrooms. Season to taste with salt and pepper.

4. Grease an ovenproof dish. Divide the stuffing between the fish and secure with a wooden cocktail stick. Arrange the fish in the dish and make two cuts in the skin of each fish. Pour the olive oil and lemon juice over them. Season with salt and pepper.

5. Bake in the centre of the oven for 25 minutes or until the flesh feels firm and the skin is lightly browned. Remove the cocktail sticks. Serve hot or cold with lemon and lime wedges.

WINE SUGGESTION: Chilled fino sherry.

Baked Haddock with Lime and Tomato Sauce

Apart from the countries with a strong African heritage, fish recipes in Latin America tend to be simple, making the most of the wonderful and plentiful variety of fish and shellfish.

Ingredients

4 x 170g/6oz haddock fillets, skinned and
pinboned

For the sauce:
3 tablespoons sunflower oil
2 red onions, finely chopped
$1/2$ tablespoon ground coriander
$1/2$ teaspoon cayenne pepper
1 red pepper, seeded and diced
1 green pepper, seeded and diced
4 tomatoes, peeled, seeded and diced
juice of 3 limes
salt and freshly ground black pepper
2 tablespoons chopped coriander

To serve: Mexican rice (see page 158)

Method

1. Preheat the oven to 190°C/375°F/gas mark 5.

2. Rinse the fish fillets well under cold water. Pat dry and set aside.

3. In a saucepan, heat the oil and cook the onions until nearly soft, about 10 minutes. Stir in the coriander and cayenne and cook for a further 2 minutes.

4. Add the chopped peppers and tomatoes and cook, uncovered, for 10 minutes. Remove from the heat, add the lime juice and season with salt and pepper.

5. Arrange the fish fillets in a buttered, shallow ovenproof dish. Cover with the sauce. Bake, uncovered, in the oven for about 20–25 minutes or until the fish flakes easily when tested with a fork.

6. Sprinkle with the chopped coriander and serve with the Mexican rice.

VARIATION: A whole emperor bream or 2 whole snappers can be used for this recipe. Clean the fish, leaving the head and tail on, and follow the recipe as above.

WINE SUGGESTION: Dry, acidic white.

Snapper with Anaheim Chilli Sauce

Anaheim or New Mexican chillies are large but mild green or red chillies. They develop an intense crispy vegetable flavour once they are grilled or roasted, and can be used to enhance the flavour of sweet red and green peppers.

Ingredients

4 x 310g/11oz whole snapper, cleaned, head
  and tail on
salt and freshly ground pepper
juice of 2 lemons

For the sauce:
3 red Anaheim chillies, halved and seeded (see
  page 194)
3 red peppers, halved and seeded
3 garlic cloves, crushed
4 tablespoons sunflower oil
2 tablespoons white wine vinegar
2 tablespoons fresh white breadcrumbs
2 tablespoons chopped coriander
salt and freshly ground pepper

Method

1. Preheat the oven to 200°C/400°F/gas mark 6. SHeat the grill to its highest setting.

2. Season the fish both inside and outside with salt and freshly ground pepper. Put the fish in an ovenproof dish in a single layer and make two cuts on the skin that is uppermost. Drizzle with the lemon juice and set aside.

3. Grill the chillies and peppers, skin side up, until they are blistered and blackened all over. Place them inside a plastic bag until they are cool enough to handle. Remove and discard the skins and chop the chillies and peppers roughly.

4. In a blender or food processor mix the chillies, peppers, garlic, oil, vinegar, breadcrumbs and coriander to a paste. Season to taste with salt and pepper.

5. Spread the paste over the fish. Bake, uncovered, in the oven for about 20 minutes or until the fish is tender.

WINE SUGGESTION: Dry, acidic white.

Fish Stew with Coconut and Shrimp Sauce

Moqueca, as this is known in Brazil, is a simple and popular fish stew. It traditionally uses thick white fish steaks, and some extra shrimps are added to the sauce for flavour. It is equally delicious when made without the coconut milk.

Ingredients

4 x 170g/6oz white fish steaks, such as cod or
    halibut
juice of 2 limes
salt and freshly ground pepper
3 tablespoons sunflower oil
2 onions, thinly sliced
1 teaspoon ground cumin
2 green peppers, seeded and thinly sliced
2 Fresno or jalapeño chillies, seeded and
    chopped (see page 194)
4 spring onions, chopped
5 tablespoons roughly chopped coriander
3 tablespoons chopped flat-leaf parsley
1 x 800g/1lb 13oz can chopped tomatoes
    with juice
200g/7oz creamed coconut, chopped
100ml/3fl oz thick coconut milk
110g/4oz shrimps, shelled and cooked

To serve: boiled rice
red chilli paste (see page 180)

Method

1. Put the fish steaks into a glass dish, add half the lime juice and season with salt and pepper. Toss the steaks well in the lime juice and set aside while making the sauce.

2. In a large, heavy-bottomed pan heat the oil and gently cook the onions for 10 minutes. Add the cumin, peppers and chillies and cook, stirring, for a further minute.

3. Mix in the spring onions, half the coriander, half the parsley, the tomatoes with their juice, the creamed coconut and coconut milk. Mix thoroughly, bring to the boil, reduce the heat and simmer gently for 20 minutes.

4. Add the fish steaks and juice to the sauce, cover and cook over medium/gentle heat for 10–12 minutes. Transfer the fish to a serving dish and keep warm.

5. Bring the sauce to the boil, add the shrimps, the remaining coriander, parsley and lime juice and cook for 3 minutes. Season to taste with salt and pepper and pour the sauce over the fish. Serve at once with boiled rice and hand the red chilli paste separately.

NOTE I: For an authentic Bahian flavour add 4 tablespoons of dendê oil (see page 277) to the sauce at the beginning of step 5.

NOTE II: An authentic accompaniment is made by adding enough sauce to toasted cassava meal (see page 247) to give it a dropping consistency.

WINE SUGGESTION: Off-dry white with good acidity.

Vegetable Dishes

VEGETABLE DISHES

When visiting a market-place in Europe, especially around the Mediterranean, it is interesting to see how many vegetables believed to be of local origin actually come from Latin America. Tomatoes, peppers, chillies, French beans, corn, avocados, all types of potatoes, to name just a few, are all 'imports' but now form an integral part of many different cuisines.

Vegetables are also an important part of the Latin American diet, and in poor areas are the only foodstuff affordable. Root vegetables, such as potatoes and cassava, are favourites and have given rise to many recipes. Cassava or manioc is restricted to Brazil since it is one of the few Brazilian Indian foods incorporated into the Portuguese and African cooking which emerged after the colonizing.

Of all the foodstuffs introduced to Europe from the New World, the potato has been the most important because of its social and culinary impact. Originally from Peru, potatoes were cultivated in the high Andes for hundreds of years before the Conquest. The Incas discovered a way of freeze-drying in order to preserve them, and the same method is still used today by Andean people. With more than 100 varieties, and colours ranging from black to bright orange, potatoes are a very important staple food in high-altitude regions, where rice and corn cannot grow.

In the late 19th century and early 20th century many South American countries received large numbers of immigrants from Japan, China, Germany, Italy and elsewhere. With them came a variety of different vegetables and fruits, which all found a place to flourish in the huge continent's many types of climate and soil. Today, food markets in São Paulo are full of vegetable stalls run by descendants of the Japanese immigrants. Further south, and in countries like Argentina, Chile and Uruguay, the European influence is most dominant. Germans and Italians settled in these areas because of the cooler climate and worked the land, just as they did in their homelands. Within a few decades their own food culture was established and they even started producing beer and wine. As with most Europeans, the staple diet is based on meat; vegetables play a smaller role in their eating habits.

The vegetable recipes that follow reflect the way in which local cooking has combined with imported cuisines. Main courses are followed by side dishes.

Unless stated otherwise, all recipes make 4 servings.

Herb Potato and Aubergine Roulade with Spicy Tomato Sauce

This roulade is very easy to make and best served hot.

Ingredients

For the roulade:
225g/8oz cold mashed potato
55g/2oz Cheddar cheese, grated
55g/2oz butter, melted
4 eggs, separated
1 tablespoon finely chopped parsley
salt and freshly ground black pepper

For the filling:
2 tablespoons sunflower oil
1 large onion, finely chopped
1 garlic clove, crushed
2 medium aubergines, cut into 1cm/$^1/_2$ inch cubes
3 tomatoes, peeled, seeded and chopped
salt and freshly ground pepper
2 tablespoons finely chopped parsley
$^1/_2$ teaspoon crushed chillies

For the garnish:
small bunch of watercress

To serve: spicy tomato sauce (see page 181)

Method

1. Preheat the oven to 190ºC/375ºF/gas mark 6. Line a 30 x 22cm/12 x 9 inch Swiss-roll tin with greaseproof paper.

2. In a large bowl mix the potato, half the cheese, the melted butter, egg yolks and parsley and season to taste with salt and pepper.

3. Whisk the egg whites until stiff but not dry and gently fold into the potato mixture.

Spread the mixture evenly into the prepared tin. Bake in the oven for 10 minutes, or until cooked, but not coloured. Turn on to a clean tea towel.

4. To make the filling, heat the oil and sweat the onion for 5 minutes or until beginning to soften. Add the garlic, aubergines and tomatoes and season with salt and pepper. Cook, uncovered, for about 20 minutes or until the aubergines are reduced to a pulp. Add the parsley and chillies and season to taste with salt and pepper. Spread the mixture over the potato roulade, then roll it up and place it, seam side down, on an oiled baking sheet. Sprinkle the remaining cheese on top.

5. Just before serving, bake the roulade in the oven until the cheese is melted and slightly browned, about 15 minutes. Serve hot with the tomato sauce and garnish with the watercress.

NOTE: The roulade can also be placed in an ovenproof serving dish and the tomato sauce poured around it. Bake until golden brown and the sauce is hot.

VARIATION: Beef picadillo (see page 92) makes a wonderful non-vegetarian filling for this roulade.

WINE SUGGESTION: Fruity red.

Root Vegetable Gratin

Any root vegetable can be used for this gratin, which makes a perfect accompaniment for roast meat and poultry.

Ingredients

285g/10oz sweet potatoes, peeled
285g/10oz celeriac, peeled
285g/10oz turnips, peeled
290ml/$^1/_2$ pint double cream
$^1/_2$ teaspoon cayenne pepper
salt and freshly ground pepper
butter for greasing
2 tablespoons grated Cheddar cheese
1 tablespoon dry white breadcrumbs

Method

1. Preheat the oven to 200°C/400°F/gas mark 6.

2. Grate the root vegetables using the coarse grater blade of a food processor or by hand.

3. In a large bowl mix the grated vegetables together with the cream and cayenne. Season with salt and pepper. Put the mixture into a greased shallow gratin dish. Cover tightly with piece of tin foil and bake in the oven for about 30 minutes or until the vegetables are cooked.

4. Heat the grill to its highest setting.

5. Take the gratin from the oven and remove the foil. Mix the cheese with the breadcrumbs and sprinkle evenly on top of the gratin. Grill until the cheese is brown and bubbly. Serve at once.

WINE SUGGESTION: Dry rosé.

Vegetable Stew with Almonds and Dried Chillies

This dish is made with what Mexicans call a *pipian*. Pipians are pesto-type sauces made with chillies, dried or fresh, and thickened with seeds.. Traditionally, they should not be salted until the moment of serving or they will separate.

Ingredients

3 tablespoons sunflower oil
1 large aubergine, cut into large cubes
2 courgettes, cut into 2.5cm/1 inch slices
2 red peppers, seeded and cut into 2.5cm/
  1 inch strips
110g/4oz French beans, topped and tailed
285g/10oz small new potatoes, washed
110g/4oz okra, washed and dried

For the sauce:
2 ancho chillies (see page 199)
1 tablespoon sunflower oil
110g/4oz blanched almonds
pinch ground cloves
$1/2$ teaspoon ground cinnamon
$1/2$ teaspoon chopped oregano
$1/2$ teaspoon ground cumin
1 teaspoon sugar
570ml/1 pint vegetable stock
salt
4 tablespoons freshly chopped coriander

To serve: spicy corn muffins (see page 240)

Method

1. Heat the oil in a large pan and brown the aubergines, courgettes and peppers in batches. Return them all to the pan when cooked, add the beans and potatoes and take off the heat while making the sauce.

2. Shake the seeds out of the chillies and rinse the pods. Tear them in pieces and put into a small bowl. Cover with hot water and soak for 20 minutes.

3. Heat the oil in a sauté pan and fry the almonds until lightly browned. Add the cloves, cinnamon, oregano, cumin and sugar and fry for 30 seconds.

4. Drain the chillies and discard the soaking liquid. In a blender mix together the chillies, almonds and spices with half the stock and process to a smooth purée.

5. Pour the purée over the vegetables, add the remaining stock, then cover and cook over a low to medium heat for 20 minutes or until the vegetables are tender.

6. Top and tail the okra. Just before serving, gently mix the okra into the sauce with the other vegetables and cook over medium heat for 8–10 minutes or until the okra are tender.

7. Season with salt and stir in the coriander. Serve hot with the corn muffins.

NOTE: This dish is also delicious served at room temperature with baked sweet potatoes or tortillas.

VARIATION: To make chicken pipian, make the sauce as described above. Cut 3 chicken breasts, boned and skinned, into large cubes. Heat 2 tablespoons sunflower oil and brown the chicken pieces in two batches. Add the browned chicken to the sauce and bring to the boil. Reduce the heat and simmer for 15–20 minutes, or until the chicken pieces are cooked. Season with salt and serve with tortillas.

WINE SUGGESTION: Medium-bodied red.

Potato, Cheese and Cayenne Puffs

Potatoes, corn and rice are the principal starchy foods in the Latin American diet – indeed, it is difficult to find a meal served without one of them. These simple, puffs are good served with roast meat, poultry or fish.

Ingredients

450g/1lb cold mashed potato
salt and freshly ground pepper
1 tablespoon each of chopped parsley, coriander
   and chives
2 tablespoons grated Parmesan cheese
1 teaspoon baking powder
3 tablespoons milk
30g/1oz butter
1 teaspoon cayenne pepper
3 eggs, separated

Method

1. Preheat the oven to 220ºC/425ºF/gas mark 7. Butter a 12-hole non-stick patty tin.

2. Season the mashed potatoes with salt and pepper. Mix in the herbs, cheese and baking powder.

3. Heat the milk, butter and cayenne in a small saucepan and add to the mashed potatoes. Mix in the egg yolks and beat thoroughly.

4. Whisk the whites to soft peaks and gently fold into the potato mixture.

5. Spoon the mixture into the patty tins and bake in the oven for about 20 minutes, or until the puffs have risen and are golden brown. Serve at once.

VARIATION: Use sweet potatoes instead of ordinary potatoes and follow the recipe as above.

NOTE: This recipe can also be baked in an oiled gratin dish until golden brown.

WINE SUGGESTION: Fruity, dry white.

Layered Polenta and Vegetable Pie

Dishes derived from corn are widely eaten, with slight variations, throughout Latin America. Polenta takes many forms and has many uses. It is eaten soft with stews and spicy casseroles, or cooled and cut into wedges with roasted meats and barbecues, or simply layered with a meat or vegetable stuffing, as in this recipe.

Ingredients

For the stuffing:
2 tablespoons olive oil
2 red onions, thinly sliced
2 garlic cloves, crushed
^{1}/$_2$ teaspoon ground coriander
1 teaspoon freshly chopped oregano
^{1}/$_2$ teaspoon crushed chillies
2 red peppers, grilled, peeled and thinly sliced
2 green peppers, grilled, peeled and thinly sliced
2 green Anaheim chillies, grilled, peeled and
   thinly sliced (see page 194)
2 tomatoes, peeled, seeded and diced
12 green olives, pitted and halved
salt and freshly ground pepper

For the polenta:
1 litre/1^3/$_4$ pints water or vegetable stock
1 teaspoon salt
140g/5oz coarse instant polenta
2 tablespoons olive oil

For the garnish:
2 tablespoons chopped parsley

To serve: spicy tomato sauce (see page 181)

Method

1. Heat the oil, add the onion and cook gently until nearly soft, about 10 minutes. Stir in the garlic, coriander, oregano and crushed chillies and cook, stirring, for a further 2 minutes.

2. Add the peppers, fresh chilli and tomatoes and mix thoroughly. Cook over low heat, uncovered, until the tomatoes become a pulp and there is little liquid left. Remove from the heat, add the olives and season to taste with salt and pepper. Set aside to cool.

3. Make the polenta: bring most of the water to the boil in a large saucepan. Slake the polenta with the remaining water (this will prevent it from forming lumps when added to the boiling liquid). Add the hot water, return to the pan and stir until thickened.

4. Reduce the heat. Continue cooking the polenta for 5-10 minutes. Season to taste.

5. Lightly oil a 2 litre/4 pint pudding basin or a round glass bowl and spread one quarter of the polenta mixture in the bottom. Put one third of the stuffing on top, leaving a 1cm/^{1}/$_2$ inch border at the sides. Continue layering, finishing with the polenta mixture. Set aside to cool.

6. When ready to serve, heat the grill to its highest setting.

7. Turn the pie on to a chopping board and cut into 6 wedges. Lightly brush a baking sheet with oil and place the wedges on it. Brush with olive oil and place under the grill until golden brown and hot.

8. Arrange the wedges on a plate and spoon the spicy tomato sauce around them. Sprinkle with chopped parsley and serve.

VARIATION: This recipe can be made using beef picadillo (see page 92) for the stuffing.

WINE SUGGESTION: Medium-bodied red.

Mexican Crêpe Gratin

Mexicans have very inventive recipes using tortillas, and this is one of them. Here, the tortillas have been substituted by crêpes, which in this case are made with cornmeal, a staple Latin American food.

Ingredients

For the batter:
110g/4oz fine cornmeal
30g/1oz plain flour
2 whole eggs
1 tablespoon sunflower oil
290ml/½ pint milk
2 tablespoons water

For the filling:
2 tablespoons sunflower oil
2 medium onions, finely chopped
1 garlic clove, crushed
1 red pepper, seeded and diced
½ teaspoon chopped oregano
675g/1½lb tomatoes, peeled, seeded and
   chopped
dash chilli sauce
salt and freshly ground pepper
4 eggs, hardboiled
170g/6oz Cheddar cheese, grated coarsely

Method

1. Preheat the oven to 220°C/425°F/gas mark 7.

2. Mix the batter ingredients in a blender. Refrigerate for 30 minutes. (This allows the starch cells to swell, and gives a lighter result.)

3. Meanwhile, make the filling. Heat the oil in a large pan. Add the onion and cook until nearly soft but not coloured, about 10 minutes. Add the garlic, red pepper, oregano and tomatoes and season well. Cook, uncovered, over medium heat for about 20 minutes. Remove from the heat, add a dash of chilli sauce and season to taste with salt and pepper.

4. Heat a pancake pan or frying pan over a moderately high heat and lightly grease with oil. When hot, pour in about 1 tablespoon of batter and swirl it about the pan until evenly spread across the bottom. Cook for 1 minute, then, using a palette knife and fingers, turn the pancake over and cook again until the underside is brown.

5. Stack 3 or 4 cooked pancakes together, roll up like a cigar and cut them into 1cm/ inch strips.

6. Peel the hardboiled eggs and cut them into rounds.

7. Oil a gratin dish. Layer the tomato sauce, egg slices, crêpe strips and cheese, finishing with a layer of cheese. Cover with the foil and bake for 10 minutes in the preheated oven.

8. Remove the foil and cook for a further 10 minutes or until the cheese is bubbly and brown. Serve at once.

WINE SUGGESTION: Medium-bodied red.

Stuffed Peppers with Tomato Sauce

This is a classic Mexican way of serving stuffed peppers. They can also be filled, dipped in batter and then fried. In this version the peppers are filled with beans and baked with a spicy tomato sauce.

Ingredients

4 large green peppers
oil for greasing
1 quantity refried beans (see page 151)
1 quantity spicy tomato sauce (see page 181)

To serve: soured cream, green rice (see
   page 156)

Method

1. Heat the grill to its highest setting. Preheat the oven to 200°C/400°F/gas mark 6.

2. Wash and pat dry the whole peppers, including the stems. Brush the skin slightly with oil and place them on a baking tray. Put the tray under the grill and cook the peppers until they are black all over.

3. Put the peppers into a plastic bag and leave until cool enough to handle. Peel off and discard the skin. Make a cut in the flesh on one side and gently remove the seeds and veins, still leaving the stems intact. Fill each pepper with the refried beans and secure with a wooden cocktail stick.

4. Pour half the tomato sauce into a medium gratin dish, arrange the peppers in it upright and pour the remaining sauce on top. Bake in the oven for about 25 minutes or until the sauce and peppers are hot. Remove the coctail sticks. Serve with green rice and hand the soured cream separately.

VARIATION: For meat-stuffed peppers use the picadillo recipe (see page 92) instead of refried beans.

WINE SUGGESTION: Full-bodied, dry red.

Ricotta and Vegetable Empanada Pie

Cornmeal is used extensively in many Latin American countries to make cakes, breads, pastries, porridge-type dishes and even drinks. This pastry used here can also be used to make sweet pies filled with apples, pears or quinces.

Ingredients

For the pastry:
170g/6oz cornmeal
170g/6oz self-raising flour
1 teaspoon salt
110g/4oz butter
30g/1oz lard
1 egg yolk
4 tablespoons cold water
1 beaten egg, for glazing

For the filling:
1 tablespoon sunflower oil
1 onion, thinly sliced
1 garlic clove, crushed
1 red pepper, seeded and finely sliced
1 green pepper, seeded and finely sliced
1 red Fresno or Kenyan chilli, seeded and sliced
   (see page 194)
$1/2$ teaspoon mild chilli powder
$1/2$ teaspoon ground allspice
1 teaspoon chopped oregano
3 tomatoes, peeled, seeded and chopped
3 tablespoons chopped parsley
salt and freshly ground pepper
255g/9oz ricotta cheese

Method

1. Preheat the oven to 200°C/400°F/gas mark 6.

2. Sift the cornmeal, flour and salt together in a large bowl. Rub in the butter and lard until the mixture looks like coarse breadcrumbs. Mix the egg yolk with the water, then add to the mixture. Mix to a firm dough, first with a knife, then with one hand. It may be necessary to add more water, but the pastry should not be too damp. Knead the dough on a lightly floured surface until smooth.

3. Divide the dough into 2 equal parts and line a 24cm/9^1/$_2$ inch flan tin with one half. Wrap the other half in cling film and chill.

4. Meanwhile, make the filling. Heat the oil, add the onion and cook over medium heat for 5 minutes. Add the garlic, peppers, chilli, chilli powder, allspice, oregano, tomatoes and parsley. Mix thoroughly, season to taste and cook over a medium heat, uncovered, for 25 minutes or until the mixture is almost dry. Transfer to a bowl and cool slightly.

5. In a bowl break up the ricotta with a fork and season with salt and pepper.

6. Spread the ricotta mixture into the pastry case. Spoon the pepper and tomato mixture on top. Roll out the remaining pastry and gently lay it on top of the flan. Press the edges together.

7. Cut a few slits in the top of the pie and brush with the beaten egg.

8. Bake in the middle of the oven for about 35 minutes or until slightly browned.

WINE SUGGESTION: Full-bodied red.

Cured Onions

Cured onions, also known as pink onions, are used as a garnish in many dishes from Ecuador, and can be added to salads, cold dishes and sandwiches. The acidity in the onions will react with metal, so it is important to use a plastic sieve or colander to degorge them or they will have a metallic taste.

Ingredients

2 red onions, sliced very finely
3 tablespoons salt
2 tablespoons lemon juice
1 teaspoon caster sugar

Method

1. Put the onions in a plastic colander or sieve and coat them evenly with salt. Leave to degorge for 20 minutes.

2. Wash the onions with plenty of cold water and pat them dry with absorbent paper.

3. Transfer the onions to a bowl and mix in the lemon juice and caster sugar. Set aside until they are pink, about 2 hours. This dish can be made up to 24 hours in advance, in which case the onions will get very pink.

Shredded Kale

This is a traditional dish to serve with *feijoada* (see page 90). Kale, or collard greens, is a very popular vegetable in Brazil.

Ingredients

900g/2lb kale or collard greens
3 tablespoons sunflower oil
1 garlic clove, crushed
salt and freshly ground pepper
juice of ½ lime

Method

1. Wash the kale thoroughly. Cut the leaves from their tough stems. Place one leaf on top of another, roll up like a cigar and shred finely.

2. Heat the oil in a large sauté pan, add the garlic and cook for 1 minute. Turn up the heat, add the shredded kale and stir for 1 minute. Cover and cook over medium heat for 5–8 minutes. Remove the lid, turn the heat to high and boil for a further 2 minutes, or until there is no liquid left. Season to taste with salt and pepper and add the lime juice. Serve hot or cold.

Sweet Potato Purée

A favourite ingredient in Latin American cuisine, the sweet potato is used widely for savoury and sweet dishes. A delicious canned purée, looking and tasting very much like chestnut purée, is sold in many countries.

Ingredients

675g/1^{1}/2lb sweet potatoes
milk and double cream
butter
^{1}/2 teaspoon ground cumin
^{1}/2 teaspoon ground coriander
^{1}/2 teaspoon crushed chillies
salt and freshly ground pepper

Method

1. Peel the sweet potatoes and cut into even-sized fairly large chunks, about 5cm/2 inches.

2. Put the potatoes into cold salted water, bring to the boil and cook over medium heat until they are soft, about 15 minutes.

3. Drain the potatoes well, return to the saucepan and stir over moderate heat for a few minutes to dry. Push the potatoes through a sieve or mince through a fine mincer plate.

4. Heat about 100ml/3 fl oz of milk with a few tablespoons of cream, then add the butter and spices. Beat this mixture into the potato.

5. Continue with more milk, cream or butter until the required consistency is reached. Season to taste with salt and pepper and serve hot.

VARIATION: This recipe is equally delicious without the milk and cream. Sweat 1 finely chopped onion in 30g/1oz butter until soft, add the spices and mix in the mashed sweet potatoes. Season well with salt and pepper and serve hot.

Fried Plantains

This is a very popular dish, usually served as an accompaniment to savoury food, but also delicious sprinkled with sugar and cinnamon and eaten as a dessert. It goes particularly well with bean dishes, is easy to make and tastes best when eaten hot.

Ingredients

4 large plantains (see page 280)
oil for frying
salt and freshly ground black pepper

Method

1. Cut the plantains in half lengthwise.

2. Heat about 2.5cm/1 inch oil in a shallow frying pan until a crumb will sizzle vigorously in it. Carefully put the plantain halves into the oil and fry until golden brown, about 2 minutes.

3. Remove with a slotted spoon and drain on absorbent paper. Season with salt and pepper and serve hot.

VARIATION: To make sweet fried plantains, mix 1 tablespoon caster sugar with 1 teaspoon ground cinnamon and sprinkle on the plantains as soon as they are fried. Serve warm with vanilla ice-cream or yoghurt.

NOTE: Plantains are used in this recipe because, unlike bananas, they keep their shape when cooked or fried.

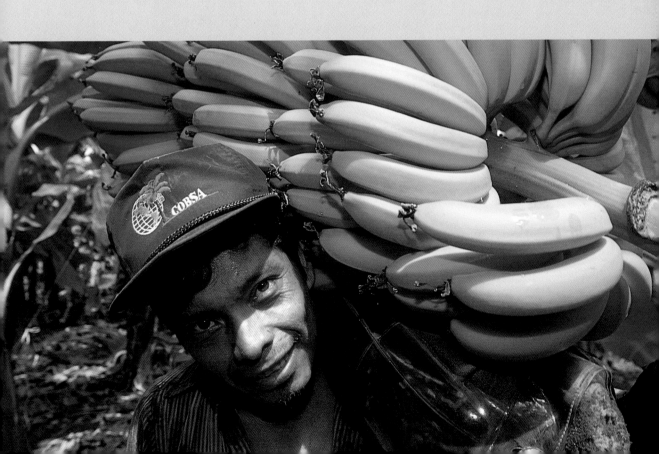

Beans and Rice

BEANS AND RICE

Beans are a staple food in almost any Latin American country, and they are served, in one form or another, at most meals. Together with maize and potatoes, beans played an important part in the diet of the Mayas and Aztecs in Mexico and Central America, and the Incas in Peru.

Black, red kidney, pink, pinto, haricot, Lima beans and peas are among the pulses native to Mexico or Peru, and were taken by the *conquistadores* back to Europe, where they were readily incorporated into the cuisines of Spain and Portugal before spreading throughout the Continent. In Latin America it is a common habit to cook large quantities of beans and store them in the refrigerator ready to be used day by day. Cooks take pride in the way they prepare and serve their beans, so canned beans are not commonly used, although I have used them for convenience in many of the recipes in this book.

Rice was introduced to the New World in the 16th century and was immediately integrated into the local diet. Together with beans, it makes a `complete protein' and is the dietary basic in much of Latin America where white long-grain rice is the variety used most frequently. Rice recipes vary from country to country, but the final result has one common characteristic: tender, fluffy and separate grains.

Unless stated otherwise, all recipes make 4 servings.

Refried Beans

The Spanish name for this dish, *frijoles refritos*, implies that the beans are fried twice, which is not true: they are first boiled and then fried. Variations of this basic recipe are numerous and there are no written rules; some people prefer their beans with a little liquid, while others prefer none at all. The same applies to texture and seasoning.

Ingredients

255g/9oz dried pinto beans
100ml/3 fl oz water
2 tablespoons sunflower oil
1 onion, finely chopped
2 tomatoes, peeled, seeded and chopped
2 garlic cloves, crushed
2 teaspoons ground cumin
2 red Fresno or Kenyan chillies, seeded and
 finely diced (see page 194)
salt and freshly ground black pepper
2 tablespoons freshly chopped coriander

Method

1. Soak the beans overnight, then cook according to the instructions on the packet. Drain and discard the cooking water.

2. In a blender or food processor purée the beans and water until smooth.

3. In a large frying pan, heat the oil and cook the onion until nearly soft, about 10 minutes. Add the tomatoes, garlic, cumin and chillies and cook, stirring, for a further 3 minutes.

4. Stir in the bean purée, season with salt and pepper and cook, stirring over medium heat, until well combined, about 20 minutes.

5. Stir in the coriander and serve hot or cold.

VARIATIONS:
• Red kidney, borlotti, black or brown beans can be used with very good results. For a bean purée with texture, process half the beans and leave the other half whole.
• If no blender or food processor is at hand, just mash the beans with a fork or potato masher as they cook with the onions.

NOTE: For a quicker version of this recipe 2 x 400g/14oz cans of pinto beans can be used.

Drunken Beans

In this recipe, the beans are left whole and cooked in a mixture of spices and beer until there is almost no liquid left. These drunken beans can replace refried beans (see page 151) as a filling for tacos, burritos, tostadas and suchlike.

Ingredients

255g/9oz dried pinto beans or 2 x 400g/14oz cans cooked pinto beans
1 tablespoon sunflower oil
3 rashers rindless streaky smoked bacon, chopped
1 large onion, finely chopped
2 garlic cloves, crushed
1 teaspoon ground cumin
1 teaspoon chilli powder or 1 teaspoon crushed chillies
1 teaspoon freshly chopped oregano
1 x 400g/14oz can chopped tomatoes
190ml/^{1}/$_3$ pint light beer
190ml/^{1}/$_3$ pint water
salt and freshly ground black pepper

Method

1. Soak the beans overnight, then cook according to the instructions on the packet. Drain and discard the cooking water.

2. In a large saucepan heat the oil and cook the bacon for 3 minutes. Add the onion, garlic, cumin, chilli and oregano and cook, stirring from time to time, until the onion is nearly soft, about 10 minutes.

3. Add the cooked beans, tomatoes, beer and water and mix thoroughly. Season with salt and pepper and bring to the boil. Reduce the heat and simmer, covered, for 30 minutes.

4. Remove the lid, stir well and simmer for a further 20 minutes or until there is very little liquid left. Season to taste with salt and pepper and serve hot.

Milky Coconut Beans

This unusual bean recipe comes from Bahia in Brazil and is delicious served with a spicy fish dish.

Ingredients

225g/8oz black beans
1 x 400g/14oz can thick coconut milk
$1/2$ teaspoon cayenne pepper
$1/2$ tablespoon caster sugar
1 teaspoon salt

Method

1. Soak the beans overnight and cook according to the instructions on the packet.

2. Drain the beans and discard the cooking water. Process the beans with the coconut milk in a blender or food processor, leaving a little texture in the beans.

3. Pour the mixture into a large saucepan, add the cayenne, sugar and salt and bring to the boil. If the mixture is too thick, add a few tablespoons of water; if not thick enough, boil until it has the consistency of creamy mashed potatoes. Serve hot or warm.

Fried Rice

Latin Americans from Mexico to Argentina immediately incorporated rice into their diets as soon as it was brought to the continent by the Spanish. As a staple food, rice forms the basis of numerous recipes, with two main types being used: white long-grain for most recipes, and pudding rice for deserts and soups.

Ingredients

225g/8oz long-grain rice
3 tablespoons sunflower or olive oil
1 garlic clove, crushed
salt and freshly ground pepper
570ml/1 pint hot water

Method

1. Wash the rice thoroughly and let it drain in a sieve for 30 minutes.

2. Heat the oil, add the rice and cook, stirring, until the rice is hot, about 5 minutes. Add the garlic and season with salt and pepper. Add the water, bring to the boil, then cover and simmer until the rice is tender and all the liquid absorbed, about 20 minutes.

3. If the rice is not cooked after 20 minutes, add a few tablespoons of hot water and cook, covered, for a further 5 minutes. The water should be completely absorbed and the rice tender with each grain separate.

VARIATIONS: This is a basic rice recipe and it can be changed in many ways.
*   The water can be substituted by chicken or vegetable stock.
*   Yellow rice: add $1/2$ teaspoon of turmeric to the rice when frying.
*   Vegetable rice: small diced carrots, courgettes, peppers and peas should be blanched and mixed in at the end.
*   Raisin and walnut rice: 55g/2oz of raisins and 55g/2oz of walnuts, coarsely chopped, can be mixed in halfway through the cooking time.

Green Rice

Originally from Mexico, this is a different and delicious way of serving rice. For an authentic appearance, oil a hole-in-the-middle mould and press the rice into it. Unmould and garnish with watercress or coriander leaves.

Ingredients

225g/8oz long-grain rice
3 tablespoons sunflower oil
4 garlic cloves, crushed
2 medium onions, chopped
3 green Fresno or jalapeño chillies, halved,
   seeded and chopped (see page 194)
570ml/1 pint hot chicken stock (see page 188)
3 tablespoons chopped parsley
3 tablespoons chopped coriander
salt and freshly ground pepper

Method

1. Wash and drain the rice thoroughly.

2. Heat 1 tablespoon of oil in a frying pan and add the garlic, onions and chillies. Fry quickly, shaking the pan until they begin to brown. Add half the stock to the pan and scrape well.

3. Transfer the liquid and onion to a blender or food processor, mix in the parsley, coriander and blend until smooth. Set aside.

4. In a large saucepan heat the remaining oil, add the rice and cook, stirring, until the rice is hot, about 5 minutes.

5. Stir in the onion mixture, the remaining stock, salt and freshly ground pepper and mix well. Bring to the boil, reduce the heat, cover and simmer for about 20 minutes or until the rice is tender and fluffy.

6. Remove from the heat but keep the pan covered for another 5 minutes before serving.

Yellow Coconut Rice

This rice makes a wonderful accompaniment to spicy dishes: the coconut milk soothes a burning palate and cleans it between mouthfuls.

Ingredients

225g/8oz long-grain rice
110g/4oz creamed coconut, chopped
570ml/1 pint hot chicken stock (see page 188)
4 tablespoons sunflower oil
2 onions, finely chopped
$^1/_2$ teaspoon ground annatto or achiote (see page 274)
$^1/_2$ teaspoon mild chilli powder
6 cloves
$^1/_2$ teaspoon ground cinnamon
salt

Method

1. Wash and drain the rice thoroughly.

2. Put the coconut into a measuring jug and add the hot chicken stock. Stir to melt.

3. Heat the oil in a large, heavy pan and add the onions. Cook until soft but not coloured. Add the annatto or achiote and the chilli and cook for a further minute.

4. Add the rice to the onions and cook, stirring, until the rice is hot, about 5 minutes.

5. Add the coconut milk, cloves, cinnamon and salt, bring to the boil and boil for 5 minutes. Lower the heat, cover and cook over gentle heat until the rice is tender and all the liquid absorbed, about 20 minutes.

NOTE: If neither annato nor achiote is available, use turmeric instead.

Mexican Rice

Grilled tomatoes, onions and garlic mixed with stock give a wonderful flavour to this recipe. If served with beans and guacamole, it makes a delicious vegetarian meal.

Ingredients

225g/8oz white long-grain rice
3 tomatoes, halved
1 onion, halved
2 garlic cloves, crushed
4 tablespoons sunflower oil
salt and freshly ground pepper
425ml/^{3}/$_4$ pint hot chicken stock (see page 188)
2 carrots, peeled and finely diced
85g/3oz frozen peas, thawed
1 green chilli, seeded and finely diced (see page 194)
^{1}/$_2$ red pepper, seeded and finely diced

For the garnish:
1 tablespoon chopped parsley

Method

1. Heat the grill to its highest setting.

2. Wash the rice in several changes of water and let it soak for 15 minutes. Drain thoroughly.

3. Place the tomatoes, onion and garlic on a baking sheet. Drizzle with 2 tablespoons of the oil and season with salt and pepper. Grill until the tomatoes and onions are lightly browned.

4. Purée the tomatoes, onions and garlic in a blender until smooth. If too thick, add a few tablespoons of chicken stock. Sieve.

5. Heat the remaining oil in a large, heavy saucepan, add the rice and cook, stirring constantly, until the rice is lightly golden but not burnt. Add the tomato mixture and cook for a further 5 minutes.

6. Stir in the carrots, peas, chilli, red pepper and chicken stock. Season with salt and pepper. Bring to the boil, reduce the heat and cook, covered, until the rice is tender and the liquid absorbed, about 20 minutes.

7. Transfer to a serving dish and sprinkle with the parsley. Serve at once.

VARIATIONS:
- Sweetcorn, courgettes, mushrooms, finely chopped French beans, celery and even diced ham and bacon can be added to this rice.
- For a delicious, homely variation cover the rice with grated cheese 5 minutes before the end of cooking time and cover tightly with a lid. When ready to serve, bring the pan to the table and remove the lid. The cheese will be completely melted and the rice moist.

Baked Red Rice

Very popular in Brazil, this rice recipe is easy to make and ideal for large gatherings, as it can be prepared well in advance and baked just before serving.

Ingredients

225g/8oz white long-grain rice
2 tablespoons sunflower oil
1 small onion, finely chopped
1 garlic clove, crushed
1 tablespoon tomato purée
1 teaspoon chopped oregano
3 tomatoes, peeled, seeded and chopped
$1/2$ teaspoon cayenne pepper
salt and freshly ground pepper
55g/2oz Cheddar cheese, grated

Method

1. Preheat the oven to 190°C/375°F/ gas mark 5. Lightly grease a medium shallow ovenproof dish.

2. Wash the rice thoroughly under cold water. Drain and cook in boiling salted water for 5 minutes. Turn into a colander and rinse with boiling water to remove the excess starch. Set aside while making the sauce.

3. Heat the oil in a frying pan, add the onion and cook over medium heat for 10 minutes. Add the garlic, tomato purée and oregano and cook for a further 2 minutes. Add the tomatoes and cayenne and season to taste with salt and pepper.

4. Toss the rice into the sauce and mix thoroughly. Pile the rice into the oiled dish and sprinkle with the cheese. Bake in the oven for 20 minutes or until the rice is tender and the cheese golden brown. Serve at once.

NOTE: Alternatively, the rice can be baked in the oven for 15 minutes, then put under a hot grill for about 2 minutes to brown the cheese.

Tortilla Dishes

TORTILLA DISHES

Tortillas are flat breads made from corn or wheat flour. Before the Spaniards introduced wheat to the Americas in the late 15th century, maize or corn was the main grain used to make breads. Corn has very little gluten, so it is difficult to make it into a leavened bread. As a result, the people of Mexico and Central America shaped corn dough into thin, unleavened cakes and cooked or toasted them briefly on a hot pottery griddle.

The Spaniards called the Mexican bread *tortilla*, the same name used for a popular round potato omelette found in Spain. With the integration of ingredients brought by the *conquistadores* into the local cuisine, wheat tortillas appeared, especially in the northern part of Mexico. The new leavened bread never replaced the tortilla in the Mexican diet, and many of the dishes tasted by the *conquistadores* are still very popular today.

Tortillas are the basis of numerous Mexican dishes, as well as being served as bread. The fillings used with them vary little; it is how the dish is assembled or cooked that makes for the variety.

Unless stated otherwise, all recipes make 4 servings.

Types of tortilla

Chalupa are oblong tortillas, a speciality of the Puebla region in Mexico.

Gorda, literally meaning `fat', is a thicker tortilla than the usual variety.

Sope is a tortilla which is thicker at the edges.

Totopos are pieces of *tortilla gorda* fried in butter and served with refried beans.

Tortilla dishes

Burritos, thought to be a North American invention, are large, wheat-flour tortillas used as a wrapper for any filling, rather like soft tacos.

Chilaquiles are usually made with stale tortillas which have been shredded, fried and layered in a casserole with cheese or vegetables. A chilli-based sauce or stock is then poured over them. They are served with radishes and slices of onions.

Chimichangas are uncooked wheat tortillas which are filled, then fried.

Enchilada are corn tortillas which are dipped in a thin savoury sauce and then in hot oil. They are then filled, rolled up like tacos, arranged in a serving dish and covered with the remaining sauce. The dish is then baked and garnished with cheese and onions.

Quesadillas are like turnovers made with uncooked corn tortillas. They usually have a savoury filling and are deep-fried or baked in the oven until crisp.

Tacos are corn tortillas wrapped around a savoury filling, which can consist of such things as meat, beans, guacamole, salsa or shredded poultry. There are two types of tacos, soft and hard. A soft taco is spread with the filling, then rolled up and eaten like a sandwich; a hard taco is filled and then fried in hot oil.

Tostadas are tortillas deep-fried or baked until crisp. They are flat or shaped into baskets and used as containers for savoury toppings and garnishes. They can also be made sweet for puddings.

Tostaditas, or tortilla chips, are wedges or strips of tortilla fried until crisp. They can be made of different types of corn, hence the dark tortilla chips, which are made of blue corn.

Classic fillings and garnishes
The most popular meat fillings are:

*   shredded chicken (poached or leftover roast chicken)
*   shredded pork (see page 103)
*   picadillo (see page 92)

Accompaniments
After selecting one type of meat, the following accompaniments are used:

*   salsa cruda (see page 176) or tomatillo sauce (see page 183)
*   shredded iceberg lettuce
*   grated cheese (Cheddar or Gouda)
*   refried beans (see page 151)
*   guacamole (see page 185)
*   soured cream
*   sliced onions and radishes
*   pickled chillies or hot chilli sauce

Corn Tortillas

Masa harina, the flour used to make tortillas, is made by boiling corn kernels with lime. The kernels are then dried and ground into flour. Masa harina is available in speciality shops and large supermarkets.

Ingredients

255g/9oz instant masa harina mix
1 teaspoon salt
about 290ml/¹/₂ pint warm water

Method

1. Combine the masa harina and salt in a bowl. Pour in two thirds of the water and mix with a knife to a doughy consistency. Add enough of the remaining water to make a soft but not sticky dough. Knead until well combined and smooth. Cover and rest for 15 minutes.

2. Divide the dough into 12 equal balls. Place each ball between sheets of greaseproof paper or cling film and use a rolling-pin to flatten them into discs about 15cm/6 inches in diameter. Peel off the paper or cling film.

3. Heat an ungreased griddle or thick sauté pan and cook the tortillas 1 at a time for about 1 minute on each side until flecked with brown.

4. Keep the cooked tortillas warm by stacking them in a clean napkin and serving them wrapped.

NOTE: The tortilla dough can also be flattened in a tortilla press – a quick, efficient gadget developed by the Spanish and found in speciality shops.

Taco Fiesta

Tacos are tortillas wrapped around a variety of savoury fillings. Traditionally, corn tortillas are served, but filled wheat-flour tortillas (called burritos) are just as delicious. All the different fillings and garnishes are put on the table and each person assembles his or her taco according to taste and eats it with their hands. Many of the garnishes can be prepared in advance and are served at room temperature. The meat and bean fillings are best served warm. Allow 2 or 3 fresh warm tortillas per person and plenty of salsa cruda and hot chilli paste on the side.

Ingredients

16 x 14cm/6 inch corn or wheat tortillas (see page 164 or 166)
2 quantities guacamole (see page 185)
1 quantity refried beans (see page 151)
1 quantity picadillo (see page 92)
2 chicken breasts, poached and shredded
$^1/_2$ iceberg lettuce, finely shredded
140g/5oz Cheddar cheese, grated
1 quantity cured onions (see page 144)
2 quantities salsa cruda (see page 176)
$^1/_2$ pint soured cream or crème fraîche
1 quantity red chilli paste (see page 180)

To serve: mixed green salad

Method

1. Preheat the oven to 170°C/325°F/ gas mark 3. To reheat the tortillas, wrap them loosely in tin foil as they are made. Place in the oven for 10 minutes before serving, then pile them on to a plate and cover with a large napkin.

2. Each person takes a tortilla and spoons on some guacamole, beans, meat or chicken, some lettuce, cheese and onions, then a small quantity of salsa cruda and soured cream on top. Roll up like a cigar – not too tightly or the filling will squeeze out of the ends when being eaten. Brave individuals can add a few drops of red chilli paste before rolling up the taco, or place a little on the plate and dip the taco into it now and again. Serve with a mixed green salad.

NOTE: Hard taco shells are not as good as freshly made tortillas, but they are good as a shortcut for a taco fiesta; allow 2 or 3 per person.

WINE SUGGESTION: Light-bodied red.

Wheat-flour Tortillas

Wheat was introduced to Mexico after the Conquest in 1519. Although wheat tortillas are common in northern parts of Mexico, they don't rival the popularity of corn tortillas.

Ingredients

310g/11oz plain flour
1 teaspoon salt
55g/2oz lard
about 190ml/¹/₃ pint warm water
1 teaspoon sunflower oil

Method

1. Sift the flour and salt into a bowl. Rub in the lard. Stir in enough water to form a soft but not sticky dough.

2. Knead the dough well on a floured surface for about 10 minutes or until smooth and elastic. Put the dough into the cleaned bowl, cover and set aside to rest for 1 hour.

3. Divide the dough into 12 equal pieces. Roll each piece on a lightly floured surface until about 20cm/8 inches wide.

4. Cook the tortillas 1 at a time in a heated comal or heavy-based frying pan until the underside is flecked with brown and bubbles appear on the surface. Turn the tortilla and cook the other side, pressing down the bubbles with a rolled-up tea towel. Grease the pan very lightly with the oil only if the tortilla is sticking.

5. Keep the tortillas warm by wrapping them in a clean cloth when they are cooked.

Crab Tostadas

This is a very good dinner party dish since all the preparation can be done in advance and the tostadas just heated up before serving. It is important not to fill them in advance or they will get soggy. The tostadas can be baked flat, but they look much nicer when cooked in a basket shape.

Ingredients

$^1/_2$ quanitity wheat-flour tortilla dough (see
    page 166)
oil for brushing

For the filling:
450g/1lb cooked crab meat
2 tablespoons sunflower oil
1 small onion, finely chopped
2 spring onions, finely chopped
3 tablespoons chopped coriander
2 tomatoes, peeled, seeded and finely chopped
3 tablespoons lime juice
salt and freshly ground pepper

To serve: $^1/_2$ iceberg lettuce, finely shredded
1 quantity refried beans (see page 151)
soured cream
1 quantity guacamole (see page 185)
1 quantity salsa cruda (see page 176)

Method

1. Preheat the oven to 130ºC/250ºF/gas
    mark 1.

2. Divide the dough into 4 equal pieces and
    shape each into a 20cm/8inch circle. Brush
    the tortillas on both sides with a little oil.
    Using inverted pudding basins or ovenproof
    cereal bowls, put the tortillas on top and
    bake for 30 minutes, or until they are crisp.
    Remove to a wire rack (they can be made
    up to a day in advance and reheated slightly
    just before serving).

3. Pick over the crab meat. In a sauté pan heat
    the oil and cook the onion for 10 minutes.

Add the spring onions, half the coriander,
the tomatoes, lime juice and crab meat.
Season with salt and pepper and cook for 5
minutes over low heat. Just before serving
mix in the remaining coriander.

4. To serve, arrange the tortillas on a plate and
    put a handful of shredded lettuce at the
    bottom of each. Layer the beans, crab
    mixture and guacamole on top, finishing
    with 1 tablespoon of soured cream. Hand
    the salsa cruda separately.

VARIATION: To make sweet tostadas, melt
30g/1oz of butter and brush each tostada. Mix
2 tablespoons of sugar with 1 teaspoon ground
cinnamon and sprinkle over the buttered
surface. Bake as above and fill with tropical fruit
salad (see page 212). Serve with plain yoghurt,
rich vanilla ice-cream (see page 229) or
cinnamon and vanilla ice-cream (see page 227).

*NOTE I: This dish is a complete meal in itself, so it
is not necessary to serve anything else with it.*

*NOTE II: The tostadas can be made finger-food
size and filled with different meats or salsas.*

*NOTE III: Picadillo (see page 92) or shredded
chicken breasts can be used instead of crab meat;
for a vegetarian tostada, substitute the meat with
grated Cheddar cheese.*

WINE SUGGESTION: Full-bodied white.

Chorizo Sausage Quesadillas

These are delicious turnovers made with uncooked tortilla dough and filled with a savoury or sweet stuffing.

Ingredients

3 Spanish chorizo sausages, skinned and
   finely chopped
30g/1oz Parmesan cheese, grated
2 tomatoes, peeled, seeded and chopped
2 spring onions, finely chopped
1 quantity wheat-flour tortilla dough (see
   page 166)
oil for brushing

To serve: mixed vegetable salad (see page 57)

Method

1. Preheat the oven to 200°C/400°F/gas
    mark 6.

2. Put the chopped sausage into a sauté pan
    and cook for about 10 minutes, stirring until
    most of the fat has come out. Using a
    slotted spoon, transfer the sausage pieces to
    a bowl and add the tomatoes and spring
    onions. Set aside to cool.

3. Divide the tortilla dough into 16 equal
    parts. Roll them on a lightly floured surface
    into 15cm/6 inch circles and place a portion
    of the filling on one half of each circle. Fold
    the other half over and pinch the edges
    together to seal. Transfer to an oiled baking
    sheet and brush the chimichangas with a
    little oil.

4. Bake in the middle of the oven for about
    15–20 minutes or until they are crisp and
    golden. Serve warm with the mixed
    vegetable salad.

VARIATIONS:
*   The quesadillas can also be deep-fried in hot
    oil until crisp.
*   Shredded chicken meat, picadillo (see page
    92), shrimps and crab meat can be used as
    alternative fillings.

WINE SUGGESTION: Full-bodied red.

Tamales

Tamales are corn husks filled with masa havina dough, then steamed. They appear in many varieties throughout Latin America: in some countries they are made with fresh corn and called humitas or pamoulas. Although they can be left unfilled, they are usually stuffed with meat, vegetables or cheese. They can be very spicy and are a good way of using up leftovers, such as picadillo or shredded beef. They also make a delicious dessert when filled with tropical fruit and nuts and served with coffee or hot chocolate.

Ingredients

70g/2^1/$_2$oz lard
225g/8oz instant masa harina (see page 279)
1^1/$_2$ teaspoons baking powder
1^1/$_2$ teaspoons salt
about 150ml/^{1}/$_4$ pint lukewarm water
12 corn husks (see note I), or 12 sheets of
 greaseproof paper measuring 22 x 10cm/
 9x4 inches

For the filling:
picadillo (see page 92)
poached and shredded chicken breasts
255g/9oz mozzarella cheese, cut into rounds

Method

1. In a bowl cream the lard with a wooden spoon.

2. Sift together the masa harina, baking powder and salt. Add 3 spoonfuls of the masa harina mixture at a time to the creamed lard, and beat with a wooden spoon until all the masa harina is thoroughly combined with the lard.

3. Slowly pour in the lukewarm water and bring the dough together with one hand. Knead lightly for 1 minute or until the dough is soft and smooth.

4. To assemble the tamales: put about 1 tablespoon of dough in the centre of a corn husk or sheet of paper and spread with the fingers into a rectangle, leaving a 2.5cm/1 inch border. Put 1 tablespoon of your chosen filling, or a piece of the cheese, in the centre of the dough. Fold one side of the wrapper a little more than halfway across the filling and bring the opposite side over the first fold. Turn the ends up to cover the seam, overlapping them across the top. Tie with a piece of string. If using corn husks, use a thin strip of husk to tie the tamales.

5. Lay the tamales in a large colander in as many layers as necessary and place the colander over a deep pan filled with hot water. Cover, reduce the heat and steam the tamales for 1 hour, adding more water to the pan if necessary. When the tamales are done, remove them from the colander with tongs, arrange on a plate and serve at once. They may be prepared in advance and reheated by steaming them again for 30 minutes.

VARIATIONS:
- Sweet tamales: Add 110g/4oz sugar, 30g/1oz ground almonds and 55g/2oz desiccated coconut to the masa harina when making the dough. Fill with 110g/4oz chopped walnuts mixed with 4 tablespoons apricot jam. Shape them half the size of the above tamales and steam for 35 minutes. Serve warm or cold.
- Using leftover plain or cheese tamales, remove the tamale from the wrapping and cut in half. Heat a little oil in a shallow frying pan and fry the tamales until golden brown. Serve at once with coffee as a snack or as part of a meal.

NOTE I: If using dried corn husks, soak in warm water for 15 minutes, then drain and pat dry before using. Greaseproof paper is a perfect substitute for the corn husks, although the appearance is not as authentic.

NOTE II: The water used for the dough can be substituted by stock, according to the filling used, or by coconut milk if making a sweet tamale.

WINE SUGGESTION: Full-bodied dry red for savoury tamales, Moscatel for sweet tamales.

Making Tamales

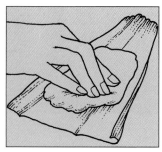

1.

2.

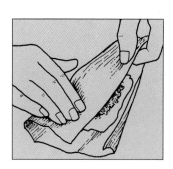

3.

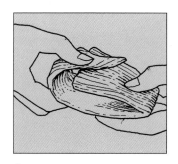

4.

5.

6.

Salsas,
Sauces and Stocks

SALSAS AND SAUCES

Literally meaning `sauce', the term *salsa* is applied to any kind of sauce in Latin America. Elsewhere, it is used to describe a sauce or relish made with freshly chopped, uncooked ingredients. The basic salsa consists of tomatoes, onions, a herb, lime juice, lemon juice or vinegar, and fresh chillies.

To keep its freshness, a salsa should be made no more than two hours before eating and all the ingredients used should be very fresh. It is essential to use good-quality vinegar, oils and spices. The other ingredients are chopped finely, but not so fine that they cannot be identified. A spoonful of salsa should contain a bit of everything.

Salsas are a healthy and delicious substitute for rich butter and cream sauces and make a change from traditional gravy. They taste good with roast, grilled, barbecued or pan-fried meat, and have the added advantage of being fresh, low in sugar and fat, and easy to make.

A good salsa has no more than three or four basic ingredients (apart from the herbs and liquid), so it keeps a clean, fresh flavour. It is best to use ingredients which are in season because they are cheaper and taste better. Although most salsas have chillies added to them, they are not essential. Different types of chilli go well with different types of food (see chilli chart, pages 195-9), so it is worth experimenting to find your preferred combination.

A salsa is a simple, quick sauce, so the tomatoes, peppers and chillies that go into it are not usually skinned. However, grilled peppers and large chillies, which have a nice, full flavour, are skinned. They add special interest to a salsa, but they lose some of their crispness in the process of grilling.

Ideally, a salsa should be made about one hour before serving and left at room temperature. Take care if using raw onions in a salsa as they can be quite strong. If you like, you can degorge the onions first (see page 277), or substitute spring onions, which have a milder flavour.

Fruit salsas are exciting and delicious with barbecues. Start with the proven combinations, like chilli and pineapple salsa with barbecued pork chops, and then move on to the more unusual salsas. Note that they do not keep as long as vegetable salsas.

Normally, the salsa is put into a serving bowl and left on the table so that people can help themselves. For a more refined presentation, small ramekins can be filled and put on individual plates.

Unless stated otherwise, each recipe makes 4 servings.

Salsa Cruda

This is also called `table salsa' because it is the basic tomato and chilli salsa served with every meal in Mexico and other Latin American countries. It goes well with meat, vegetables, rice and potatoes, and is even used as a salad dressing!

Ingredients

6 red tomatoes, seeded and diced small
1 red onion, finely chopped
2 salad onions, white and green parts, roughly chopped
2 tablespoons finely chopped coriander
1 green Dutch or Westland chilli, seeded and finely chopped (see page 194)
$1/2$ teaspoon finely chopped oregano
pinch sugar
juice of 1 lime or 2 lemons
3 tablespoons sunflower oil
salt and freshly ground black pepper

Method

1. Combine all the ingredients well. Season to taste with salt and pepper, and serve at room tmperature.

NOTE: The fresh green chilli can be substituted by a few drops of hot chilli sauce or $1/2$ teaspoon chilli powder.

Mango and Avocado Salsa

This salsa goes particularly well with grilled and barbecued chicken, fish and lamb.

Ingredients

1 large mango, peeled and finely diced
$1/2$ red onion, finely chopped
$1/2$ green pepper, diced
$1/2$ red pepper, diced
3 tablespoons white wine vinegar
2 tablespoons lime juice
2 tablespoons roughly chopped coriander
5 tablespoons sunflower oil
1 tablespoon roughly chopped chives
1 small avocado, diced
salt and freshly ground black pepper

Method

1. Mix together all the ingredients, except the avocado, in a bowl. Season to taste with salt and pepper, then gently toss in the avocado.

Three Pepper Salsa

The grilling of the peppers and Anaheim chilli gives this salsa a unique flavour, which complements roasted or barbecued meat and fried fish recipes. Unlike other fresh salsas, this recipe will keep for a few hours in the refrigerator.

Ingredients

1 red pepper, grilled, peeled and finely diced
1 yellow pepper, grilled, peeled and finely diced
1 green pepper, grilled, peeled and finely diced
2 green Anaheim chillies, grilled, peeled and finely diced (see page 194)
100ml/3 fl oz sunflower oil
4 tablespoons white wine vinegar
1 garlic clove, crushed
pinch sugar
2 tablespoons finely chopped flat-leaf parsley
2 tablespoons finely chopped coriander
1 teaspoon chopped oregano
dash Tabasco sauce
juice of 1 lime
salt and freshly ground black pepper

Method

1. Mix all the ingredients together in a bowl. Season to taste with salt and pepper and set aside for 1 hour to develop the flavours.

2. Just before serving, remove the garlic clove.

Jalapeño and Lime Salsa

This salsa has a clean, vegetable flavour. It goes well with any type of roast, and the lime and lemon juice give it a slightly sharp edge.

Ingredients

1 large onion, finely chopped
1 teaspoon salt
juice of 2 limes
juice of 1 lemon
$1/2$ garlic clove, crushed
2 green jalapeño or Fresno chillies, seeded and finely chopped (see page 194)
2 tablespoons chopped flat-leaf parsley
1 teaspoon freshly chopped marjoram or oregano
salt

Method

1. Mix the onion with the salt, place in a plastic colander and leave to degorge for 5 minutes. Rinse the onion in cold water and drain well.

2. In a non-metallic bowl mix together the onions, lime and lemon juice, garlic, chillies, parsley and marjoram. Season to taste with salt and leave at room temperature for 1 hour. Serve with grilled or barbecued fish, chicken or pork.

Pineapple and Chilli Salsa

This salsa is delicious with barbecued pork sausages or roast pork.

Ingredients

1 small red onion, finely chopped
1 teaspoon salt
boiling water
3 tomatoes, seeded and finely diced
1 dried ancho chilli, seeded and finely chopped
  (see page 194)
1 tablespoon roughly chopped coriander
1 red pepper, skinned, seeded and finely diced
juice of 3 limes
$1/2$ fresh ripe pineapple, peeled, cored and
  finely diced
salt

Method

1. Put the onion into a plastic sieve or colander and sprinkle with the salt. Leave to stand for 10 minutes and rinse well with boiling water.

2. In a large bowl combine the onion with all the other ingredients and mix well. Season with salt and refrigerate for at least 30 minutes before using.

NOTE: *Lightly heat the ancho chilli under the grill for a more intense, deeper flavour.*

VARIATION: To make melon and chilli salsa, use half a honeydew melon, diced, instead of the pineapple.

Scotch Bonnet and Papaya Salsa

Scotch bonnet, Jamaican hot and habañero chillies are all from the same family; in fact, they look and taste very similar. They are the hottest chillies in the world, so should be handled with care and eaten with caution.

Ingredients

1 large onion, finely chopped
1 green Scotch bonnet or habañero chilli, seeded and finely chopped (see page 194)
1 ripe papaya, peeled, seeded and diced
1 small garlic clove, crushed
juice of 2 limes
3 tablespoons white wine vinegar
2 tablespoons chopped flat-leaf parsley
salt

Method

1. Put the onion in a sieve, rinse with hot water and drain.

2. Mix the onion with the remaining ingredients in a bowl and leave at room temperature for 1 hour. Season with salt and serve with seafood or fish.

Creoja Sauce

This is more of a dressing than a salsa, and delicious as a substitute for gravy with roast pork or veal. It can also be used to marinate and baste barbecued meat.

Ingredients

juice of 2 limes
4 tablespoons olive oil
1 tablespoon roughly chopped coriander
1 tablespoon roughly chopped flat-leaf parsley
1 teaspoon freshly chopped thyme
$1/2$ garlic clove, crushed
$1/2$ teaspoon red chilli paste (see page 180)
salt and freshly ground black pepper

Method

1. Thoroughly combine all the ingredients in a mixing bowl and season to taste with salt and pepper.

NOTE I: The hot chilli paste can be substituted by $1/2$ teaspoon crushed chillies or hot chilli sauce.

NOTE II: When using this salsa to baste meat for barbecues, tie 3 or 4 large sprigs of rosemary and/or thyme together and use as a brush. It will impart a delicate flavour to the meat.

Spicy Avocado Salsa

In Venezuela a finely chopped hardboiled egg is added to this salsa; the result is called *guasacaca*. It is delicious served as a dip with tortilla chips or with spicy chicken wings (see page 71).

Ingredients

5 tablespoons groundnut oil
3 tablespoons white wine vinegar
juice of 1 lime
$1/2$ teaspoon hot chilli powder
2 small tomatoes, seeded and diced
2 avocados, peeled and cut into 2.5cm/1 inch cubes
$1/2$ yellow pepper, seeded and finely diced
$1/2$ red pepper, seeded and finely diced
2 tablespoons finely chopped parsley
1 tablespoon chopped spring onion, white and green parts
salt and freshly ground pepper
hot chilli sauce (optional)

Method

1. Combine the oil, vinegar, lime juice and chilli powder in a large bowl and mix well with a wooden spoon. Add the diced tomatoes, avocados, yellow and red peppers, parsley and spring onions. Mix thoroughly and season to taste with salt, pepper and a few drops of hot chilli sauce.

Fresh Chilli Paste

A good thick sauce for chilli growers or lovers, this is also an invaluable seasoning companion for the daring cook.

Ingredients

200g/7oz fresh red chillies (Fresno or jalapeño), seeded and halved (see page 194)
hot water
2 teaspoons tomato purée
1 garlic clove, crushed
4 tablespoons groundnut oil
1 teaspoon ground cumin
1 tablespoon chopped fresh oregano
100ml/3fl oz chicken stock (see page 188)

Method

1. Rinse the chillies and drain. Put them in a bowl and cover with boiling water. Leave to stand for 1 hour, then drain.

2. Process the chillies, tomato purée, garlic, oil, cumin, oregano and stock until smooth.

3. In a small saucepan simmer the chilli purée, uncovered, for about 10 minutes or until the mixture is thickened. Season to taste with salt. When cold, store in a glass jar.

NOTE: This paste is also called salsa roja and can be made using small, fiercely hot red chillies, like tabasco or Thai chillies. Keep covered in the refrigerator for up to 2 weeks and use to flavour dips, stews and soups.

Thick Mango and Chilli Sauce

This sauce is very good with lean and not too strongly flavoured meat or fish. The sweetness of the mango and the heat from the chillies make a perfect match.

Ingredients

2 ripe mangoes
2 tablespoons sunflower oil
1 large onion, chopped
1 teaspoon ground cumin
1 tablespoon finely chopped fresh oregano
2 red Thai or Indian chillies, seeded and chopped (see page 194)
3 tablespoons white rum
3 tablespoons white wine vinegar
2 tablespoons soft light brown sugar
salt

Method

1. Peel the mangoes and cut the flesh into chunks.

2. Heat the oil in a large pan. Add the onion and cook until soft but not coloured, about 12 minutes.

3. Add the cumin, oregano, chillies and mangoes and cook over medium heat for about 10 minutes.

4. Add the rum, vinegar and sugar and bring to the boil. Reduce the heat and simmer for 15 minutes or until the mangoes are completely soft. Remove from the heat and season to taste with salt.

5. Transfer to a blender or food processor and process. The sauce should have the consistency of a soft purée. If is too thick, add a little water. Serve warm or cold.

Spicy Tomato Sauce

This sauce, which tastes and smells delicious, can be used in many different ways. It can be made up to two days in advance, refrigerated and reheated when needed.

Ingredients

1 x 1.8kg/1lb 13oz can chopped tomatoes
3 tablespoons sunflower oil
2 Kenyan or Fresno red chillies, seeded and finely chopped (see page 194)
2 garlic cloves, crushed
$1/2$ teaspoon ground cinnamon
$1/2$ teaspoon ground cumin
$1/2$ teaspoon ground coriander
good pinch cayenne pepper
good pinch paprika
1 tablespoon tomato purée
3 tablespoons chopped parsley
4 spring onions, white and green parts, chopped
$1/2$ teaspoon sugar
salt and freshly ground black pepper

Method

1. Mix all the ingredients together in a large, thick-bottomed pan and gently bring to the boil. Season with salt and pepper, reduce the heat, and cook, uncovered, for 30 minutes.

2. Taste, adjust the seasoning if necessary, and serve hot or cold.

NOTE: For a smooth sauce, purée the mixture at the end of cooking. It can be made up to 2 days in advance, then refrigerated and reheated when needed.

Yellow Chilli Paste

Pale yellow chillies can vary greatly in heat since there are quite a few different varieties. The most common ones are the Hungarian wax or the Cera, but any of the other varieties can be used. Just make sure to taste for heat.

Ingredients

1.75 litres/3 pints water
24 wax chillies (see page 196)
2 tablespoons sunflower oil
2 tablespoons white vinegar
2 tablespoons salt

Method

1. Bring the water to the boil in a large saucepan. Add the whole chillies and boil, uncovered, for 5 minutes. Drain and refresh under cold water.

2. Split the chillies in half, remove the seeds and discard (see page 194).

3. In a blender or food processor, mix the chillies, oil, vinegar and salt and process to a smooth purée. Transfer to a bowl, cover, and use as a substitute for fresh mild chilli.

Red Dried Chilli Paste

This is the basic recipe for a good chilli paste that will keep in the refrigerator for up to a month. It's easy to make and ideal as a table salsa for the more adventurous.

Ingredients

55g/2oz dried tabasco or hot red chillies (see page 199)
150ml/¼ pint boiling chicken stock (see page 188)
5 tablespoons olive oil
1 garlic clove, crushed
salt

Method

1. Break the chillies in half and brush out the seeds. Place the chillies and boiling stock in a bowl and leave for 2 hours.

2. In a blender or food processor, blend the chillies with the stock, oil and garlic. Season to taste with salt and process to a smooth purée. Transfer to a bowl, cover and refrigerate.

NOTE: This chilli paste is a good substitute for fresh chillies and will keep for up to a month if refrigerated. It can be used as a flavouring for dressings, mayonnaise, dips and sauces.

Chipotle Chilli Salsa

Chipotles are smoked, dried jalapeño chillies. They have a wonderful nutty flavour that goes well with stews, soups and salsas.

Ingredients

3 chipotle chillies (see page 198)
150ml/^{1}/$_4$ pint cider vinegar
6 tomatoes, seeded and finely diced
1 red pepper, seeded and finely diced
pinch sugar
2 tablespoons chopped parsley
^{1}/$_2$ teaspoon chopped oregano
salt

Method

1. Halve the chillies and brush out the seeds. Finely chop the flesh.

2. In a small saucepan bring the vinegar to the boil and remove from the heat. Add the chillies and set aside for 30 minutes.

3. Transfer the chillies and vinegar to a bowl and add all the remaining ingredients. Mix thoroughly and season to taste with salt.

Tomatillo and Apple Salsa

Tomatillos, also known as husk tomatoes, are small, green Mexican tomatoes with a distinctive tart flavour. Very popular in Mexico, they are sold fresh or in cans at speciality shops and can be substituted by green gooseberries.

Ingredients

5 fresh tomatillos, roughly chopped, or 12 gooseberries
1 yellow pepper, seeded and diced
1 small green apple, unpeeled, cored and finely diced
1 small onion, finely chopped
3 tablespoons roughly chopped coriander
2 tablespoons olive oil
2 tablespoons lime juice
2 green chillies, Fresno or jalapeño, seeded and finely chopped (see page 194)
^{1}/$_2$ teaspoon salt

Method

1. Mix all the ingredients together in a bowl. Season to taste with salt and leave at room temperature for 1 hour before serving.

Escabeche Sauce

Escabeche is a vinegar-based sauce and is also the name given to recipes where food is marinated or pickled in vinegar. It is a commonly used sauce for fried fish, but is also delicious with cooked vegetables. This recipe is easy to make and the chillies and peppers can be added to taste.

Ingredients

55ml/2 fl oz olive oil
3 medium onions, thinly sliced
3 tomatoes, peeled, seeded and cut into strips
1 green pepper, seeded and cut into strips
1 green jalapeño or Fresno chilli, seeded and
   thinly sliced (optional, see page 194)
$1/2$ teaspoon ground cumin
55ml/2 fl oz white wine vinegar
55ml/2 fl oz warm water
salt and freshly ground black pepper
12 green olives, stoned

Method

1. In a large saucepan heat the oil and cook the onions over medium heat until they are nearly soft, about 10 minutes.

2. Add the tomatoes, green pepper, chilli and cumin and cook for a further 5 minutes, stirring once or twice and taking care not to crush the tomatoes.

3. Add the vinegar and water and season with salt and pepper. Bring to the boil, remove from the heat and add the olives. Transfer to a serving dish and serve hot or cold.

NOTE: For a classic serving, fried fillets of white fish are placed on a bed of lettuce, the escabeche sauce is poured over and chopped coriander is used as a garnish.

Guacamole

Guacamole is a dip so well known outside Latin America that it scarcely needs an introduction. In Mexico the cooks put the avocado stone on top of the guacamole as it is believed to prevent the avocado from discolouring. Try it and see!

Ingredients

2 very ripe avocados
juice of 1 lime
1 small onion, finely chopped
1 teaspoon salt
boiling water
2 medium tomatoes, peeled, seeded and
    chopped
2 red jalapeño or Fresno chillies, seeded and
    finely chopped (see page 194)
dash Tabasco sauce
2 tablespoons chopped coriander
salt and freshly ground pepper

Method

1. Halve the avocados, remove the stone and roughly mash the flesh in the skin using a fork. Transfer to a bowl and add the lime juice. Mix thoroughly to prevent discolouring.

2. Put the onion into a non-metallic sieve, sprinkle with the salt and leave for 10 minutes. Pour boiling water over the onions and drain well. Pat dry with absorbent paper.

3. Add the onions, tomatoes, chillies, Tabasco and coriander to the avocados and mix well. Season to taste with salt and pepper and add a little more Tabasco if not hot enough.

4. Keep covered at room temperature until required.

Peanut, Chilli and Ricotta Cheese Dip

A versatile recipe, this can be used as a sandwich filling or dip.

Ingredients

225g/8oz smooth peanut butter
4 tablespoons double cream
4 tablespoons milk
55g/2oz ricotta or cottage cheese
4 tablespoons sunflower oil
3 tablespoons chopped coriander
salt and freshly ground pepper
1 teaspoon mild chilli powder

Method

1. Mix all the ingredients except the seasoning together in a blender or food processor and process until smooth.

2. Taste and season with salt, pepper and chilli powder.

Mayonnaise

This is a basic mayonnaise recipe which can be flavoured with chilli purées for a Latin twist and used in salads, sandwiches and dips.

Ingredients

2 egg yolks
salt and freshly ground white pepper
1 teaspoon mustard
290ml/^{1}/$_2$ pint olive oil, or 150ml/^{1}/$_4$ pint each
   olive oil and salad oil
squeeze of lemon juice
1 tablespoon white wine vinegar

Method

1. Put the yolks into a bowl with a pinch of salt and the mustard and beat well with a wooden spoon.

2. Add the oil literally drop by drop, beating all the time. The mixture should be very thick by the time half the oil is added.

3. Beat in lemon juice to taste.

4. Resume pouring in the oil, going rather more confidently now, but alternating the dribbles of oil with small quantities of vinegar.

5. Add salt and white pepper to taste.

VARIATION: To make spicy red pepper mayonnaise, grill 2 red peppers and 1 red Kenyan or jalapeño chilli, skin side up, until blistered and black. Peel, then process or chop finely to a pulp. Make the mayonnaise as above, seasoning with 1 teaspoon mild chilli powder instead of the mustard, and mix the purée in once the mayonnaise is made.

NOTE: *If the mixture curdles, another egg yolk should be beaten in a separate bowl, and the curdled mixture beaten into it drop by drop.*

Stocks

Most cooking in Latin America is done on top of the stove. In fact, it is not unusual, especially in Mexican recipes, for meat or poultry to be poached before being added to a sauce for further cooking, leaving behind valuable stock to be used in other dishes. As in most countries, however, stock cubes are frequently used – sometimes added to the water for boiling pasta, rice and beans. Most cooks would not dream of making fresh stock for a specific dish, mainly because many sauces are tomato or pepper based.

The secret of making good stocks is slow, gentle simmering. If the liquid is the slightest bit greasy, vigorous boiling will produce a murky, fatty stock. Skimming, especially of meat stocks, is vital. As fat and scum rise to the surface, they should be lifted off with a perforated spoon, perhaps every 10 or 15 minutes.

Vegetables, particularly onions, carrots and celery, add flavour and colour to stocks; leeks, tomato skins and seeds, and mushroom stalks can also be used if you like. The total weight of vegetables should be equal to or less than the weight of the bones.

A good way of storing a large batch of stock is to boil it down to double strength and to dilute it with water when using it. Alternatively, it can be boiled down to a thick syrupy glaze, which can be used like stock cubes. Many cooks freeze the glaze in ice-cube trays, then transfer the frozen cubes to a plastic box in the freezer. They will keep for at least a year if fat-free.

Chicken Stock

Ingredients

onion, sliced
celery stick, sliced
carrot, sliced
chicken bones
parsley
thyme
bay leaves
peppercorns

Method

1. Put all the ingredients into a saucepan. Cover generously with water and bring to the boil slowly. Skim off any fat and/or scum.
2. Simmer for 2–3 hours, skimming frequently and topping up the water level if necessary. The liquid should reduce to half the original quantity.

3. Strain, cool and lift off all the fat.

Brown Stock (Beef)

Ingredients

900g/2lb beef bones
1 onion, peeled and chopped (remove the skins)
2 carrots, cut into 4
1 tablespoon oil
parsley stalks
2 bay leaves
6 black peppercorns

Method

1. Preheat the oven to 220°C/425°F/
    gas mark 7.

2. Put the beef bones into a roasting tin and
    brown in the oven. This may take up to 1
    hour.

3. Heat the oil in a large stock pot and brown
    the onion and carrots. It is essential that
    they do not burn.

4. When the bones are well browned, add
    them to the vegetables with the onion skins,
    parsley stalks, bay leaves and black
    peppercorns. Cover with cold water and
    bring very slowly to the boil, skimming off
    any scum as it rises to the surface.

5. When clear of scum, simmer gently for 3–4
    hours, or even longer, skimming off the fat
    as necessary and topping up with water if
    the level gets very low. The longer it
    simmers and the more the liquid reduces by
    evaporation, the stronger the stock will be.

6. Strain, cool and lift off any remaining fat.

NOTE: To make glace de viande (concentrated
beef stock), boil the fat-free stock in a heavy-
bottomed saucepan over a steady heat until thick,
clear and syrupy. Pour into small pots. When cold,
cover with polythene or jam covers and secure.
This stock will keep in the refrigerator for several
weeks, or can be frozen in an ice-cube tray.

Fish Stock

Ingredients

onion, sliced
carrot, sliced
celery, sliced
fish bones, skins, fins, heads or tails
crustacean shells, e.g. prawn or mussel
parsley stalks
bay leaf
pinch chopped thyme
black peppercorns

Method

1. Put all the ingredients into a saucepan,
    cover with cold water and bring to the boil.
    Reduce the heat to a simmer and skim off
    any scum.

2. Simmer for 20 minutes if the fish bones are
    small, 30 minutes if large. Strain.

NOTE: The flavour of fish stock is impaired if the
bones are cooked for too long. Once strained,
however, it may be strengthened by further boiling
and reducing.

Chillies

CHILLIES

Archaeological evidence in Mexico shows the presence of chillies as far back as 6,000 years ago. All chillies belong to the *Solanaceae* family, as do tomatoes, potatoes and aubergines. The genus *Capsicum* (from the Latin *capsa*, meaning 'case') includes all peppers, from the sweet bell pepper to the hottest of chillies. There are 20 to 30 separate species of *Capsicum*: the *Annuum* includes almost all the most common chillies like Ancho, Ball, Cayenne, Jalapeños, Pasilla, Serrano. Most of the chillies found in South America, Like the Aji, belong to the *Baccatum* species, while the Hebanero and New Mexican or Anaheim chillies belong to the *Chinense* species. Given the widespread use of chillies in modern times, it is hard to believe that until the end of the 15th century, the people of Central and South America were the only ones using them in their cuisine. The Spanish and Portuguese took chillies to their colonies in Africa, Asia and India, where they were immediately incorporated into the local cuisines. By the end of the 16th century, chillies were known around the world and had become a major source of flavouring for millions of people.

There are hundreds of chilli varieties throughout the world, and one variety can have several different names, which is a source of confusion for the occasional chilli buyer. In North America, chillies tend to keep their Spanish Mexican or South American names. In the UK, chillies come via Africa or the Far East, where they are named differently. To confuse things even further, supermarkets tend to name the chillies by their country of origin, hence Thai, Indian and Kenyan.

Outside places like Mexico, India, South America and Spain, where they are part of a gastronomic heritage, chillies are often considered only as a source of heat. The variety of subtle flavours and the uses of fresh and dried chillies are just beginning to be discovered and appreciated. The `heat' comes from capsaicin, a bitter alkaloid concentrated mostly in the seeds and internal ribs or veins, which is measured in units called Scovilles. A mild chilli, such as Anaheim, rates 300–600 Scoville units, while the hottest of all the chillies, the habañero, rates 200,000–350,000 Scoville units. As a general rule, the smaller the chilli, the hotter it will be. Small chillies also tend to have lots more seeds and veins. As a rough guideline, expect the same heat from fresh and dried chillies, but as with dried fruit, dried chillies have a more intense and richer flavour, especially the mild large ones.

Fresh chillies are a very good source of vitamin C, while powdered chilli is rich in vitamin A. Chillies have been used in folk medicine for centuries and are believed to cure numerous illnesses, including bronchitis. They are also believed to help digestion and relieve congested noses. One of the reasons for their success in the hot areas of the world is that their spiciness makes people perspire, which lowers the body temperature.

While it cannot be said that chilli-eating is addictive, the palate does get used to the burning sensation they produce, so regular consumption means that hotter and hotter food is needed to give any impact.

Cooking with chillies

It is important to remember the following points when cooking with chillies.

1. The longer the chilli is cooked in a dish, the hotter the result. Capsaicin is not destroyed by heat or freezing, so start with very little chilli and adjust at the end of cooking.

2. Chilli pods of the same variety from the same tree vary in hotness, so taste a little piece before adding to a dish.

3. Chillies vary enormously in flavour, as well as in heat, so if possible, find out which variety you are using (see chilli chart, pages 195-9). There is no way of decreasing the heat once the dish is cooked, although adding sugar is believed to help. But since one can add just so much sugar to a savoury dish, it is best to taste the chilli beforehand.

4. Commercially made chilli sauces tend to contain too much vinegar and too many spices; they make up with heat what they lack in flavour. Home-made chilli paste and sauces are very easy to make and keep for a long time in the refrigerator. They can be used in a variety of dishes, such as dips, dressings, pasta, potatoes, rice, soups, stews and sandwiches, to name just a few.

5. Sensitivity to hot food varies enormously; what is unbearably hot for some is quite mild for others. To sooth the burning sensation of chillies, dairy products are useful. Try a little yoghurt, milk or soured cream to take away the heat. Alternatively, a mouthful of bland food, such as tortillas, rice, beans or potatoes, will also help `wash off' the heat from chillies.

Capsaicin, the chemical responsible for the hotness of chillies, dissolves in milk fat or alcohol, so contrary to popular belief, high-alcohol drinks, such as tequila or vodka, are more cooling than beer. (Alcohol also acts as a painkiller.) Very cold drinks (and that is where the beer comes in) are also thought to be a good antidote, simply because they numb the taste-buds and make the `burning' less obvious. The only drink that makes the burning worse is water, so avoid it!

6. To reduce the heat of chillies before cooking, remove the seeds and veins, which contain around 80 per cent of their heat. Soak the flesh in 3 parts vinegar to 1 part salt for 1 hour, rinse and follow the recipe.

Buying, storing and drying chillies

How to prepare chillies

WARNING Capsaicin, the substance in chillies responsible for their heat, can cause a very painful burning sensation if it comes into contact with the eyes, mouth or sensitive skin. Be sure to follow the instructions below.

Fresh chillies

Buy firm, smooth-skinned chillies with a bright colour. If the skin is wrinkled, the chillies have lost their moisture and will quickly start to decay where soft spots appear. Fresh chillies lose their flavour and moisture quickly, so avoid buying large quantities. Store wrapped in a cool, dry place, preferably the vegetable drawer in the refrigerator.

Dried chillies

Look for clear, plastic packaging so that the chillies can be checked. Large dried chillies should be supple and fragrant, a sign that their natural oils have not been lost during the drying process. Once opened, small or large dried chillies should be put into an airtight container and kept in a cool place. Alternatively, they can be frozen and defrosted just before being used. If they are dusty, just wipe them with a dry cloth.

Drying chillies

If you have a large amount of chillies at hand, they can be dried at home very easily. Most chilli varieties are suitable for drying, but only fully matured and preferably red chillies should be used. Using a large needle with heavy cotton thread, string the pods through their flesh close to their stems and hang in a warm, dry place inside, or a sunny, breezy place outside for a week, or until they are completely dry. They can then be crushed, powdered, frozen or kept in an airtight container.

PREPARING FRESH CHILLIES

Wearing rubber gloves, cut the chilli in half and wash under running water, discarding the seeds. To improve the flavour, and because the skin can be tough and bitter, chillies can be peeled. Grill or roast them until their skin is black, or, if using a small quantity, char them over an open gas flame using tongs or a fork. Once the skin is black, put the chillies in a plastic bag until they are cool enough to handle. Still using rubber gloves, remove the skins and discard. Any surfaces that came into contact with chillies should be washed very carefully.

PREPARING DRIED CHLLIES

Large dried chillies are safe enough to handle until they have been soaked, after which they should be handled as fresh chillies. To prepare a dried chilli, snap off the stalk and cut the pod in half lengthways. Brush out and discard the seeds, removing the internal ribs or veins. Tear the chilli into small pieces or snip with scissors, place in a bowl and cover with hot water or stock. Set aside to soak for at least 20 minutes. The smaller varieties of dried chilli should be handled with care and gloves should be worn. They do not need soaking and can be added directly to soups, stews and sauces.
Dried chillies develop a depth of flavour and increase their pungency if roasted or grilled for 5 minutes in a medium-hot oven or 3 minutes under a hot grill. They can also be dry-roasted in a non-stick frying pan until they begin to soften, about 2 minutes on each side. Overdoing it will make the chillies taste better.

FRESH CHILLIES

Fresh Chillies

1. Anaheim

2. Red Fresno

3. Jalapeños

4. Habañeros

5. Dutch or Westland

6. Wax

7. Thai or Indian

Fresh Chillies

NAME/CHARACTERISTICS	COLOURS	USES	SUBSTITUTES	HEAT SCALE
AJI or orange Thai chilli (*Capsicum baccatum*) Aji is a generic name for any chilli in South America. It measures 7–13cm/3–5 inches long and 1cm/$^{1}/_{2}$ inch wide with thin flesh. It has a fruity flavour and is quite hot. When dried it is called canagueño.	Yellow to orange.	In all Peruvian dishes, particularly ceviches. It is also good pickled in any Thai or Malayan dishes.	Brazilian malagueta (smaller and hotter) or 2 Indian chillies to 1 Aji.	
ANAHEIM or New Mexican (*Capsicum chinense*) 10–15cm/4–6 inches long, 2.5cm/1 inch wide and flattish. Smooth medium-thick flesh and a mild, sweet, vegetable flavour. The red Anaheim is sweeter than the green and also known as chilli Colorado.	Green and red.	Very versatile chilli. Flavour is improved by roasting, a delicious addition to roasted sweet pepper salads, sandwich fillings & green chilli sauces.	New Mexico green or red are a little bit hotter, but a good substitute.	
CAYENNE (*Capsicum annuum*) 7–13cm/3–5 inches long. Long, thin, sharply pointed. The many varieties include Hot Portugal or Ring of Fire, grown for their heat.	Green, red, yellow.	Primarily used for grinding into cayenne pepper or in bottled sauces.	Thai or Indian	
DUTCH or HOLLAND RED chilli, or Red or Green Westland chilli 10cm/4 inches long with a curved, tapering point; it has a thick flesh with a strong, fresh flavour.	Bright red or green.	Salsas, pickles, stews, soups and pipians (see glossary, page 280).	Red Thai or frescos.	
FRESNO or Kenyan (*Capsicum chinense*) 5cm/2 inches long, 2.5cm/1 inch wide on the shoulders, tapering to a round end. Sometimes mistaken for a red jalapeño, fresno has a medium-thick flesh with a sweet flavour.	Light green, red.	Good in everything, raw, cooked or grilled. Used in salsas, ceviches, soups and stir-fries.	Jalapeño, red or green, although less hot, make a perfect substitute.	
HABAÑERO, or Jamaican hot, Scotch bonnet, rocoto, rocotillo (*Capsicum chinense*) These chillies are all of the same family and have a very similar shape and taste. They are 5cm/2 inches long and roundish with an irregular shape which resembles a bonnet. The habañero and its cousins are the hottest chillies in the world with an intense, fruity flavour.	Deep green to orange and light red.	Its fierce heat goes really well with seafood and shellfish. Good for flavouring oils, vinegars, salsas and pickles.	Any *Capsicum chinense* will be a perfect substitute, although the heat varies slightly.	
JALAPEÑO (*Capsicum chinense*) The most used chilli in the USA. About 5–7cm/2–3 inches long, 2.5cm/1 inch wide and tapered to a round end. Juicy, thick-fleshed and rather stringy, with a clean, fresh vegetable flavour.	Grass green to dark green or red.	A very popular and versatile chilli which can be stuffed or grilled and used in anything from salsas to pickles, marinades to curries.	Fresno, even though slightly hotter, is a good substitute when roasted for salsas.	

CHILLIES ~ KEY: 🌶🌶🌶🌶 = VERY HOT   🌶 = FIERCELY HOT

NAME/CHARACTERISTICS	COLOURS	USES	SUBSTITUTES	HEAT SCALE
PIMIENTO (*Capsicum annuum*) 10cm/4 inches long, 7.5cm/3 inches wide, with almost a heart shape. It is a mild chilli, with thick flesh and found mostly canned or pickled. Once powdered it becomes paprika, a well-known spice.	Scarlet.	As a substitute for red peppers, pimentos can be stuffed, used in sauces and marinades, or grilled and cut into strips for sandwich fillings, salads or pasta dishes.	Hungarian sweet chilli has a paler colour but similar flavours and uses.	🌶
POBLANO (*Capsicum annuum*) 12cm/5.5 inches long, 7.5cm/3 inches wide on the shoulders, looking like a triangle with a tapered point. The poblano has a thick flesh with a mild but rich flavour. It is the most popular of the fresh chillies in Mexico.	The green-fleshed poblano has an aubergine skin colour, this becomes deep red brown when ripe.	The green variety is not eaten raw, but is always roasted and skinned and used mainly for stuffing. Poblanos also make good *mole* sauces and pipians (see glossary, page 280).	Although hotter, New Mexico red can be used.	🌶
SERRANO or Mountain Chilli (*Capsicum annuum*) Small, bullet-shaped chillies with a rounded end. Measuring 3–5cm/1–2 inches long, serranos have a thick, smooth flesh with a hard appearance. They are high in acidity with a pungent flavour.	Bright green and scarlet red	Used in salsas, pickles and relishes; thinly sliced to flavour stews, curries and other slow-cooking dishes, and also as a decoration chilli.	Thai chillies or ajis. (1 Thai to 3 Serranos)	🌶🌶🌶
TABASCO (*Capsicum frutescers*) 2.5cm/1 inch long, these small tapered chillies have a smooth skin and thin flesh. With a very hot and sharp flavour they constitute the main ingredient of the world-famous McIlhenny Tabasco pepper sauce.	Bright yellow, orange or red.	Soups, stews and flavouring oils.	Brazilian malagueta or Thai chillies (Indian in the UK).	🌶🌶🌶🌶
THAI or Indian chilli in the UK (*Capsicum annuum*) 2.5–5cm/1–2 inches long, slender with a pointed end. These are thin-fleshed with lots of seeds.	Bright red and dark green.	Used extensively in Asian cuisines, the Thai chilli is very good for flavouring oils and as a decorative element in soups, stews, stir-fries and noodle dishes.	Serranos or Brazilian malagueta (a bit hotter than the Thai).	🌶🌶🌶🌶
WAX chillies (*Capsicum annuum*) Includes chillies with very different characteristics, such as Hungarian wax, banana, caribe, Santa Fe, Cera, Gierro. Sizes vary from 7.5–10cm/3–4 inches long and the heat varies from medium to hot. They usually have a sweetish, waxy taste.	Pale yellow green to pale yellow.	Good for salsas (grilled, skinned and cut into strips) and for chilli purées.	Use any light yellow chilli with thick flesh, but make sure to taste a small piece before using any of them, as hotness can vary.	🌶🌶

197

DRIED CHILLIES

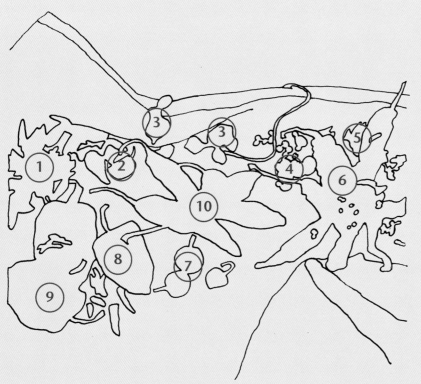

Dried Chillies

1. Cayenne

2. Chipotle

3. Habanero

4. Tepin

5. Bird's Eye

6. Pasilla

7. Cascabel

8. Ancho

9. Mulato

10. Guagillo

Dried Chillies

NAME/CHARACTERISTICS	USES	HEAT SCALE
ANCHO or DRIED POBLANO Dark mahogany in colour, 10–12cm/4–5 inches long and 7cm/3 inches on the shoulders. It is the sweetest dried chilli, with a mild flavour of prunes.	Stuffed rajas (strips), *moles*, salsas, soups, stews, chilli paste.	🌶🌶
BIRD'S EYE, Pequin, Chilli Pequeño or Piquin 1cm/$\frac{1}{2}$ long, small, bright orange to bright red, usually oval or arrowhead-shaped. Thin-fleshed with a smoky, sweet flavour.	Ideal for flavouring oils and vinegars, or in stews and soups.	🌶
CASCABEL, Little Rattle or Chilli Bola Round in shape, about 3.5cm/1$\frac{1}{2}$ inches long. Dark reddish-brown in colour, thick-fleshed and smooth-skinned with lots of seeds. Nutty, woody flavour, slightly acidic and tannic.	Soups, salsas, chilli paste with nuts.	🌶🌶
CAYENNE, Ginnie Pepper 5–10cm/2–4 inches long, tapering to a point. Bright red, thin-fleshed. Cayenne chillies have an acidic, tart flavour.	Most used in powdered form and in bottled sauces. Good for flavouring oils and vinegars.	🌶🌶🌶🌶
CHIPOTLE, Chilli Ahumado or Meco Chipotle is a smoked, dried red jalapeño. 2.5cm/1 inch long, 1cm/$\frac{1}{2}$ inch wide, dark brick to coffee colour with cream veins and ridges. A distinctive smoky and hot flavour.	Chipotle is good with everything; its smoky flavour gives an interest to all dishes, especially soups, salsas and stews.	🌶🌶🌶
GUAJILLO 10–15cm/4–6 inches long, 3.5cm/1 inches wide, slightly curved and tapered at the end. Shiny dark cherry in colour with thin skin and slightly tannic taste.	Guajillo is widely used in Mexico, mainly in sauces, soups and stews.	🌶
HABAÑERO 2.5cm/1 inch round, golden orange in colour. Thin-fleshed with intense heat, aroma and flavour. Dried or fresh, the habañero is the hottest chilli available. Its rich fruity flavour can be tasted even through all its heat.	It goes particularly well with fish soups and in stews, salsas and in chilli pastes. A little goes a long way.	🌶
MULATO 10–13cm/4–5 inches long, 5–7.5cm/2–3 inches wide. Dark brown in colour, the mulato is similar to the ancho, but larger and flatter. It has a medium-thick flesh and a smoky, pungent flavour with hints of tobacco and liquorice.	Very good stuffed, in salsas and mixed with mulato and pasilla for mole sauces.	🌶
PASILLA or Chilli Negro 13–15cm/5–6 inches long, 2.5cm/1 inch across. Shiny graphite colour, with twisted, tapered body. Liquorice and earthy flavour. It can be used instead of ancho, but it has a more pungent flavour.	Ideal chilli for any seafood. Pasilla is also used in powdered form and can be used in any salsa.	🌶🌶

Chilli-flavoured Oil

This oil can be used to make salad dressings, drizzled over potatoes or rice, used as a cooking oil or in marinades. You will need a 570ml/1 pint glass bottle.

Ingredients

425ml/³/₄ pint groundnut oil
10 dried tabasco or bird's eye chillies (see page 199)
1 teaspoon coriander seeds
1 teaspoon cayenne pepper
1 marjoram sprig or 1 teaspoon dried marjoram

Method

1. Place the glass bottle in a pan filled with water; make sure the bottle fills with water and bring to the boil. Boil for at least 10 minutes, remove from the water, drain and leave to dry completely.

2. Warm the oil in a large saucepan. Add the chillies, coriander seeds, cayenne and marjoram, mix carefully and simmer for 5 minutes.

3. Strain the oil through a funnel into the sterilized bottle. Add some of the chillies to the bottle for a decorative effect, but discard the remaining flavourings.

4. Cover and keep in a cool place. Alternatively, the chillies and herbs can be left in the oil and the bottle topped up with fresh oil as you use the original contents. This however, will gradually dilute the flavour.

Desserts and Ice-creams

DESSERTS AND ICE-CREAMS

Although fresh fruit is the dessert most commonly served on a daily basis in Latin America, there are numerous recipes for special and festive occasions. Of these, crème caramel and milk pudding are the undisputed favourites. The former, probably the first dessert a young cook will learn to make, is intensely sweet and may be flavoured with vanilla, chocolate, sweetcorn, cheese, nuts or coffee. Milk pudding is, if anything, even sweeter and, traditionally, a labour of love. Sugar and milk are boiled together for hours and must be stirred constantly. It is no exaggeration to say that the biggest gastronomic advance in Latin America has been the introduction of sweetened condensed milk in cans. Now milk pudding can be produced by boiling an unopened can of condensed milk for a mere $1^1/_2$ hours. Of course, purists and mothers-in-law deride this method...

The flavourings used in sweet dishes are many and various. Chocolate, a product native to Mexico, is used in desserts, cakes and drinks, but chocolate bars, as eaten in the northern hemisphere, take second place to the wide range of sweets made with coconut, sweet potatoes, nuts, caramel and candied fruit. Milk fudges, with nuts or coconut and amazingly bright food colourings, are sold in the streets and markets, usually by children, and are a feast for the eyes as well as the stomach.

Cream is very rarely used as an ingredient for making desserts, and seldom served with them; the only exception is ice-cream, which generally contains more fruit than cream anyway.

Sugar is used very heavily, mainly because of its keeping properties in hot climates, but also because Latin American countries are large producers of cane sugar, which makes it cheap and readily available.

The following recipes are a mixture of updated classics and new inventions inspired by the variety of fruits, nuts, seeds and flavourings found in Latin America. Many, such as charlottes, mousses and ice-creams, resemble their European ancestors but have an added tropical twist.

Unless stated otherwise, all recipes make 4 servings.

Flambé Bananas with Vanilla Ice-cream

Flambé bananas is a very popular dessert in South America and is usually served with a lot of panache in good restaurants.

Ingredients

6 large bananas
grated zest and juice of 1 lime or lemon
$1/2$ teaspoon ground cinnamon
pinch ground cloves
$1/2$ teaspoon ground allspice
55g/2oz butter
30g/1oz soft dark brown sugar
grated zest and juice of 1 orange
3 tablespoons Grand Marnier or Curacao

To serve: vanilla ice-cream (see page 229)

Method

1. Peel the bananas and slice them in half lengthwise. Toss them in the lime or lemon juice to prevent them discolouring.

2. Place the spices in a large frying pan and cook, stirring, for 1 minute. Add the butter and mix thoroughly. When the butter is melted and hot, add the bananas with the lime juice. Using two wooden spoons, turn the bananas gently, taking care not to crush them. Add the sugar, the orange juice and zest and the lime zest, and gently toss the bananas in the liquid.

3. Turn up the heat and allow the bananas to get some colour without stirring; just shake the pan gently from time to time.

4. Place the Grand Marnier or Curaçao in a ladle, heat it over a flame, then pour over the bananas. Light a match, stand back and set the alcohol alight. Shake the pan gently until the flames subside.

5. To serve: put 2 banana halves on a plate, add a generous serving of vanilla ice-cream and spoon the remaining sauce over the bananas. Serve at once.

Nut and Coffee Tart with Coffee Cream

Latin American desserts tend to be very sweet but not particularly rich. In this recipe, however, sugar and nuts meet with a vengeance, to make a deliciously rich and sweet confection with just a hint of coffee.

Ingredients

170g/6oz flour quantity rich shortcrust pastry
  (see page 251)

For the filling:
2 tablespoons instant coffee granules
4 tablespoons hot water
85g/3oz soft dark brown sugar
3 large eggs
4 tablespoons light golden syrup
juice of 1 lime
110g/4oz unsalted butter, melted and cooled
pinch salt
85g/3oz walnuts, roughly chopped
85g/3oz Brazil nuts, roughly chopped
85g/2oz pine nuts

To serve: 150ml/$^1/_4$ pint double cream
1 teaspoon icing sugar

Method

1. Preheat the oven to 200°C/400°F/gas mark 6.

2. Roll out the pastry and line a 24cm/9$^1/_2$ inch loose-bottomed flan tin. Chill in the refrigerator for 20 minutes.

3. Bake the pastry `blind' (see page 274), then reduce the oven temperature to 180°C/350°F/gas mark 4.

4. Dissolve the instant coffee in a large bowl with the hot water and save 1 teaspoon for flavouring the cream. Whisk in the eggs, golden syrup, lime juice, butter and salt. Scatter the nuts on to the pastry base and gently pour the egg mixture over the nuts.

5. Bake in the middle of the oven until set, about 30 minutes. Remove from the oven and transfer to a rack to cool.

6. Lightly whip the cream, add the reserved coffee essence and sugar and mix well. Serve with the tart.

Pineapple Charlotte

This is a very popular dessert in Brazil, where it is made using pineapples, peaches or prunes and layered on a flat dish instead of in the traditional deep charlotte mould.

Ingredients

570ml/1 pint water
255g/9oz caster sugar
$1/2$ pineapple, peeled, cored and cut into
   2.5cm/1 inch cubes
4 tablespoons water
2 scant tablespoons powdered gelatine
570ml/1 pint milk
4 egg yolks
110g/4oz caster sugar
55g/2oz flour
5 tablespoons white rum
24 sponge finger biscuits
55g/2oz desiccated coconut

Method

1. Mix the 570ml/1 pint of water with the sugar in a large saucepan. Cook over a low heat until the sugar is dissolved, then add the pineapple chunks. Cook gently for 20 minutes or until the pineapple is soft. Drain and reserve the syrup.

2. Put the 4 tablespoons of water into a small, heavy saucepan. Sprinkle over the gelatine and leave to soak for 10 minutes.

3. Scald the milk. In a bowl, lightly beat the yolks with the sugar, add the flour and mix thoroughly to form a paste. Pour the hot milk on to the mixture, mix well and pour it back into the pan. Cook over gentle heat for 2 minutes or until it thickens slightly to form a custard.

4. Dissolve the gelatine over gentle heat, and when clear, stir in half the rum. Add to the custard and mix well.

5. Add the remaining rum to the syrup.

6. Line a charlotte mould or soufflé dish (16cm/$6^1/2$ inches wide x 8cm/3 inches deep) with cling film. Dip one biscuit at a time into the syrup and line the sides of the mould. Put half the pineapple chunks at the bottom of the mould and pour in half the custard. Sprinkle with half the coconut and add the remaining diced pineapple. Cover with the remaining custard and finish with a layer of biscuits.

7. Cover with a piece of oiled cling film, then put a plate and a 225g/8oz weight on top. Refrigerate for at least 6 hours.

8. Unmould and decorate the top with the remaining coconut.

VARIATIONS: Prune charlotte: Poach 110g/4oz dried prunes in syrup until soft, then follow the recipe.
- Peach charlotte: Finely slice the contents of a 400g/14oz can of peaches, then follow the recipe.
- Add 110g/4oz toasted and ground peanuts to the custard and dip the biscuits in 290ml/ $1/2$ pint coffee mixed with the rum. Sprinkle the top with toasted ground peanuts instead of coconut.

NOTE: When making this recipe in a flat dish, layer the syrup-dipped biscuits alternately with the custard, finishing with a layer of custard. Sprinkle the whole surface with desiccated coconut, then cover and chill.

Lime and Lemon Mousse with Pistachio Praline

Lemons are not easily found in South America, but limes are extensively used. Since limes have a sourer taste than lemons, they help balance the sweetness in this recipe in a very delicious way.

Ingredients

1 x 400g/14oz can sweetened, condensed
   skimmed milk
grated zest and juice of 3 limes
grated zest and juice of 2 lemons
3 egg whites
pinch salt
1 tablespoon caster sugar
$^1/_4$ pint double cream

For the praline:
30g/1oz pistachio nuts, unsalted and shelled
55g/2oz granulated sugar

Method

1. In a large bowl, whisk the condensed milk, juice and zest of the limes and lemons until thick, about 1 minute.

2. In another large bowl whisk the egg whites with a pinch of salt until stiff but not dry. Add the sugar and whisk until shiny, about another minute.

3. Lightly whip the cream.

4. Using a large metal spoon, fold the whipped cream and then the whisked egg whites into the lime and lemon mixture. Taste and add more lemon juice if not sharp enough. Pile the mousse into individual glasses or into a large glass dish and chill for at least 4 hours.

5. Meanwhile, make the praline: grease a baking sheet. Put the pistachio nuts and sugar into a thick-bottomed saucepan and place over gentle heat. As the sugar begins to melt, stir carefully with a metal spoon to coat the nuts. Continue cooking until the mixture is thoroughly caramelized (browned). Quickly tip on to the oiled tray and leave to cool. When completely cold, break into fragments or pound to a coarse powder in a mortar or blender. It can be stored up to a week in an airtight container.

6. Just before serving, cover the mousse completely with a very fine layer of the praline and serve at once.

NOTE: This mousse should have a very sharp lime/lemon taste to balance the sweetness of the pistachio praline.

Crunchy Banana Dessert

Bananas are so delicious in the tropics that they are usually eaten fresh. They are sometimes cooked to prevent discoloration, but even then they tend to become quite brown. This recipe is best if using very ripe bananas with lots of flavour.

Ingredients

6 ripe bananas
110g/4oz soft dark brown sugar
juice of 1 lime
3 tablespoons water
Greek yoghurt
190ml/^{1}/$_3$ pint double cream

For the crunchy topping:
55g/2oz butter
5 tablespoons white breadcrumbs
55g/2oz soft light brown sugar
1^1/$_2$ teaspoons ground cinnamon

For the garnish:
1 tablespoon icing sugar

Method

1. Peel the bananas and mash with a fork. In a large skillet mix the mashed bananas with the sugar, lime juice and water and cook until well blended, about 5 minutes. Transfer to a large bowl, add the yoghurt and mix well.

2. Whip the cream till it falls in ribbons, then gently fold it into the banana mixture. Taste and add some lemon juice if too sweet. Pour into a glass bowl or individual glasses and refrigerate.

3. To make the crunchy crumbs: melt the butter in a frying pan and very slowly fry the breadcrumbs in it, stirring frequently until they have absorbed most of the butter and are golden and crisp. Mix in the soft brown sugar and cinnamon and stir until the crumbs are coated with caramelized sugar. Transfer to a plate to cool.

4. Just before serving, sprinkle the banana cream with the sweet breadcrumbs and dust with icing sugar. Serve at room temperature.

Mexican Bread Pudding

This is a richer and sweeter version of bread and butter pudding. It is delicious warm or cold. If making it for children, replace the rum with apple juice.

Ingredients

200g/7oz raisins
140g/5oz dried prunes, roughly chopped
55ml/2 fl oz white rum
310g/11oz stale white bread cut into 2.5cm/
    1 inch pieces
140g/5oz walnuts, roughly chopped
290ml/^{1}/$_2$ pint single cream
290ml/^{1}/$_2$ pint milk
340g/12oz apple sauce (see page 222)
110g/4oz caster sugar
85g/3oz unsalted butter, melted
3 large eggs, beaten
1 teaspoon ground cinnamon
^{1}/$_2$ teaspoon ground nutmeg
30g/1oz soft light brown sugar

Method

1. Combine the raisins, dried prunes and rum in a bowl and set aside to marinate for 1 hour. Drain and discard the liquid.

2. Preheat the oven to 180°C/350°F/gas mark 4.

3. Generously butter a 28cm/11 inch oblong dish and scatter the drained raisins and prunes at the bottom. Put the bread pieces and chopped walnuts on top.

4. Place the cream, milk, apple sauce, sugar, melted butter, eggs, cinnamon and nutmeg in a large bowl and mix well.

5. Strain the mixture over the bread and cover the dish with tin foil. Bake in the preheated oven until the centre of the pudding is firm, about 1 hour. Serve warm or cold.

6. Heat the grill to its highest setting. Sprinkle the brown sugar evenly over the pudding and place under the grill until the sugar is slightly caramelized. Serve hot or warm.

Tropical Fruit Salad with Cinnamon Crème Chantilly

Fruit salads are very popular everywhere in South America, and the leftovers are usually puréed in a blender with some orange juice to make a fresh fruit shake. Throughout Brazil fruit bars specialize in making fresh fruit drinks in almost any combination of flavours to suit the customer's taste.

Ingredients

1 ripe mango
2 small, ripe papayas
2 bananas
$1/2$ fresh pineapple
1 honeydew melon
2 oranges
1 pink grapefruit
4 passion-fruit, halved
1 x 2.5cm/1 inch root ginger, peeled and grated
150ml/$1/4$ pint coconut milk (see page 276)
1 tablespoon white rum (optional)

For the crème Chantilly:
290ml/$1/2$ pint double cream
few drops vanilla essence
1 tablespoon icing sugar
good pinch ground cinnamon

To serve: ginger tuiles (see page 250)

Method

1. Peel the mango, papaya, bananas, pineapple and half the melon, and cut into 3.5cm/$1^1/2$ inch cubes.

2. Peel and segment the oranges and grapefruit and mix with the prepared fruit in a large bowl.

3. In a blender purée the remaining melon with the passion-fruit pulp, ginger, coconut milk and rum until smooth. Sieve and add to the fruit. Mix thoroughly, cover and refrigerate.

4. Meanwhile make the crème Chantilly. Mix the cream, vanilla essence, icing sugar and cinnamon and whip to soft-peak consistency.

5. To serve: spoon a generous amount of crème Chantilly over individual bowls of fruit salad. Hand the ginger tuiles separately.

Peruvian Coffee Chocolate Pots

The combination of chocolate and coffee appears in many recipes for desserts, baked goods and drinks. This is a deliciously rich and creamy dessert which develops a better flavour if made a day in advance.

Ingredients

290ml/$\frac{1}{2}$ pint full-fat milk
290ml/$\frac{1}{2}$ pint single cream
1 vanilla pod, split in half lengthwise
2 tablespoons instant coffee granules
55g/2oz granulated sugar
100ml/3 fl oz water
85g/3oz dark chocolate, finely chopped
3 egg yolks
55g/2oz caster sugar

For the garnish:
chocolate shavings

Method

1. Preheat the oven to 150°C/300°F/gas mark 2.

2. In a small saucepan bring the milk, cream and vanilla pod to the boil. Add the instant coffee, stir well and set aside.

3. Put the granulated sugar into a heavy pan with half the water and allow to melt slowly. When the sugar has melted completely, boil rapidly until it has turned to caramel. Imediately tip in the remaining water (it will splutter dangerously, so stand back). Stir until dissolved, then remove from the heat. Add the chocolate, stirring until melted. Strain the infused milk into the caramel/chocolate mixture and mix well.

4. In a bowl mix the egg yolks and the caster sugar and beat until pale with a wooden spoon. Pour the milk mixture on to the yolks and mix thoroughly.

5. Strain the mixture into 6 individual ramekins or 1 large soufflé dish and cover with tin foil. Put the pots in a shallow baking tin and add enough hot water to reach one third of the way up the sides of the pots. Bake for 25 minutes (35 minutes if using one large dish) or until just set. Remove from the oven, uncover and leave to cool. Refrigerate overnight or for at least 4 hours before serving.

6. Garnish with chocolate shavings.

Grilled Pineapple Skewers with Coconut Ice-cream

Pineapple is a very popular fruit in tropical America, used mainly in sweets, puddings, ice-creams and drinks. Large slices of freshly cut pineapple are sold on market stalls as a fruit snack.

Ingredients

1 large fresh pineapple
1 tablespoon cornflour
30g/1oz butter

For the marinade:
grated zest and juice of 2 limes
2 tablespoons soft dark brown sugar
1 teaspoon ground cinnamon
1/2 teaspoon ground allspice
2 tablespoons clear honey
2 tablespoons rum
grated zest and juice of 1/2 orange

For the garnish:
mint leaves

To serve: coconut ice-cream (see page 226)

Method

1. Peel the pineapple, cut into 4 lengthwise pieces, then remove the core. Cut the flesh into 5cm/2 inch cubes.

2. Mix all the marinade ingredients together in a large bowl, add the pineapple chunks and toss them well. Cover and leave to marinate at room temperature for 1 hour.

3. Heat the grill to its highest setting. Brush a baking sheet with oil.

4. Thread the pineapple cubes on to 4 large or 8 small skewers and baste with some of the marinade. Put the skewers on the oiled baking sheet. Grill for 5 minutes on each side, or until the pineapple has some colour.

5. Meanwhile, mix the cornflour with 2 tablespoons of the marinade. Put the remaining marinade into a small pan and bring to the boil. Add the cornflour mixture and cook, stirring, until slightly thickened.

6. Whisk in the butter with a fork or small balloon whisk until the sauce is shiny and the butter completely melted.

7. To serve: spoon some of the sauce on to a plate, add 2 small scoops of coconut ice-cream on one side and arrange the pineapple skewer on the other side. Garnish with a sprig of mint and hand any remaining sauce separately.

Pineapple and Star Anise Compote

This easy-to-make recipe is sometimes cooked until the compote almost sets; it can then be rolled into small balls, dusted with sugar and served as petits fours or used as a stuffing for stoned prunes. In any form it is simply delicious.

Ingredients

1 large, ripe pineapple
caster sugar (see step 1)
2 whole star anise
grated zest and juice of 1 lemon
$1/2$ teaspoon ground cloves
pinch ground cinnamon

To serve: coconut ice-cream (see page 226)
light groundnut oil cake (see page 237)

Method

1. Peel, core and cut the pineapple into chunks. Weigh the fruit, then measure out the same weight of caster sugar.

2. In a blender process half the sugar with the whole star anise until the sugar is powdery and the star anise is finely ground.

3. In a large saucepan mix both sugars, pineapple chunks, lemon zest and juice, ground cloves and cinnamon and leave to stand for 30 minutes.

4. Bring the mixture to the boil and cook over medium heat, stirring constantly, until the pineapple breaks up into shreds and there is almost no liquid left, about 25 minutes.

5. Serve warm with coconut ice-cream or use to sandwich the groundnut oil cake. This is also delicious served well chilled with plain yoghurt.

VARIATION: For a Caribbean flavour add 85g/3oz freshly grated coconut at step 3.

'Burnt' Coconut Crème Caramel

Crème caramel, known as *flan* in Spanish, is a favourite dessert throughout Latin America, where it is made in a variety of flavours, including cheese, walnut, chocolate, sweetcorn and coffee. It is usually made using sweetened condensed milk and is much sweeter than its European counterpart.

Ingredients

85g/3oz desiccated coconut
110g/4oz granulated sugar
4 eggs
2 tablespoons caster sugar
570ml/1 pint full-fat milk

Method

1. Preheat the oven to 180°C/350°F/gas mark 4.

2. Put the coconut on a baking sheet and place in the oven for 20 minutes or until lightly toasted.

3. Turn the oven down to 150°C/300°F/gas mark 2. Put a 1.14 litre/2 pint hole-in-the-middle mould or gratin dish in the oven for 10 minutes.

4. Place the granulated sugar in a heavy pan with 4 tablespoons of water and allow it to melt slowly over low heat. When the sugar has melted completely, boil rapidly until it becomes a rich brown caramel. Add half the toasted coconut, then pour into the warmed mould, tilting it carefully to coat the inside. Leave to cool completely.

5. In a bowl, beat the eggs and caster sugar with a wooden spoon until pale.

6. Scald the milk with the remaining toasted coconut and stir into the egg mixture. Mix thoroughly and strain into the caramel-coated mould.

7. Fill a deep baking dish with hot water and put the mould in the middle. Bake for about 1 hour or until the custard has set. Remove from the oven and leave to cool in the mould. Refrigerate overnight or for at least 4 hours before unmoulding it.

VARIATIONS:
- Walnut: Add 110g/4oz ground walnuts before scalding the milk at step 6, then follow the recipe as above. Unmould the pudding and decorate with walnut halves.
- Chocolate: Add 85g/3oz cocoa powder before scalding the milk at step 6, then follow the recipe. After unmoulding the pudding, decorate with chocolate shavings.

NOTE: Heating the mould slightly helps the caramel coating to stick more easily and evenly.

Quince Purée

Quinces belong to the apple and pear family; in fact, they look very much like apples, with firm, pale yellow, dry flesh, but are not eaten raw. When cooked, the flesh becomes pale pink. Quinces are used to make a very popular fruit paste called *membrillo* in Spain, *marmelada* in Portugal and *pâté de coing* or *cotignac* in France, which is usually eaten with soft cheese. They can also be used with apples, or as a substitute for them, in tarts, pies and pork dishes.

Ingredients

450g/1lb quinces
85g/3oz caster sugar
150ml/^{1}/$_4$ pint black grape juice
2 teaspoons ground allspice
juice and 2 strips of peel from 1 lemon

To serve: Brazil nut shortbread (see page 246)

Method

1. Peel, core and slice the quinces finely.

2. Place the slices in a large, heavy pan with the sugar, grape juice, allspice, lemon peel and juice and mix thoroughly. Bring to the boil, reduce the heat and simmer gently until the quince is very soft, about 35 minutes.

3. Remove the lemon peel and mash the fruit with a potato masher or fork, leaving a bit of texture. If still too watery, boil rapidly until all the liquid has evaporated. Serve warm or cold with Brazil nut shortbread.

NOTE: The puree can be served with yoghurt, crème fraîche or cakes.

French Pancakes (Crêpes)

Many classic French recipes, such as this, are now part of the cosmopolitan cook's repertoire. Crêpes are most commonly used in savoury dishes, but are delicious served with sweet fillings.

Ingredients

110g/4oz plain flour
pinch salt
1 egg
1 egg yolk
290ml/$^1/_2$ pint milk, or milk and water mixed
1 tablespoon oil
oil for cooking

Method

1. Sift the flour and salt into a small bowl, then make a 'well' in the centre, exposing the bottom of the bowl.

2. Place the egg and egg yolk in the well with a little of the milk.

3. Using a wooden spoon or whisk, mix the eggs and milk, gradually drawing in the flour from the sides.

4. When the mixture reaches the consistency of single cream, beat well and stir in the oil.

5. Add the rest of the milk; the consistency should now be that of thin cream. (The batter can also be made by placing all the ingredients in a liquidizer for a few seconds, but take care not to over-blend or the mixture will be bubbly.)

6. Cover the bowl and refrigerate for about 30 minutes. (This allows the starch cells to swell, giving a lighter result.)

7. Prepare a pancake pan or frying pan by heating well and wiping with oil. Pancakes are not actually fried in fat – the purpose of the oil is simply to prevent sticking.

8. When the pan is ready, pour in about 15ml/1 tablespoon of batter and swirl about the pan until evenly spread across the bottom.

9. Place over the heat for 1 minute, then use a palette knife and your fingers to turn the pancake over and cook the other side until brown. (Pancakes should be extremely thin, so if the first one is too thick, add a little extra milk to the batter. The first pancake is unlikely to be perfect, and is often discarded.)

10. Make up all the pancakes, turning them out on to a clean tea towel or plate.

Crème Anglaise

This custard sauce is an essential part of many puddings, such as charlottes and tarts, but it is equally delicious served on its own.

Ingredients

290ml/$\frac{1}{2}$ pint milk
1 vanilla pod, split in half lengthwise
2 egg yolks
1 tablespoon sugar
4 drops vanilla essence (optional)

Method

1. Heat the milk and split vanilla pod. Bring slowly to the boil.

2. Mix the egg yolks and sugar in a bowl. Remove the vanilla pod from the pan and pour the milk on to the egg yolks, stirring steadily. Mix well and return to the pan.

3. Stir over gentle heat until the mixture thickens enough to coat the back of a spoon; this will take 8–10 minutes. Do not boil. Pour into a cold bowl.

4. Add the vanilla essence, if using.

VARIATIONS: To flavour the crème anglaise add any of the following to the milk instead of the vanilla pod.
- grated zest of 1 orange plus 2 tablespoons Grand Marnier.
- 2.5cm/1 inch root ginger, peeled and grated plus 1 teaspoon ground ginger.
- 1 cinnamon stick plus $\frac{1}{2}$ teaspoon ground cinnamon.
- 1 tablespoon instant coffee.

At the end of the cooking time you can add the sieved pulp of 4 passion-fruit plus 1 tablespoon rum.

Milk Pudding

Milk pudding is made by cooking milk and sugar over a low heat until the mixture thickens and becomes toffee-coloured. This popular dessert is called *dulce de leche* or *leche quemada* in Spanish-speaking countries, and *doce de leite* in Brazil.

Although easy to make, milk pudding is time-consuming to prepare and it needs constant stirring to prevent it from catching at the bottom of the pan. It can be cooked to various consistencies; at the 'spoon' stage it has the consistency of soft-set jam, but it may be cooked until it is solid enough to cut, like a fudge. It can be made by boiling an unopened can of sweetened condensed milk in water for $1\frac{1}{2}$ hours, but the result, even though delicious, does not have the same delicate texture and flavour achieved by the slow cooking method.

Two versions of milk pudding are given opposite: one is a traditional recipe and the other a short cut taken from *The Book of Latin American Cooking*, by Elisabeth Lambert Ortiz.

Traditional Milk Pudding

Ingredients

1.75 litres/3 pints full-fat milk
590g/1lb 5oz granulated sugar
1 teaspoon bicarbonate of soda

Method

1. Mix the milk and sugar and soda together in a large, heavy saucepan and bring to the boil, stirring continuously. Once the milk has boiled, reduce the heat to a gentle simmer and cook, uncovered, stirring every 5 minutes until the mixture is reduced by one third, about 1$\frac{1}{2}$ hours.

2. Increase the heat slightly and stir constantly with a wooden spoon until the mixture is light toffee-coloured and thick enough for you to see the bottom of the pan when the spoon is drawn across it, about 45 minutes to 1 hour.

3. Remove from the heat and beat the mixture with a balloon whisk until creamy and cool, about 2 minutes. Keep refrigerated for up to 3 weeks or indefinitely in sterilized jam jars. The mixture can be used as a filling for cakes or served on its own.

NOTE: This recipe is very good for using lsrge quantities of milk and the ratio is 200g/7oz granulated sugar for each 570ml/ 1 pint milk. The zest of 1 lime or $\frac{1}{2}$ an orange can be added to the milk at the beginning of cooking for a nice flavour and chopped nuts or raisons soaked in liquuer can be added at the end for variation.

Colombian Milk Pudding

This Colombian recipe is a compromise between the traditional method and the 'boil in the can' one. The result is a creamy milk pudding.

Ingredients

1 x 400g/14oz can evaporated milk
1 x 400g/14oz can skimmed, sweetened condensed milk

Method

1. Mix the ingredients together in a heavy saucepan and bring to the boil. Reduce the heat and simmer, stirring constantly, until the mixture is thick and toffee-coloured, about 25 minutes.

2. Transfer to a bowl and refrigerate until needed. It will keep up to a week in the refrigerator, but indefinitely if poured into sterilized jars while still hot.

NOTE: A traditional way of serving milk pudding is with a thick slice of cheese (mozzarella, Gouda or Edam) and a cup of strong black coffee.

Apple Sauce

A slight variation on traditional apple sauce, this version can be used as an ingredient in other recipes or eaten on its own with yoghurt or ice-cream.

Ingredients

450g/1lb cooking apples
finely grated zest of 1 lime
$^1/_2$ teaspoon ground allspice
3 tablespoons water
2 teaspoons sugar
15g/$^1/_2$oz butter

Method

1. Peel, quarter, core and slice the apples.

2. Place in a heavy saucepan with the lime zest, allspice, water and sugar. Cover with a lid and cook very slowly until the apples are soft.

3. Beat in the butter, cool slightly and add extra sugar if required. Serve hot or cold.

Poaching Syrup

This is a basic recipe for syrup which can be used to poach any fruit and flavoured in many ways. Cinnamon sticks, star anise, citrus rind and herbs such as rosemary and thyme can all be used with tasty results.

Ingredients

285g/10oz granulated sugar
570ml/1 pint hot water

Method

1. Put the sugar and water into a wide-bottomed sauté pan and place over low heat until the sugar has dissolved. Add any spices or flavourings to taste.

2. Bring to the boil without stirring.

3. Boil until the syrup reaches the required concentration.

4. Use as required.

NOTE: Strirring causes sugar crystals to form on the sides of the pan. Should this happen, dip a clean pastry brush into hot water and brush the side of the pan to dissolve the crystals.

Mango and Passion-fruit Ice-cream

Mangoes are commonly used to make ice-creams, but passion-fruit is more often used for ice lollies. The mixture of both is certain to please Latins and Europeans alike!

MAKES 860ML/1½ PINTS

Ingredients

3 large, very ripe mangoes
4 passion-fruit
85g/3oz icing sugar
juice of 1 lemon
70g/2½oz sugar
110ml/4 fl oz water
6 egg yolks
290ml/½ pint double cream

Method

1. Peel the mangoes and remove all the flesh. Cut the passion-fruit in half and scoop out the inside. Process the mangoes, passion-fruit, icing sugar and lemon juice to a purée. Push through a sieve and set aside.

2. Place the sugar and water in a saucepan and dissolve over gentle heat. When completely dissolved, boil the mixture to the thread stage (see page 282). Cool for 1 minute.

3. Pour the sugar syrup on to the egg yolks and whisk until the mixture is thick and mousse-like. Do not allow the syrup to come into contact with the whisk when adding it to the yolks, or it will soildify

4. Lightly whip the cream, then fold in the mango purée and egg mixture. Pour into freezer containers, chill and freeze.

5. When half-frozen, rewhisk and refreeze.

Peanut Crunch Ice-cream

Peanut recipes are great favourites in many Latin American countries, especially when they appeal to the nations' sweet tooth.

MAKES 1.14 LITRES/2 PINTS

Ingredients

85g/3oz granulated sugar
4 tablespoons water
85g/3oz unsalted, shelled and toasted peanuts
425ml/^{3}/$_4$ pint milk
290ml/^{1}/$_2$ pint double cream
3 tablespoons smooth peanut butter
140g/5oz caster sugar
6 egg yolks
few drops vanilla essence

Method

1. Grease a baking sheet. Put the granulated sugar into a heavy pan with the water and allow to dissolve slowly. When it has dissolved completely, boil the liquid rapidly until it turns to caramel. Remove the pan from the heat, add the peanuts, then quickly tip the mixture on to the greased tray and leave to cool.

2. Put the milk, double cream, peanut butter and sugar into a heavy saucepan and bring slowly to the boil. Beat the yolks with the vanilla in a large bowl.

3. Pour the scalding milk mixture on to the yolks, whisking as you do so. Pour into a roasting pan or 2 ice trays. Leave to cool.

4. Freeze the ice-cream until solid but still soft enough to give when pressed with a finger.

5. When the peanut and caramel crunch is completely cold, break it into fragments, using a rolling pin.

6. Tip the ice-cream into a cold bowl, break it up, then whisk with a rotary beater until smooth, pale and creamy. Fold in the peanut and caramel chunks and refreeze. Remove from the freezer 20 minutes before serving.

Guava, Cinnamon and Ginger Ice-cream

Guava is popular in all tropical countries; its delicate flavour and strong aroma make a delicious ice-cream.

MAKES 860ML/1½ PINTS

Ingredients

2 x 400g/14oz cans guava halves in syrup
1 strip lemon zest
1 teaspoon ground cinnamon
30g/1oz icing sugar
2.5cm/1 inch ginger root, peeled and grated
juice of 1 lime
290ml/½ pint double cream, lightly whipped

Method

1. Put the guava halves and their syrup into a saucepan, add the lemon zest, cinnamon, icing sugar, grated ginger and lime juice and bring to the boil.

2. Simmer, covered, for 20 minutes. Remove the lemon rind and liquidize the mixture until smooth. Sieve and allow to cool.

3. Fold the lightly whipped cream into the guava purée. Taste, and if too sweet, add a few more drops of lime juice.

4. Chill, then freeze. When half-frozen, whisk well and return to the freezer.

NOTE: If fresh guavas are available, use 450g/1lb. Wash and peel the fruit with a potato peeler. Halve and poach gently in sugar syrup (see page 223) with the lemon rind and cinnamon until they are very soft. Remove the guavas from the syrup and boil the syrup to the thread stage (see page 282). Process the guavas with 100ml/3 fl oz of the syrup and follow the recipe as above.

Coconut Ice-cream

If one ingredient can represent the essence of tropical food, it has to be the coconut. This fruit is used for drinks, ice-creams, puddings, savoury dishes, biscuits and cakes and is delicious when mixed with other fruits in combinations invariably called `tropical' or `exotic'. It is essential to use fresh coconut in this recipe.

MAKES 860ML/1½ PINTS

Ingredients

285g/10oz finely grated fresh coconut (see page 276)
570ml/1 pint coconut milk
1 egg
1 egg yolk
110g/4oz caster sugar
570ml/1 pint double cream

Method

1. Heat the fresh coconut with the coconut milk in a small pan.

2. Place the egg, yolk and sugar in a basin set over, not in, a pan of simmering water and whisk until light and fluffy.

3. When the milk and coconut mixture has nearly boiled, pour it on to the egg mixture and whisk well. Allow to cool.

4. Whip the cream lightly and fold it into the coconut mixture. Transfer it to another bowl, if necessary.

5. When half-frozen, rewhisk and refreeze.

Cinnamon and Vanilla Ice-cream

Dark brown sugar gives this ice-cream a beautiful colour, which is enhanced by the distinctive flavours of cinnamon and vanilla – simply irresistible!

MAKES 1.14 LITRES/2 PINTS

Ingredients

1 vanilla pod, split in half lengthwise
290ml/$^1/_2$ pint double cream
425ml/$^3/_4$ pint milk
30g/1oz caster sugar
3 cinnamon sticks, broken
1 teaspoon ground cinnamon
6 egg yolks
85g/3oz soft dark brown sugar

Method

1. In a large saucepan, mix the vanilla pod, double cream, milk, sugar, cinnamon sticks and ground cinnamon. Bring to the boil, stirring. Remove from the heat, cover and set aside for 30 minutes to infuse.

2. Beat the yolks with the dark brown sugar until well combined. Gradually strain in the milk mixture. Pour the mixture back into the same pan and cook over low heat, stirring constantly, until the mixture thickens slightly.

3. Pour into a freezer-proof container and chill. Freeze the mixture until solid but still soft enough to give when pressed with a finger, about 3 hours.

4. Tip the ice-cream into a cold bowl, break it up, then process or whisk until smooth, pale and creamy. Refreeze.

5. Remove from the freezer 20 minutes before serving.

Sweetcorn Ice-cream

Corn is used in so many Latin American dishes that it comes as no surprise to find sweetcorn ice-cream. It has a creamy, rich texture with a fresh, clean flavour of corn.

MAKES 1.14 LITRES/2 PINTS

Ingredients

4 large corn cobs, uncooked
290ml/$^1/_2$ pint double cream
570ml/1 pint milk
6 egg yolks
110g/4oz sugar
$^1/_2$ teaspoon vanilla essence

Method

1. Scrape the kernels from the cobs with a sharp knife. Process the kernels in a blender with the double cream and milk until smooth. Pour into a large saucepan, bring to the boil and set aside to cool completely.

2. Strain the mixture, pressing the kernels with the back of a spoon to extract all the liquid.

3. Beat the egg yolks and sugar with a wooden spoon until thoroughly mixed. Add the milky liquid and whisk together. Return it to the pan and cook over low heat, stirring constantly, until the custard coats the back of the spoon. Do not boil. Add the vanilla essence.

4. Strain into a shallow tray and allow to cool. Freeze.

5. Once frozen, take the ice-cream out of the freezer and allow to soften at room temperature. Process or whisk to remove the ice crystals.

6. Place the ice-cream back in the container and refreeze.

Pineapple Ice-cream

Pineapples have a high acid content, so they freeze better in cream-based ice-creams than sorbets.

MAKES 860ML/1 ½ PINTS

Ingredients

1 large pineapple
425ml/$^3/_4$ pint water
170g/6oz caster sugar
4 egg yolks
290ml/$^1/_2$ pint double cream, lightly whipped
3 tablespoons white rum

Method

1. Peel the pineapple, remove the core and cut the flesh into large chunks.

2. Put the water and sugar into a wide-bottomed saute pan and place over low heat until the sugar has dissolved. Add the pineapple chunks and bring to the boil, then reduce the heat and simmer until the pineapple is cooked, about 30 minutes. Strain and put the liquid back into the pan.

3. Boil the liquid rapidly to the thread stage (see page 282). Cool for 1 minute. Whisk the egg yolks and gradually pour in the sugar syrup, making sure it does not touch the beaters or it will solidify. Whisk until the mixture is very thick and leaves a ribbon trail. Cool for 2 minutes.

4. Process or blend the pineapple to a purée. Add the purée, cream and rum to the mousse mixture and mix thoroughly. Pour into a container, chill, then freeze.

5. When half-frozen, tip the ice-cream into a cold bowl, break it up, then whisk until smooth, pale and creamy. Refreeze.

6. Remove from the freezer 15 minutes before serving.

VARIATION: For a hint of coconut, reduce the double cream to 190ml/$^1/_3$ pint and blend 110g/4oz creamed coconut together with the pineapple chunks.

NOTE: For a more intense pineapple flavour use pineapple juice instead of water.

Rich Vanilla Ice-cream

This is a basic vanilla ice-cream recipe to which fruit purées, chopped nuts or liqueurs may be added (see variations below).

MAKES 570ML/1 PINTS

Ingredients

70g/2oz granulated sugar
8 tablespoons water
1 vanilla pod, split in half lengthwise
3 egg yolks
425ml/³/₄ pint double or single cream

Method

1. Put the sugar, water and vanilla pod into a saucepan and dissolve the sugar over gentle heat, stirring.

2. Beat the egg yolks well. Half whip the cream.

3. When the sugar has completely dissolved, bring the syrup up to boiling point and boil to the thread stage (see page 282). Allow to cool for 1 minute, then remove the vanilla pod, scrape out the black seeds and return the pod to the syrup.

4. Whisk the egg yolks and gradually pour in the sugar syrup, making sure it does not touch the beaters or it will solidify. Whisk until the mixture is very thick and leaves a ribbon trail.

5. Cool, whisking occasionally. Fold in the cream and freeze.

6. When the ice-cream is half frozen, whisk again and return to the freezer. (If you wish to add other flavourings, do so at this stage, then refreeze.)

VARIATIONS: Almost anything can be added to this basic recipe: try chopped prunes soaked in port, caramelized almonds, passion-fruit purée or coffee liqueur.

Cakes, Breads, Biscuits and Pastry

CAKES, BREADS, BISCUITS AND PASTRY

Cakes and pastries are very popular throughout Latin America, not as desserts but as mid-morning or afternoon snacks. Many sweet dishes are based on traditional Spanish and Portuguese recipes, and some are still made in identical circumstances. For example, in Spain enormous quantities of egg whites were used in the making of sherry, and the leftover yolks were donated to convents, where they were transformed into cakes and confectionery. Even though sherry was never produced in the New World, Spanish nuns took the tradition of convent baking with them when they went as missionaries to Mexico and Peru, the two most important countries in colonial times. The tradition continues to this day, with nuns, novices and orphan girls producing elaborate hand-made cakes and sweets – a source of income and pride for the convents involved. Their wedding cakes are also very sought-after, not only for their exquisite sugar work, but also because they are believed to bring good fortune to newlyweds.

Brazilian desserts and pastries are invariably very sweet and rich in eggs– a legacy from the Portuguese. While Mexican baking also uses large quantities of sugar and eggs, it shows more Spanish influence in its use of nuts, particularly almonds. With time, most recipes began to incorporate native ingredients, such as chocolate, vanilla, cashew nuts and peanuts.

Most cakes are simple creations: Swiss rolls filled with milk pudding or guava paste, and sponge cakes made with almonds, walnuts, chocolate, cornmeal and coconut. Although sweeter than European cakes, they are not as rich and they rarely include buttercream or icing.

Breads, on the other hand, are almost completely European in style. While the indigenous unleavened *tortilla* bread rules the roost in Mexico and Central America, Spanish, Portuguese and French varieties can be found everywhere else. Bakers also have the European tradition of baking at least twice a day.

Sweet pastries tend to be small turnovers and pies (*empanadas* and *pastelzitos*) rather than open tarts. They are usually filled with fruit or nuts, but the flavouring varies from country to country.

The recipes within this chapter have been chosen for their simplicity, yet all will give you an authentic flavour of Latin American baking.

Coffee, Cocoa and Cinnamon Cake

Cocoa is commonly used in baked goods and puddings in South America. This is a light, not-too-rich cake which goes well with ice-creams and fruit compotes, but is also delicious on its own with a cup of coffee.

Ingredients

oil for greasing
190ml/$\frac{1}{3}$ pint strong black coffee
2 tablespoons cocoa powder
200g/7oz caster sugar
85g/3oz butter, softened
$\frac{1}{2}$ teaspoon vanilla essence
2 eggs
140g/5oz plain flour
$\frac{1}{2}$ teaspoon bicarbonate of soda
1 teaspoon baking powder
1 teaspoon ground cinnamon

To serve: icing sugar
cinnamon and vanilla ice-cream (see page 227)

Method

1. Preheat the oven to 200°C/400°F/ gas mark 6. Grease a 20cm/8 inch moule-à-manqué tin and line the base with a disc of greased greaseproof paper. Dust it lightly with sugar and flour.

2. In a small saucepan mix the coffee, cocoa and half the sugar and bring to the boil. Reduce the heat and simmer, uncovered, for 10 minutes. Cool completely.

3. Cream the butter and remaining sugar in a mixing bowl until light and fluffy. Stir in the vanilla essence. Add the eggs gradually, beating well after each addition. Add a little of the flour, if necessary, to prevent the mixture from curdling.

4. Sift the remaining flour with the other dry ingredients twice and combine with the butter mixture. Fold in the coffee and cocoa liquid until the mixture is smooth and well blended.

5. Pour into the prepared cake tin and bake in the centre of the oven for 20 minutes. Turn the oven temperature down to 180°C/350°F/gas mark 4 and bake for a further 15 minutes, or until the sides have shrunk away from the tin slightly and the top springs back when pressed lightly with a fingertip. Remove from the oven and allow to cool in the tin.

6. Turn out, dust with icing sugar and serve.

Chocolate, Orange and Prune Cake

Dried and canned prunes are widely used in South American cuisine. They appear frequently in desserts, stuffings, canapés, petits fours and cakes.

Ingredients

oil for greasing
150ml/¹/₄ pint orange juice
110g/4oz prunes, stoned and halved
3 eggs, separated
salt
110g/4oz caster sugar
110g/4oz butter, soft but not melted
110g/4oz plain flour
2 tablespoons cocoa powder
2 teaspoons baking powder

For the icing:
140g/5oz good-quality dark chocolate, cut into
   small pieces
150ml/¹/₄ pint double cream
1 teaspoon ground cinnamon

To serve: orange crème anglaise (see page 220)
   or vanilla ice-cream (see page 229)

Method

1. Preheat the oven to 180°C/350°F/gas mark 4. Grease a 22cm/9 inch cake tin and line the bottom with a disc of greaseproof paper.

2. In a small saucepan heat the orange juice, remove from the heat, then add the prunes and leave to soften for 10 minutes.

3. Whisk the egg whites with a pinch of salt until stiff. Still whisking, add the sugar spoonful by spoonful until the mixture is stiff and shiny. Whisk in the egg yolks, then gently mix in the soft butter.

4. Sift together the flour, cocoa powder and baking powder twice. Using a large metal spoon, carefully fold the flour into the egg mixture.

5. Fold in the prunes and orange juice and turn the mixture into the prepared tin. Bake in the centre of the oven for about 30 minutes or until the cake feels firm to the touch. Leave to cool for a few minutes, then loosen with a palette knife around the sides and turn on to a wire rack to cool completely.

6. To make the icing, gently heat together the chocolate, cream and cinnamon. Stir until all the chocolate has melted and the mixture is smooth and shiny. Allow to cool and thicken to a coating consistency before pouring over the cake.

7. Allow the icing to harden for at least 2 hours. Serve with chilled orange crème anglaise or vanilla ice-cream.

Carrot Cake

The unusual combination of carrots and chocolate works really well in this light cake. It's a favourite with children.

Ingredients

310g/11oz carrots, peeled and roughly chopped
150ml/¼ pint sunflower oil
4 eggs
225g/8oz caster sugar
225g/8oz plain flour
pinch salt
1 tablespoon baking powder
1 teaspoon ground cinnamon
good pinch ground cloves

For the icing:
50g/2oz caster sugar
110ml/4 fl oz milk
55g/2oz butter
55g/2oz cocoa powder

Method

1. Preheat the oven to 200°C/400°F/gas mark 6. Lightly grease a 23cm/9 inch square cake tin and line the base with a piece of greased greaseproof paper.

2. In a blender or food processor blend the carrots, oil and eggs to a pulp. Add the sugar and mix well.

3. Sift the flour, salt, baking powder, cinnamon and cloves together. Add to the carrot mixture and blend for a few seconds or until the flour is completely incorporated. Pour into the prepared tin and bake in the centre of the oven for 35 minutes or until a sharp knife inserted into the centre of the cake comes out clean. Remove from the oven and allow to cool.

4. Combine all the icing ingredients in a saucepan and boil until syrupy, about 10 minutes. Pour the hot liquid on top of the cake and leave to cool completely.

5. Cut into 7.5cm/3 inch squares and serve.

Light Groundnut Oil Cake

This cake uses oil instead of butter and the result is a light cake with good keeping qualities. A more fragrant oil, such as walnut or hazelnut oil, can be used for a more distinctive flavour.

Ingredients

oil for greasing
200g/7oz plain flour
2 teaspoons baking powder
4 eggs, separated
200g/7oz caster sugar
$\frac{1}{2}$ teaspoon vanilla essence
4 tablespoons groundnut oil
1 x 170g/6oz can evaporated milk

To serve: icing sugar or quince purée (see page 218)

Method

1. Preheat the oven to 180°C/350°F/ gas mark 4. Grease a 20cm/8 inch moule-à-manqué or cake tin and line the base with a disc of greased greaseproof paper.

2. Sift together the flour and baking powder.

3. In a bowl beat together the egg yolks, sugar and vanilla essence until light and fluffy. Incorporate the groundnut oil and condensed milk, then carefully fold in the sifted flour.

4. Whisk the egg whites until they stand in soft peaks, then fold them into the mixture using a large metal spoon. Pour into the prepared tin and bake for about 30 minutes or until a sharp knife or skewer inserted into the centre comes out clean. Remove from the oven and cool in the tin for 10 minutes.

5. Turn out the cake and, just before serving, dust it with icing sugar. Serve with squash and orange compote or quince purée.

Walnut and Ground Rice Cake

Walnuts are to South Americans what almonds are to Europeans – a versatile ingredient used in many cakes, sweets and puddings. This intensely flavoured cake contains no flour.

Ingredients

oil for greasing
110g/4oz butter, at room temperature
85g/3oz caster sugar
3 eggs, separated
110g/4oz ground rice
85g/3oz ground walnuts
1 teaspoon baking powder
3 drops vanilla essence

To serve: 2 tablespoons icing sugar pineapple
and star anise compote (see page 215)

Method

1. Preheat the oven to 200°C/400°F/gas mark 6. Grease a 20cm/8 inch cake tin and line the base with a disc of greased greaseproof paper.

2. Cream the butter and sugar together in a mixing bowl until light and fluffy. Add the egg yolks one by one and beat well.

3. Mix the ground rice, walnuts and baking powder together. Add to the butter mixture and beat until smooth. Add the vanilla essence.

4. Whisk the egg whites to medium peaks and fold into the mixture using a large metal spoon. Pour into the prepared tin.

5. Bake in the centre of the oven for 25 minutes or until the sides have shrunk away from the tin slightly and the top springs back when pressed lightly with a fingertip.

6. Remove from the oven and allow to cool in the tin for 10 minutes, then turn out on to a wire rack and leave to cool completely.

7. Dust the cake heavily with the icing sugar and serve the pineapple and star anise compote separately.

VARIATION: When the cake is cold, split it in 3 horizontally using a serrated knife, and sandwich the parts together using half a quantity of Colombian milk pudding (see page 221). Dust the top of the cake with icing sugar before serving.

Easy Cornmeal, Coconut and Prune Cake

This is an all-in-one recipe, which produces a moist and delicious cake.

Ingredients

oil for greasing
55g/2oz desiccated coconut
190ml/$^1/_3$ pint hot water
110g/4oz butter, cut into small cubes
85g/3oz prunes, quartered
110g/4oz polenta or coarse cornmeal
55g/2oz self-raising flour
1 teaspoon baking powder
110g/4oz caster sugar
3 eggs, beaten
juice of $^1/_2$ lime

Method

1. Preheat the oven to 180°C/350°F/
    gas mark 4. Grease a 900g/2lb loaf tin and
    line the base with greased greaseproof
    paper. Dust it lightly with sugar and flour.

2. In a medium bowl, mix together the
    coconut, hot water, butter and prunes until
    the butter has completely melted.

3. In a large bowl sift the polenta, flour and
    baking powder together. Mix in the sugar.

4. Add the coconut mixture, eggs and lime
    juice to the flours and mix thoroughly with
    a wooden spoon until all the ingredients are
    well combined. Pour into the prepared tin
    and bake in the middle of the oven for 30–
    35 minutes or until the sides have shrunk
    away from the tin slightly and the top
    springs back when pressed lightly with a
    fingertip. Remove the cake from the oven
    and allow to cool slightly before turning out
    on to a plate. Serve warm or cold.

NOTE: This cake is very good the next day, cut into
slices, lightly toasted and buttered.

Spicy Corn Muffins

Using three of the best-loved ingredients in Latin America – corn, chillies and coriander – this recipe is very quickly made. Although muffins are North American in origin, similar shaped buns are found in many South American countries.

Ingredients

200g/7oz sifted plain flour
70g/2$\frac{1}{2}$oz yellow cornmeal
1 tablespoon baking powder
pinch salt
4 tablespoons chopped coriander
2 Fresno or jalapeño chillies, seeded and finely
  chopped (see page 194)
30g/1oz soft light brown sugar
6 tablespoons water
3 large eggs
70ml/2$\frac{1}{2}$ fl oz sunflower oil

Method

1. Preheat the oven to 180°C/350°F/
    gas mark 4 and warm a baking tray. Place
    paper cases in a 12-hole patty tin.

2. Sift the flour, cornmeal, baking powder and
    salt together twice and put into a large
    bowl. Stir in the coriander, chillies and
    sugar.

3. In a jug mix together the water, eggs and
    oil. Add this liquid to the dry ingredients
    and mix, using a round-tipped knife, until
    well combined. Fill each paper case about
    two-thirds full, then sit the tin on the
    warmed baking tray. Bake in the oven for
    about 15–20 minutes or until a sharp knife
    inserted into the centre comes out clean.

4. Remove from the oven and allow the
    muffins to cool in the tin for 5 minutes.
    Serve warm.

VARIATION: For sweet cornmeal muffins, omit the chillies and coriander, use milk instead of water and add 1 teaspoon ground cinnamon to the flour.

NOTE: This batter can also be baked in a well-greased cake tin or gratin dish and sliced before serving.

Cuban White Bread

This delicious bread is baked in an unusual way, but with great results.

Ingredients

15g/^{1}/$_2$oz fresh yeast or 7g/^{1}/$_4$oz easy-blend
  yeast
290ml/^{1}/$_2$ pint warm water
1 teaspoon sugar
2 teaspoons salt
450g/1lb strong white flour
55g/2oz cornmeal

Method

1. In a small bowl thoroughly mix the fresh
    yeast with 2 tablespoons of the warm
    water and the sugar.

2. Sift the salt and flour into a large bowl. Stir
    in the easy-blend yeast, if using.

3. Add the fresh yeast and water to the flour
    and mix to a sticky dough. Remove the
    dough to a lightly floured surface and knead
    for 10–15 minutes or until smooth and
    elastic. Form the dough into a ball.

4. Lightly oil a bowl, put the ball of dough into
    it and turn to coat with oil. Cover the bowl
    with cling film. Leave to rise in a warm,
    draught-free place for 1–1^1/$_2$ hours or until
    doubled in size.

5. Turn the dough on to a lightly floured
    surface and shape into a round or long loaf.
    Sprinkle a baking sheet with half the
    cornmeal and put the shaped bread on top.
    Allow to rise for 5 minutes.

6. Slash two diagonal lines in the top of the
    dough with a sharp knife, brush the whole
    loaf with water and sprinkle the remaining
    cornmeal on top. Place in a cold oven. Set
    the oven to 200°C/400°F/gas mark 6 and
    place a roasting tin filled with hot water at
    the bottom of the oven.

7. Bake until the bread is crusty and the
    underside sounds hollow when tapped.
    Transfer to a wire rack to cool slightly and
    serve warm or cold.

Corn Bread

There are numerous recipes for corn bread as it is very popular throughout Latin America. It can be made using cornmeal or polenta flour and, when available, fresh corn kernels are also added to the mixture. Corn bread is best served warm or straight from the oven.

Ingredients

oil for greasing
425ml/^{3}/$_4$ pint milk
30g/1oz butter
1 teaspoon salt
1 teaspoon sugar
^{1}/$_2$ teaspoon chilli powder
^{1}/$_2$ teaspoon paprika
85g/3oz instant polenta or cornmeal
1^1/$_2$ teaspoons baking powder
3 eggs
1 x 340g/12oz can sweetcorn, drained and
   roughly chopped

Method

1. Preheat the oven to 190°C/375°F/
    gas mark 5. Grease a 1.75 litre/3 pint
    capacity shallow ovenproof dish.

2. In a large saucepan mix together the milk,
    butter, salt, sugar, chilli and paprika and
    bring to scalding point.

3. Sift together the cornmeal and baking
    powder.

4. Remove the milk from the heat and slowly
    add the cornmeal, stirring with a wooden
    spoon to prevent lumps forming. Add the
    eggs and sweetcorn and mix thoroughly.
    Pour the mixture into the prepared dish and
    bake for about 30 minutes or until lightly
    brown and set.

VARIATIONS:

*   Finely chop 1 onion and 1 red pepper and
    sweat in 2 tablespoons olive oil until nearly
    soft, about 10 minutes. Add to the mixture
    at step 4.

*   Scrape the kernels from 2 ears of corn and
    use instead of the canned sweetcorn.

*   Grate 85g/3oz Cheddar or Red Leicester
    cheese on the coarse side of the grater and
    add to the mixture at step 4.

*   Very quick cornbread: In a bowl or food
    processor mix together 170g/6oz cornmeal,
    85g/3oz melted butter, ^{1}/$_2$ teaspoon salt,
    1 teaspoon sugar, 1 teaspoon aniseed,
    2 teaspoons baking powder and 190ml/^{1}/$_3$
    pint milk. Pour into an oiled 23cm/9 inch
    square cake tin and bake for about 40
    minutes at 190°C/375°F/gas mark 5, or
    until a sharp knife or skewer inserted into
    the centre comes out clean.

*   Richer cornbread: Use 290ml/^{1}/$_2$ pint
    buttermilk mixed with 150ml/^{1}/$_4$ pint soured
    cream instead of the milk and follow the
    recipe as above.

Sun-dried Banana and Walnut Bread

Latin American baking is similar to that of Spain and France – lots of white crusty bread but almost no brown breads. However, the ever-growing number of vegetarians and health-conscious people is changing things, so in recent years it has become easier to find wholemeal bread, although mainly in healthfood shops.

Ingredients

oil for greasing
140g/5oz sun-dried bananas, roughly chopped
140g/5oz caster sugar
110g/4oz plain oats
85g/3oz wholemeal flour
30g/1oz plain flour
2 teaspoons baking powder
$^1/_2$ teaspoon salt
$^1/_2$ teaspoon bicarbonate of soda
150ml/$^1/_4$ pint concentrated orange juice
1 egg
2 tablespoons sunflower oil
140g/5oz walnuts, roughly chopped

Method

1. Preheat the oven to 180°C/350°F/gas mark 4. Brush a 900g/2lb loaf tin with oil.

2. Put the chopped bananas in a small bowl, cover with boiling water and set aside for 10 minutes. Drain the bananas and discard the water.

3. In a large bowl combine the sugar, oats, both flours, baking powder, salt and bicarbonate of soda.

4. Mix the orange juice, egg and oil together and add to the dry ingredients. Mix in the bananas and walnuts. Pour the mixture into the prepared tin and bake in the preheated oven until the edges begin to brown and a skewer inserted comes out clean, about 1 hour. Cool in the pan for 15 minutes, then turn on to a rack to cool completely.

Polenta

Polenta is eaten in many Latin American countries. Being filling and cheap, it is basically a poor man's food and is normally served with saucy dishes, such as chicken and okra casserole (see page 68). It is very rarely fried and can be eaten cold with milk and sugar as a dessert.

Ingredients

2 litres/3^1/$_2$ pints water
2 teaspoons salt
285g/10oz coarse cornmeal, maize flour or
  polenta
oil

Method

1. Put the water and salt into a large saucepan and bring to the boil.

2. Remove from the heat and sprinkle in the cornmeal, whisking quickly to avoid lumps.

3. Return the pan to a reduced heat and cover it to prevent spattering.

4. Continue cooking until the polenta is thick, approximately 20–25 minutes, stirring often to prevent sticking and burning. Serve hot, piled high on a plate.

NOTE: The water can be substituted by chicken or beef stock to give the polenta a savoury flavour.

Brazil Nut Shortbread

Delicious on its own with a cup of coffee or hot chocolate, this shortbread recipe is easy to make and keeps for a long time. Biscuits are very popular in Latin American countries, with arrowroot, coconut, cocoa, peanut and cream biscuits being some of the favourites.

Ingredients

110g/4oz butter
55g/2oz caster sugar
55g/2oz Brazil nuts
110g/4oz plain flour
30g/1oz ground rice
$^1/_2$ teaspoon ground cinnamon

Method

1. Preheat the oven to 170°C/325°F/ gas mark 3.

2. Grind the Brazil nuts finely in a food processor.

3. Beat the butter until soft, add the sugar and mix thoroughly.

4. Sift in the flour, ground rice, cinnamon and Brazil nuts and work to a smooth paste.

5. Place a 15cm/6 inch flan ring on a baking sheet and press the shortbread paste into a neat circle inside it. Remove the flan ring and flatten the paste slightly with a rolling pin. Crimp the edges and prick thoroughly with a fork.

6. Mark the shortbread into 8 wedges, sprinkle slightly with a little extra sugar and bake for 40 minutes until a pale biscuit colour. Remove from the oven, recut the wedges and leave to cool for 2 minutes. Lift on to a cooling rack and cool completely. Store in an airtight container.

NOTE: If a food processor is not available, chop the nuts finely.

Toasted Cassava Meal

Cassava or manioc meal plays the part of bread in a Brazilian meal, where it is sprinkled over juicy dishes to soak up the liquid. It has a bland taste, so for special occasions it is fried in butter and a variety of ingredients are added to it. Cassava meal is also known as *gari* in Indian food stores.

Ingredients

85g/3oz butter
285g/10oz cassava meal
salt and freshly ground pepper

Method

1. In a frying pan, over medium heat, melt the butter. Stir in the cassava meal and cook, stirring constantly, until golden brown and dry. This will take about 10 minutes. Season to taste with salt and pepper and serve hot or cold.

VARIATIONS:
• Festive cassava: Add 1 medium onion to the butter and cook until soft. Mix 55g/2oz raisins and 55g/2oz green olives (pitted and halved) with the cassava meal and fry for 10 minutes. Serve hot.

• With eggs: Cook 1 small chopped onion in the butter, add 2 beaten eggs and cook for 1 minute. Add 5 tablespoons of cassava meal and cook, stirring frequently, for 8 minutes, or until the meal becomes golden. Season with salt and pepper and stir in 2 tablespoons chopped parsley. Serve hot or cold.

Hazelnut and Lemon Biscuits

A legacy from the Spanish kitchen, these biscuits are easy to make and delicious.

Ingredients

oil for greasing
225g/8oz ground hazelnuts
85g/3oz caster sugar
55g/2oz plain flour
grated zest and juice of 1 lemon
1 egg

Method

1. Preheat the oven to 180°C/350°F/ gas mark 4. Lightly grease a baking sheet.

2. In a bowl mix the ground hazelnuts with the sugar and add the flour and lemon zest.

3. Beat the egg and lemon juice together and add to the mixture.

4. Place teaspoonfuls on the greased baking sheet and bake in the preheated oven until the biscuits are brown and crisp. Transfer to a wire rack to cool.

Triple Chocolate Cinnamon Biscuits

From North America to Argentina cinnamon is the all-time favourite spice for sweets and baking. Here it is combined with the much-loved walnut and chocolate.

Ingredients

oil for greasing
30g/1oz plain flour
30g/1oz cocoa powder
1 1/2 teaspoons ground cinnamon
1/4 teaspoon baking powder
pinch salt
85g/3oz unsalted butter, softened
100g/3 1/2oz caster sugar
3 eggs
225g/8oz bitter dark chocolate, melted and cooled
140g/5oz walnuts, roughly chopped
170g/6oz milk chocolate, finely chopped

Method

1. Preheat the oven to 180°C/350°F/ gas mark 4. Lightly grease 1 or 2 baking sheets.

2. Sift together the flour, cocoa, cinnamon, baking powder and salt.

3. In a large bowl beat the butter, sugar and eggs until smooth. Stir in the melted chocolate and mix well. Add the flour mixture and mix thoroughly. Finally, stir in the nuts and chopped milk chocolate.

4. Drop tablespoons of the mixture on to greased baking sheets and bake until the biscuits look dry and cracked but feel soft when lightly pressed, about 11 minutes.

5. Transfer to a wire rack to cool.

Ginger Tuiles

Ginger is used in savoury dishes on the north-east coast of Brazil, but the rest of the country uses it mostly in sweets, biscuits and baking.

Ingredients

15g/^{1}/$_2$oz butter, melted, for greasing
55g/2oz unsalted butter, softened
55g/2oz caster sugar
pinch salt
^{1}/$_2$ teaspoon ground ginger
1 size 3 egg white, room temperature
55g/2oz plain flour, sifted
2 tablespoons finely chopped crystallized ginger

Method

1. Preheat the oven to 190°C/375°F/ gas mark 5. Brush two baking sheets heavily with the melted butter, dust lightly with flour and put in the freezer.

2. Warm a bowl in the oven for 5 minutes. In the warmed bowl mix the softened butter, sugar, salt and ground ginger with a hand whisk until thoroughly combined.

3. Gently mix in the egg white and flour. Chill for 30 minutes before using.

4. Spread teaspoonfuls, well apart, on the chilled baking sheets. Sprinkle with the chopped ginger and bake in the oven until pale brown, 5–6 minutes.

5. Shape the tuilles by bending them around an oiled rolling-pin or the handle of a large wooden spoon.

6. When cold, store in an airtight container.

NOTE: Silicone paper can be used instead of brushing the baking sheet with butter.

Fresh Herb Pastry

Latin Americans are very fond of savoury pastries such as empanadas, and flavouring the pastry itself is also very popular.

Ingredients

225g/8oz plain flour
pinch salt
$^{1}/_{2}$ teaspoon cayenne pepper
110g/4oz butter, chopped
30g/1oz lard
1 tablespoon finely chopped fresh oregano
2 tablespoons finely chopped parsley
5 tablespoons very cold water

Method

1. Sift the flour with the salt and cayenne pepper.

2. Rub in the butter and lard until the mixture resembles breadcrumbs. Stir in the herbs and mix well.

3. Add the cold water and mix to a firm dough, first with a knife, then with one hand. It may be necessary to add more water, but the pastry should not be too damp.

4. Wrap and chill for 30 minutes before using.

Sweet Rich Shortcrust Pastry

Sweet tarts made with this type of pastry are found in the southern countries of South America, where the food has a stronger European influence.

Ingredients

225g/8oz plain flour
pinch salt
110g/4oz butter, chopped
1 tablespoon caster sugar
1 egg yolk
3 tablespoons very cold water

Method

1. Sift the flour with the salt.

2. Rub in the fat until the mixture resembles coarse breadcrumbs. Stir in the sugar.

3. Mix the egg yolk with the water, then add to the mixture. Mix to a firm dough, first with a knife, then with one hand. It may be necessary to add more water, but the pastry should not be too damp.

4. Wrap and chill for 30 minutes before using.

VARIATION: To make a plain rich shortcrust, omit the sugar.

Puff Pastry

Although more often bought frozen than made at home, puff pastry is really quite easy to make.

Ingredients

225g/8oz plain flour
pinch salt
30g/1oz vegetable shortening
150ml/¼ pint very cold water
140–200g/5–7oz butter

Method

1. If you have never made puff pastry before, use the smaller amount of butter: this will give a standard puff pastry. If you have some experience, more butter will produce a lighter, very rich pastry.

2. Sift the flour with a pinch of salt. Rub in the vegetable shortening. Add the water and mix with a knife to a doughy consistency. Turn the dough on to the table and knead quickly until just smooth. Wrap and leave to relax in the refrigerator for 30 minutes.

3. Lightly flour the work surface or a board and roll the dough into a rectangle about 10 x 30cm/4 x 12 inches.

4. Tap the butter lightly with a floured rolling-pin to form a flattened block measuring about 9 x 7.5cm/3 x 3 inches. Place the butter on the rectangle of pastry. Fold the third of the pastry closest to you over the butter then bring down the top third. Press the sides together with the rolling-pin to prevent the butter escaping. Give the pastry parcel a 90° anticlockwise turn so that the folded edge is on your left.

5. Tap the pastry parcel with the rolling-pin to flatten the butter a little, then roll out quickly and lightly until the pastry is three times as long as it is wide. Fold it very evenly in three as before and press the edges firmly with the rolling-pin. Turn the pastry anticlockwise so the folded edge is on your left. Roll out again to form a rectangle as before.

6. The pastry has now had two rolls and folds, or `turns' as they are called. Leave to rest in a cool place for 30 minutes or so. The rolling and folding must be repeated twice more, the pastry again rested, and then again given two more `turns'. This makes a total of six. if the butter is still very streaky, roll and fold the pastry once more. Use as required.

Pastelzitos

Pastelzitos are small savoury pastries which are popular throughout Latin America. This recipe comes from Ecuador, but the Chinese in Brazil had a reputation for making the lightest and nicest pastelzitos.

Ingredients

For the pastry:
225g/8oz plain flour
$^1/_2$ teaspoon salt
$^1/_2$ teaspoon baking powder
55g/2oz butter, cut into cubes
5 drops lemon juice
4 tablespoons water
sunflower oil for frying

For the filling:
1 quantity picadillo (see page 92)

Method

1. Sift the flour, salt and baking powder into a large bowl. Rub in the butter until the mixture resembles coarse breadcrumbs.

2. Mix the lemon juice into the water and add enough to the flour to form a soft but not sticky dough.

3. Knead until elastic, about 3 minutes, cover and rest for 30 minutes.

4. Divide the dough into 12 equal parts. On a floured surface, roll each piece of dough into a 13cm/5 inch circle. Put 2 teaspoons of picadillo in the centre of each circle, brush the edges with water and press together to form a semi-circle. Seal the ends well.

5. Heat the oil in a frying pan untill a crumb will sizzle vigorously in it. Fry the pastelzitos until golden brown and crisp. Drain on absorbent paper. Serve at once.

VARIATIONS:

*   Sweetcorn: Mix a 200g/7oz can of drained sweetcorn with 150ml/$^1/_4$ pint soured cream, season well with salt and freshly ground black pepper and follow the recipe as above.

*   Hearts of palm: Slice the hearts of palm from a 400g/14oz can and mix with 55g/2oz grated Cheddar and 4 tablespoons double cream. Season with salt and freshly ground black pepper and follow the recipe as above.

*   Cheese: Mix 55g/2oz grated Cheddar with 55g/2oz grated Parmesan and $^1/_2$ teaspoon paprika. No salt is needed since both cheeses are quite salty. Follow the recipe as above.

NOTE: The lemon juice is sometimes substituted by a few drops of white rum or vodka. It is believed to give the pastry a crisp, light texture when fried.

Drinks

DRINKS

Latin America produces a variety of alcoholic drinks, ranging from home-brewed *chiche* to spirits such as *tequila*, *cachaca* and *pisco* and excellent wines from Chile and Argentina. Very good beer is also produced and consumed in great quantities throughout the continent.

This chapter includes recipes for classic cocktails such as margaritas, describes the traditional way of drinking tequila and provides guidelines on how to match wine with chilli-flavoured dishes.

The most popular non-alcoholic drink in Latin America is undoubtedly coffee, followed by chocolate and maté tea. The history of all these drinks makes fascinating reading, and the recipes using them make delicious drinking.

Wine

by Elizabeth Morcom

South America has been producing wine since the arrival of the Spanish *conquistadores* in the 16th century. European vines were first planted in Mexico and spread rapidly southwards. After Europe, South America produces more wine than any other continent. Although Chilean wine enjoys the most international acclaim, Argentina and Brazil produce greater quantities – to satisfy a huge home consumption. Wine is also made in Uruguay, Peru, Bolivia and even a little in Colombia, Ecuador and Venezuela. In Central America, Mexico is an important producer.

ARGENTINA AND BRAZIL

In the past, poor grape varieties predominated, yielding indifferent wine. Although major investment in wine is still comparatively new, premium grape varieties are now being planted in these two major producing countries and their wineries updated, with exciting prospects for the future, especially in Argentina. The vineyards there are mainly in the western province of Mendoza, in the foothills of the Andes and just a short hop over the mountains from Chile's wine areas. The vineyards of Brazil are mainly in the south of the country, bordering Uruguay.

Although Spain and Portugal have influenced the past development of wine in these countries, the grape varieties now being planted are definitely `international' and, as in many New World countries, a truly individual wine `identity' is largely lacking. Argentina has the aromatic, white torrontes grape variety with its grapy, muscat aromas, but chardonnay and semillon are now common too. The malbeci – a less well-known Bordeaux grape variety, also found in Cahors but not much elsewhere – used to be widely planted for red wines and is a good match for the local beef, but better-known cabernet and merlot are now exciting more interest. Brazil has greater problems than Argentina in producing good-quality wine, but it too is making progress with classic, premium varietals, and investment from abroad is considerable.

CHILE

Of the main producers, Chile has made the speediest progress and is already making world-class wines. Most of the vineyards are in the Central Valley to the south of the capital, Santiago, where the climate is almost ideal for wine-making. Plantings of classic, premium grape varieties, such as sauvignon, chardonnay and semillon, cabernet, merlot and, to a lesser extent, pinot noir, have been extensive, and interest from foreign investors, including owners of Bordeaux châteaux, has been keen. Chilean wines for export are increasingly well made: characterful, clean and fruity. Most are made for drinking within two or three years. Above all, they are excellent value for money.

MEXICO

Mexico is Latin America's fourth most important producer of wine, with vineyards mainly in the north of the country. The climate is not ideal, but premium grape varieties have now been planted, largely along Californian lines, and there has been some foreign investment, especially in brandy and sparkling wine production.

MATCHING WINE WITH LATIN AMERICAN FOOD

As it is with colours, so it is with food and wine – certain combinations, such as fish and tannic red wine, do not work well, while others, such as lamb and claret, work like a dream. However, there are no hard and fast rules; much is down to personal choice. The secret is to try to pair like with like, which is what I have attempted to do in my wine recommendations for the recipes in this book. Ideally, there should be no clash and no domination of flavours. Both wine and food should show each other off to advantage.

Intensity of flavour is as important as the type of flavour and, of course, there is quality; an `everyday' dish should not be paired with an expensive, top-class wine and vice versa. Colour association also plays its part: pale dishes are often more successfully matched with white wines and rich, dark dishes with reds.

As in any cuisine, there are `problem' ingredients, such as vinegar, avocado, egg, chocolate and, of course, spices such as chilli, but a successful match can usually be found.

The position of a particular dish within a meal can also affect wine choice. Because our senses become gradually dulled during the course of a meal, lighter wines are usually served before fuller-bodied wines, whites before reds, dry wines before sweet and younger wines before older wines.

WINES AND CHILLIES

Just as there are many varieties of grape, so there are different varieties of chilli, with different aromas and flavours. These can often coincide. Fresh jalapeños or serranos, for example, can have herbal, green olive or vegetal characteristics, as do many wines. Dried chillies, on the other hand, have smoky, tobacco or chocolate overtones, which are also found in red wines such as pinot noirs, with their ripe fruit and earthy, sometimes smoky flavour, and reds aged in American oak, such as Rioja and many New World cabernets. (Avoid those with harsh, mouth-drying tannins, which tend to intensify the heat of chillies.)

Although dry white wines may be overwhelmed by hotter chillies, those with citrus flavours, such as chardonnays and semillons, seem to work well with milder chilli dishes, especially those containing fish. Distinctive sauvignons, such as those from New Zealand, can be perfect matches for dishes with green and red peppers as well as chilli.

When it comes to hot and very hot chillies, a wine is needed which will match the flavours of the dish and sooth the heat. Spirits help, but often a rounded, full-bodied, fruity red or a mouth-filling, smooth, off-dry white, such as a chenin blanc, gewürztraminer or riesling will work well. Sparkling wine is often a good choice too. A delicate, dry white would be overwhelmed by very hot chillies, even if it quenches the thirst. Lager works only as a thirst quencher and heat soother – it does little to harmonize with other flavours. A carefully chosen wine should cope with the heat of the chilli and complement the flavours of the dish.

Spirits and Cocktails

This section describes the more well-known alcoholic drinks made of native ingredients in Latin American countries.

Cachaça is a Brazilian rum made from sugar cane. It is considered 'the drink of the poor', but is used extensively in many mixed drinks and is the main ingredient of *caipirinha*, the national drink of Brazil. It is also drunk on its own in small glass cups.

Chicha is an Indian fermented beer-like drink made from maize according to centuries-old tradition: a pot is filled with chewed corn kernels and left to ferment for three days. Once strained, the liquid has a cloudy appearance and sour taste. Chicha is popular in Mexico and all the Andean countries of South America.

Pisco is a Peruvian type of brandy made from distilled muscat wine. It is also very popular in Bolivia and Chile.

Pulque, from Mexico, is another fermented beer-type of drink. It is made from the sap of the maguey or century plant.

Tequila is a Mexican distilled drink made from the *Agave azul tequilana*, a relative of the maguey plant. The roots of the plant are ground, mixed with water, fermented and distilled twice, resulting in a colourless drink. Tequila can also be aged and will then have a light straw colour. One of the traditional ways of drinking tequila is with lime and salt. In one hand a good pinch of salt is put in the space between the thumb and index finger, and half a lime is held with the same hand. With the glass in the other hand, the salt is licked, all the tequila is swallowed at once and then the lime juice is sucked. The lime can be substituted by an orange slice or a lime-rubbed slice of cucumber.

Fruit Drinks

Fruit is the dessert *par excellence* in Latin American countries and fresh fruit juices are consumed in great quantities. Fruit bars are as common in Brazil as pubs are in England, and serve mainly made-to-order fruit drinks. Freshly squeezed orange juice or milk are used as the bases for a variety of drinks, the most common ones being avocado, milk, lime juice and sugar blended to a thick milk shake consistency, and papaya shake, using orange juice or milk. The combinations are endless and the *batidas* or *vitaminas*, as they are called, are frequently drunk as a mid-morning or afternoon snack.

Margarita

This classic Mexican drink is made with tequila.

Ingredients

1 slice lime
salt in a saucer
55ml/2 fl oz lime juice
150ml/¼ pint tequila
55ml/2 fl oz triple sec
crushed ice

Method

1. Chill 4 tumblers or cocktail glasses in the freezer for 10 minutes.

2. Moisten the rim of the glasses with the slice of lime and dip into the saucer of salt until lightly frosted.

3. Shake the lime juice, tequila, triple sec and crushed ice well, pour into the glasses and serve.

Unless stated otherwise, all recipes make 4 servings.

Pisco Sour

This is a very popular drink in Peru, Bolivia and Chile. The egg white is added to create a foam.

Ingredients

300ml/11 fl oz pisco (see page 259)
4 teaspoons caster sugar
juice of 1 lime
4 ice cubes, crushed
1 egg white

Method

1. Chill 4 tumblers or cocktail glasses in the freezer for 10 minutes.

2. In a bowl mix together the pisco, sugar and lime juice. Transfer to a cocktail shaker, add the egg white and shake vigorously 9 or 10 times.

3. Strain into the chilled glasses and serve.

Coconut Punch

Drinks using milk are very popular in Brazil. This one is made using thick coconut milk and lime. The *cachaça* can be substituted by white rum.

Ingredients

1 x 400g/14oz can thick coconut milk
juice of 2 limes
55g/2oz caster sugar
100ml/3 fl oz *cachaça* or white rum.
6 ice cubes, crushed

Method

1. Put all the ingredients into a food processor or blender and process for 1 minute. Pour into chilled tumblers or cocktail glasses and serve at once.

VARIATIONS: To make a fruity coconut punch add any of the following before processing it:
• the pulp of 3 passion-fruits.
• 2 fresh guavas, peeled and seeded.
• $1/2$ fresh mango, peeled and flesh cut into cubes.
• $1/2$ fresh pineapple, peeled, cored and cut into cubes.

Caipirinha

The national drink of Brazil is traditionally made straight in the glass with *cachaça*, but can also be made with vodka.

Ingredients

4 limes, washed and cut into chunks
4 tablespoons caster sugar
225ml/8 fl oz *cachaça*
8 ice cubes, crushed

Method

1. Divide the limes between 4 tumblers and add the sugar. Using a spoon, mix the limes and sugar together, crushing the limes to extract the juice and oil from the skin.

2. Divide the *cachaça* and crushed ice between the glasses, stir well and serve.

Sangrita

This is a drink from Mexico which is made with tequila, orange and tomato juice and chilli sauce.

Ingredients

55ml/2 fl oz fresh orange juice
juice of 1 lime
290ml/$\frac{1}{2}$ pint tomato juice
190ml/$\frac{1}{3}$ pint tequila
2 teaspoons hot chilli sauce
pinch salt

Method

1. Chill 4 tumblers in the freezer for 10 minutes.

2. Mix together all the ingredients and pour into the chilled tumblers. Serve as an aperitif.

Yugeno

This is a Peruvian drink made with pisco and orange juice.

Ingredients

190ml/$\frac{1}{3}$ pint fresh orange juice
190ml/$\frac{1}{3}$ pint pisco (see page 259)
8 ice cubes, crushed

Method

1. Chill 4 tumblers or cocktail glasses.

2. Mix together the orange juice, pisco and ice, pour into the chilled glasses and serve at once.

Avocado, Lime and Milk Batida

Strange as it may sound, this is a delicious and very nutritious drink.

Ingredients

2 ripe avocados
1 litre/1$\frac{3}{4}$ pints very cold milk
juice of 1 lime
3 tablespoons caster sugar (to taste)

Method

1. Blend all the ingredients together in a food processor or blender. Add sugar to taste and serve at once.

VARIATION: Substitute the avocados with 3 large, ripe bananas.

NOTE: Very frequently 3 tablespoons fine oats will be added to the banana or avocado batida, making it a complete and delicious meal.

Papaya and Orange Batida

This is a particularly good recipe for using over-ripe papayas.

Ingredients

2 small, very ripe papayas, peeled, seeded and diced
1 litre/1$^3/_4$ pints freshly squeezed orange juice
juice of $^1/_2$ lime

Method

1. Combine all the ingredients together in a blender or food processor . Add sugar to taste and serve at once.

NOTE: The orange juice can be substituted by cold milk; both versions are very popular.

Mixed Fruit Batida

Any fruit, or even leftover fruit salad, can be used for this batida, and the orange juice can be substituted by milk.

Ingredients

1 banana, peeled and sliced
$^1/_2$ pineapple, peeled and cut into large cubes
$^1/_2$ papaya, peeled and cut into cubes
1 litre/1$^3/_4$ pints orange juice
squeeze of lime juice

Method

1. Mix all the ingredients together in a food processor or blender and process to a smooth drink. Serve at once.

VARIATION: To make this drink into a healthy meal, add a few tablespoons of yoghurt.

Tropical Limeade

This unusual drink is delicious; a dash of rum can be added for an extra kick.

Ingredients

5 limes, thoroughly washed and sliced
handful of ice cubes
1 litre/1$^3/_4$ pints very cold water
4 tablespoons caster sugar (to taste)
4 mint leaves

Method

1. Mix all the ingredients together in a food processor or blender until the ice is completely crushed and the limes become a pulp. Pass through a coarse strainer and serve immediately.

NOTE: This drink can also be made using half lemons, half limes, although lemon skins are more bitter.

Coffee

Although coffee is African (Ethiopian) in origin, Latin America is the world's largest producer today. Coffee was introduced to the Caribbean in the 18th century by the French and plantations quickly spread throughout Central and South America. By this time, coffee drinking was already an established habit in Europe, especially in England, Paris and Vienna, where coffee houses had flourished since the mid-17th century.

Coffee grows best in the regions situated between the tropics of Cancer and Capricorn, hence its large production in African and Latin American countries. It is a labour-intensive crop, and in most countries the picking is still done by hand. There are three main varieties of coffee.

Arabica is considered the best of the three varieties and represents 70 per cent of the world's production. It makes a rich, smooth and aromatic coffee with the lowest caffeine level.

Robusta has a rougher, more intense flavour and has almost double the caffeine content of Arabica. It is a much cheaper bean and is normally used to make instant coffee and cheaper coffee blends.

Liberica is produced in large quantities, but it has a very insignificant taste.

There are many types of coffee, mostly named after their country of origin. The best known are Colombian, Costa Rican, Brazil Santos, Guatemalan, Jamaican, Kenyan and Mocha, all being of the Arabica variety. As with grapes, the soil, altitude and weather play an important part in determining the taste and aroma of coffee beans. The other important factors are the roasting and blending. Roasting develops the aroma, flavour and body of the coffee beans and determines the delicacy or richness of a brew. The most common types of roasting are as follows:

Light or pale roast has a delicate, yet full taste and is the most suitable to drink with milk.
Medium roast has a stronger flavour and aroma, but no bitterness. It is good with or without milk and makes a good after-meal coffee.
Dark roast has a strong flavour and aroma, a deep colour and is best served black.
Continental roast has a very strong, bitter taste. It is used mainly with cheap beans, since most of the beans' oils are destroyed during roasting. It is drunk black in small cups and is definitely an acquired taste.

Since the taste for coffee differs so much from country to country, roasting and blending are traditionally undertaken by the importers rather than the producers. All coffee beans have qualities that are remedied or enhanced by mixing them with other types of bean, and to achieve a good blend, up to eight types are sometimes used. The perfect balance is achieved when flavour, body and aroma are in complete harmony. It is, of course, a matter of personal taste, but modern consumers are extremely discerning in their choice.

To achieve a good brew it is important to have the correctly ground coffee for the method used:

Percolators – coarse grind
Cafetière – medium grind
Espresso pots and machines – espresso grind
Filter – fine grind

Ideally, the coffee should be ground just before

being used in order to preserve all its qualities. The volatile molecules present in the coffee are responsible for its flavour; richness escapes when the beans are exposed to air.

Vacuum-packed ground coffee retains most of the qualities of freshly ground coffee, but once opened, the packet should be tightly sealed or kept in an airtight container in the refrigerator, where it will hold its freshness for about one week. Storing whole beans in the same way will keep them fresh for up to three weeks. Coffee, ground or whole, freezes well if put inside an airtight container; the beans can then be ground from frozen and used at once.

Instant coffee is usually made with poorer quality Arabica beans from Brazil and intensively produced Robusta beans from Africa. A strong brew of freshly roasted and ground coffee is made. This brew is then spray-dried, leaving behind the coffee powder. The heat needed to evaporate the water destroys the coffee's natural oils, the result being a drink that resembles coffee, but does not have the characteristic taste or aroma of freshly made ground coffee.

Instant freeze-dried coffee retains more freshly made coffee qualities and is the best of the instant coffees. A strong brew is made, then frozen and ground into particles. The water is then removed with a very small amount of heat, which leaves the fresh coffee taste almost intact.

Decaffeinated coffee is made by `washing' the caffeine off the coffee beans using water or an organic solvent (methylene chloride). Neither method alters the coffee's final taste, but the water process is usually preferred to the chemical one.

There are a few rules to follow to get the most out of freshly ground coffee:

1. If not brewed enough, the result will be weak and tasteless coffee. If brewed for too long, the coffee will taste bitter and the fragrance will be destroyed. To make weak coffee it is better to make a normal brew and then dilute it with water; to make strong coffee, increase the amount of coffee, not the brewing time.

2. Coffee-making equipment should be clean and free of any residue, as the oils left in the pot will turn rancid and make the new brew taste bitter.

3. Water should be fresh and cold to start with and brought almost to boiling point.

4. The distinctive coffee fragrance is released only while the coffee is hot, so warm the pot and cups with hot water to prolong the coffee's wonderful aroma.

5. The longer the water is in contact with the coffee, the less ground coffee is needed; Cafetières therefore need less coffee than filters. As a general rule, one rounded tablespoon of ground coffee per coffee cup is used, but it varies according to the method of making and personal taste.

6. Avoid buying coffee in bulk or beans stored in open bins; when exposed to air over a period of time they lose most of their delicious smell.

COFFEE-DRINKING IN LATIN AMERICA

Almost all Latin Americans, including children, start the day with a large cup of strong coffee diluted with hot milk and almost invariably very sweet. In Mexico, brown sugar, cinnamon and cloves are added to the breakfast *cafe con leche*. For the rest of the day, small cups of strong black coffee are consumed at regular intervals. It is said that an average Latino will drink about 20 of these small cups a day, while real addicts may drink as many as 40 cups. Towards the end of the afternoon, a small piece of cake or some sweets will be eaten with coffee. Black coffee drinking goes on until the end of the evening and is believed by many people to promote a good night's sleep! Until recently, most people had never heard of decaffeinated coffee.

In most households, coffee is made ready sweetened. Water and sugar are brought to the boil, ground coffee is added and the brew is passed through a paper or cloth filter straight into a warmed coffee pot or thermos.

Instant coffee is mostly used in countries that do not produce coffee themselves, such as Chile and Argentina. In coffee-producing nations, even poor landworkers or *peons* grow enough coffee in their back gardens to supply their family needs, and use traditional methods of roasting and grinding. In Brazil, the unstable economy sometimes makes the price of coffee prohibitive for most of the population, but people are prepared to give up all other foodstuffs in order to have their beloved coffee.

Chocolate

Until recently, cocoa, the seed of the fruit of the cacao tree, was believed to be a native of the rainforest regin of South America. However, new evidence shows that it originated in Mexico and spread to Central America long before the arrival of the Spaniards. *Chocolatl*, as it was called by the Aztecs, was a very important part of the economy and the beans were used as currency. The drink made from cocoa, a sort of hot chocolate made with water and flavoured with honey, chilli, allspice and vanilla, was reserved for the aristocracy and apparently prohibited to women. It was not much different from the chocolate drunk in Mexico today.

After the Conquest, foodstuffs brought back from Mexico and Peru, such as tomatoes, potatoes, peppers and corn, began to be cultivated in the Mediterranean area. Cocoa was the only crop that could not be transplanted to Europe, since it needed a tropical climate in which to grow. Most of the producing areas were Spanish colonies, so Spain kept the monopoly on production and consumption for more than 100 years.

Between 1600 and 1660 chocolate drinking became an established habit throughout Europe, although it was superseded by tea in England and Russia – a pattern that persists to this day. When it was the main breakfast drink, however, great pains were taken to get it just right. Spices, sugar, cream and milk were all added, producing a drink not much different from what the Aztecs drank. The French food writer Anthelme Brillat-Savarin, in his book *The Physiology of Taste* (1825), gives his recipe for perfect hot chocolate, and the painstaking attention to detail shows its importance in a society already introduced to coffee and tea.

A cocoa tree is small and will produce about 20 pods in each harvest. Each pod weighs around 450g/1lb and contains 20–40 seeds or beans. The beans are the size of almonds and need to go through a long process before they are transformed into something palatable. When removed from the pod, the seeds have a white pulp covering them which drains away after they have fermented for a few days. They are then dried naturally in the sun or artificially. When completely dry, the beans are roasted, cracked and ground. The process used for grinding melts down the cocoa butter, which constitutes 50 per cent of the beans. The butter cools to a solid brown block, called `mass', which is the raw material for all chocolate products. Cocoa is made by removing 70–80 per cent of the butter from the `mass'.

For 300 years after being brought to Europe chocolate was always thought of as a drink. It wasn't until the 19th century and the invention by Rodolphe Lindt of a process called `conching', which enhances the texture and taste of chocolate, that it also became a confectionery. Conching is a very costly process and the chocolate found today in many Latin American countries is still made without it. The result is a less rich, coarser chocolate, where gritty bits of sugar, spices and sometimes almonds can still be tasted.

Mexican Coffee

This is a sweetened after-dinner coffee flavoured with allspice.

Ingredients

570ml/1 pint water
45g/1^1/$_2$oz granulated sugar
1 teaspoon ground allspice
55g/2oz ground coffee

Method

1. Bring the water, sugar and allspice to the boil. Add the coffee, mix thoroughly and leave to stand for 5 minutes.

2. Strain into a warmed coffee pot or cups and serve.

Brazilian Black Coffee

This is a pleasant way of preparing an after-lunch or after-dinner coffee with a hint of cocoa.

Ingredients

570ml/1 pint water
30g/1oz caster sugar
1 teaspoon cocoa powder
55g/2oz ground coffee

Method

1. Bring the water and sugar to the boil. Warm up a coffee pot or small coffee cups.

2. Mix the cocoa with the ground coffee and add to the water as soon as it comes to the boil. Remove from the heat, leave to stand for 4 minutes and strain into the cups or pot. Serve at once.

NOTE: If using a cafetière, add the cocoa to the coffee and pour the hot water on top. If using a filter, follow the first method.

Mexican Hot Chocolate

If Mexican chocolate is not available, this recipe makes a very good, rich substitute.

Ingredients

225g/8oz dark chocolate, chopped
1 tablespoon water
$^1/_2$ teaspoon ground cinnamon
2 tablespoons caster sugar
pinch ground cloves
30g/1oz ground almonds
1 litre/1$^3/_4$ pints milk
few drops vanilla essence

Method

1. Melt the chocolate with the water, cinnamon, sugar and cloves over very gentle heat.

2. Bring the almonds and milk to the boil.

3. Take the melted chocolate off the heat and mix in half the milk.

4. Return to the heat and slowly add the remaining milk, whisking continuously to form a froth. Add the vanilla essence and more sugar to taste and serve at once.

NOTE: A quicker way to make this is to put the chocolate and half the milk mixture into a blender; with the motor running, add the remaining milk slowly until all is well blended and frothy.

Champurrado

Champurrado is a drink from Guatemala made with chocolate, coffee and milk and thickened with coarse polenta or cornflour. This is a quicker version which uses cocoa instead of chocolate.

Ingredients

570ml/1 pint milk
425ml/$^3/_4$ pint black filter coffee
4 tablespoons cocoa powder
55g/2oz polenta or cornmeal
30g/1oz caster sugar
2 teaspoons ground cinnamon
$^1/_2$ teaspoon ground cloves
few drops vanilla essence

Method

1. Mix all the ingredients, except the vanilla, in a food processor or blender and pour into a thick-bottomed saucepan.

2. Whisking continuously, cook over medium heat for 20 minutes or until slightly thickened. Add the vanilla essence and more sugar to taste and serve at once.

Menu Suggestions

1. Sweet potato, corn and green chilli soup

    Beef casserole in dried chilli sauce

    Grilled pineapple skewers with coconut ice- cream

2. Peanut soup

    Tropical fruit salad with cinnamon crème Chantilly

3. Avocado, papaya and grapefruit salad

    Turkey escalopes with chilli cream sauce

    Cinnamon and vanilla ice-cream with hazelnut and lemon biscuits

4. Fried aubergines with salsa cruda

    Fresh tuna steamed with fruit juice

    Peruvian coffee chocolate pots

5. Courgette and French bean salad

    Salt cod cakes with red pepper salsa

    Mango and passion-fruit ice-cream

6. Tortilla salad with watercress and chilli dressing

    Lamb brochettes with mango and avocado salsa

    Mexican bread pudding

7. Hearts of palm flan with herb pastry

    Grilled snapper with mango chilli sauce

    Flambé bananas with vanilla ice-cream

8. Chilled hearts of palm and avocado soup

    Pork chops with pineapple and lime salsa

    Passion-fruit and mango mousse

9. Ceviche

    Garlic-roasted chicken with sweet potatoes

    Lime and lemon mousse with pistachio praline

10. Two-bean chilli with vegetables

    Mexican rice

    Fresh mangoes and pineapples

11. Brazilian meat and black bean stew

    Crème caramel

12. Tortilla soup

Layered polenta and vegetable pie

`Burnt' coconut crème caramel

13. Chickpea soufflé cakes with red pepper mayonnaise

Vegetable stew with almonds and dried chillies

Tropical fruit salad

14. Creamy chicken gratin

Brazil nut shortbread with pineapple and star anise compote

15. Crab gratin

Turkey blanquette with coconut milk and chillies

Mango and passion-fruit ice-cream

16. Taco fiesta

Fresh papaya with lime juice

17. Corn and spring onion fritters with guacamole

Baked stuffed trout

Nut and coffee tart with coffee cream

18. Herb potato and aubergine roulade with spicy tomato sauce

Marinated vegetable salad

Crunchy banana dessert

Glossary

GLOSSARY

Acaraje A typical Afro-Brazilian food, *acaraje* are black-eyed pea dumplings fried in dendea oil; they may be served on their own or filled with a variety of spicy stuffings.

Aji The generic name for chillies in Peru, Bolivia, Ecuador and other South American countries.

Allspice Also called Jamaican pepper, allspice is native to tropical America. It resembles large brown peppercorns and tastes like a mixture of cloves, cinnamon and nutmeg. Best bought whole and ground when needed, allspice is widely used in Caribbean and Central American cooking. Jamaica is the world's largest producer.

Annatto or **Achiote** Also called *urucu*, annatto is a food colouring made from the small, bright red seeds of an evergreen tree found in the Caribbean and throughout South America. The powder made from the seeds is used in all sorts of dishes, sweet and savoury, and is also used to colour cooking oil. The seeds are exported to England, where they are used for colouring Leicester and Red Cheshire cheeses.

Antichudos A typical Peruvian food, sold in the streets as a snack. Chunks of ox heart are skewered, marinated in spicy vinegar sauce and grilled. They are usually very spicy.

Arrowroot A fine flour made from the dried roots of a tropical plant. It is mainly used to make biscuits and as a thickening agent.

Atole or **Pozol** A Mayan dish of ground maize spiced with chillies which is eaten for breakfast; a sort of spicy porridge.

Avocado A fruit native to tropical America. Its name is a corruption of the local word *ahucatl*. There are three main varieties: West Indian, Guatemalan and Mexican. Also known as the alligator pear, the avocado is second only to olives in containing the highest percentage of fat, 79 per cent of which is mono-unsaturated. Avocados are a good source of vitamins A, B and C and a moderate source of potassium; they contain no cholesterol.

Bacalao or **Bacalhau** Dried salted cod.

Bahian cooking Bahia is a state on the northeast coast of Brazil, where the African influence on people and cuisine predominates. The mixture of West African ingredients, dishes and culture with that of the native Indians and the Portuguese has resulted in a unique and diverse cuisine.

Bain-marie A baking tin half-filled with hot water in which terrines, custards, etc. stand while cooking. The food is protected from direct fierce heat and cooks in a gentle, steamy atmosphere. Also a large container that will hold a number of pans standing in hot water, used to keep soups, sauces, etc. hot without further cooking.

Bake blind To bake a flan case while empty. In order to prevent the sides falling in or the base bubbling up, the pastry is usually lined with paper and filled with `blind beans' (see below).

Baste To spoon over liquid (sometimes stock, sometimes fat) during cooking to prevent drying out and to promote flavour.

Batida A generic term in Brazil for blended cocktail drinks, alcoholic or not.

Blanch Originally, to whiten by boiling, e.g. briefly to boil sweetbreads or brains to remove traces of blood, or to boil almonds to make the brown skin easy to remove, leaving the nuts white. Now commonly used to mean parboiling, as in blanching vegetables when they are parboiled prior to freezing, or precooked so that they have only to be reheated before serving.

Blind beans Dried beans, peas, rice or pasta used to fill pastry cases temporarily during baking.

Braise To bake or stew slowly on a bed of vegetables in a covered pan.

Brazil nut Also known as Para or cream nuts, Brazils come from one of the largest trees in the Amazon forest. They are easy to open if chilled for 10 minutes, and easier to slice if boiled shelled for 5 minutes and allowed to cool.

Burrito A wheat-flour tortilla used as a wrapper for a variety of fillings.

Cacao A bean, native to South America, which grows on a tall tree that grows wild in the rain forests along the Orinoco and Amazon rivers. The seeds are the size of almonds and have to be fermented and treated in order to become cocoa and chocolate. Cacao is now cultivated in most tropical regions of the world and is a major source of income for many developing countries (see page 266).

Cachaça A Brazilian colourless rum made from sugar cane, used extensively in mixed drinks or drunk on its own.

Caipirinha The national drink of Brazil, made with limes blended with cachaça or rum, ice and sugar.

Cancha Toasted corn.

Caramel Sugar cooked to a toffee.

Caruru An Afro-Brazilian stew made with shrimp, okra and fish.

Cashew A fruit indigenous to Brazil. Eaten ripe, it is delicate and delicious, but it is mainly used to make concentrated juice. It is hard to find outside the producing countries. Better known are the nuts attached to the fruits. The Portuguese introduced them to warm areas of the world, including Goa in India, which is today the biggest producer of cashew nuts.

Cassareep A syrup made from the boiled-down juice of cassava or manioc, used extensively in Caribbean cooking.

Cassava or **Manioc** Also called *yuca*, this tuber is native to Brazil, but was taken to Africa in the 16th century, where it became a staple starch. There are two main varieties, one of which is poisonous until washed. There are many by-products of cassava, including tapioca, cassava meal and cassareep.

Cassava meal or **Manioc meal** A seasoning served throughout Latin America. *Farinha de mandioca*, as it is known in Portuguese, may be eaten plain, sprinkled on juicy food to soak up the liquid, or lightly toasted in butter and mixed with herbs, sultanas, sweetcorn, etc. Together with the basic tomato salsa, it stays on the dining table for every meal and is particularly good with beans.

Chancho A South American term for pig or pork.

Charqui Originally dried llama meat, but today it may also be donkey and mule meat. It is eaten mainly in Andean countries.

Chicha A fermented, beer-like drink made from maize; it has a cloudy appearance and sour taste. Very popular in the Andean countries of South America, particularly Peru and Bolivia.

Chilaquiles A casserole made with fried stale tortillas layered with vegetables and covered with a chilli sauce or stock.

Chillies These are hot members of the Capsicum family, of which all peppers are part. There are hundreds of varieties of chilli, and as a general rule, the smaller the chilli the hotter it will be. Green chillies also tend to be hotter than the red variety, and dried chillies are just as hot as fresh ones. (See also pages 192-201.)

Chimichangas Uncooked wheat tortillas which are filled, then fried.

Chorizo A spicy sausage made with pork, garlic

and red chilli powder. Originally from Spain, it is found throughout Latin America.

Chunos Also known as *papa seca*, these are freeze-dried potatoes, made by an ancient technique invented by the Andean Indians. The same method is still used today (see page 19).

Churrasco A barbecued meat feast, usually prepared outdoors, with a variety of meat cuts. A tradition in Argentina, southern Brazil and Uruguay.

Churros A deep-fried, long, doughnut-like pastry, filled with *doce de leite* and tossed in sugar and cinnamon. They are eaten in Chile, Argentina, Brazil and other South American countries.

Coconut The fruit of the coco-palm. It has a brown fibrous husk covering thick white flesh and a hollow core containing coconut water. The flesh and its various products play an important part in the cuisines of many countries, being used in both sweet and savoury dishes. The various forms of coconut may be bought ready-prepared from supermarkets, but it is relatively easy to make them yourself from fresh coconuts (see below).

Fresh Coconut

When buying fresh coconut, choose those which feel heavy and when shaken appear to have plenty of liquid inside. The `eyes' – three dark round spots on top of the coconut – should be clean of mould and moisture.

Method

1. With a skewer or screwdriver pierce the `eyes' and drain the cloudy liquid into a bowl or cup. (Coconut water, as this liquid is called, is usually drunk cold or mixed with alcohol. Coconut milk is the liquid extracted from pressing grated coconut flesh that has been mixed with water or milk for at least 30 minutes.)

2. To break the shell, cover the coconut with a tea towel and hit it with a hammer. Alternatively, put the whole nut into a preheated oven, 200°C/400°F/gas mark 6, for 5 minutes. The heat makes the shell easier to break and leaves the flesh free once the nut is cracked.

3. Coconut flesh has a thin dark skin on the outside which must be removed. Use a potato peeler or sharp knife to peel it off.

4. Using a metal grater or the appropriate blade on a food processor, grate the flesh to the desired coarseness.

To make coconut milk

1. Place the grated coconut in a food processor or liquidizer and cover with hot water or hot milk. Blend well and leave to cool. Strain through a fine sieve or a muslin cloth, making sure to extract all the liquid from the pulp.

NOTE: Follow the same instructions to make coconut milk from desiccated coconut. If using creamed coconut, follow the instructions on the packet.

Comal A pottery griddle used to cook tortillas.

Coriander A herb, originally from the Mediterranean, which is the most commonly used herb in Latin American cuisine. Its unique flavour is slowly destroyed by heat, so add half the amount stated in any recipe at the beginning of cooking and mix in the remainder just before serving.

Cream To beat ingredients together, such as butter and sugar, when making a sponge cake.

Crêpes Thin French pancakes.

Cuy An Andean rodent, this guinea pig is found mainly in Peru and Bolivia, where it is the biggest source of protein in the diet.

Deglaze To loosen and liquefy the fat, sediment and browned juices stuck at the bottom of a frying pan or saucepan by adding liquid (usually stock, water or wine) and stirring while boiling.

Degorge To extract the juices from meat, fish or vegetables, generally by salting. Usually done to remove indigestible or strong-tasting juices.

Dendea oil Oil extracted from the fruit of the oil palm; it varies in colour from yellow to deep orange and red and gives a distinctive taste to Bahian food. It is widely used in Brazil, and also in West Africa, where it is called red palm oil. An acquired taste, it can be substituted by adding a little paprika to the cooking oil of any Bahian dish.

Devein To remove the fine black vein in the flesh of prawns. First peel the prawns, then use a small sharp knife to cut a slit along the back and lift the vein out. Rinse the prepared prawns under running water and dry on absorbent paper before using.

Doce de leite Milk boiled with sugar until it becomes a thick, golden-brown paste with a light caramel taste. A staple sweet in all Latin American countries, it can be eaten on its own or used as filling for cakes, pies, churros, etc. The consistency varies from soft set to a hard paste, and coconuts, nuts or prunes can be added to it. It is also called *dulce de leche, leche quemada* or *manjar* (see page 220).

Dried shrimps Very small pink shrimps with a strong flavour and smell of seafood. They are used as a seasoning in many African–Bahian dishes from Brazil, and are also used in Chinese and Southeast Asian cooking. They can be bought in oriental food shops.

Egg wash Beaten raw egg, sometimes with salt, used for glazing pastry to give a shine when baked.

Empanadas Small savoury pasties or turnovers made by wrapping a white flour dough around a filling of meat, chicken, cheese, hearts of palm or sweetcorn, depending on the region in which they are made. They are called empadas or empadinhas in Brazil and are very popular in Chile, Argentina, Uruguay and other South American countries.

Enchiladas Tortillas dipped in a thin red or green tomato sauce and quickly fried. They are then rolled up like a taco with a cheese or meat filling and the remaining sauce is poured over before serving.

Epazote A perennial herb, also known as ambrosia in English. It is used as a flavouring in Mexican cooking, especially with beans. It has a strong and bitter flavour and is hard to find outside Mexico.

Escabeche Term used to describe foods marinated or pickled in vinegar. Of Arab origins, this method of preserving food was introduced to Latin America by the Spanish.

Escalope A thin slice of meat, sometimes beaten out flat to make it thinner and larger.

Farinha de mandioca See Cassava meal.

Farofas A typical Brazilian dish made with cassava meal fried in butter and a variety of added ingredients, such as eggs, olives, raisins, cheese, prunes, bacon, chopped meat, carrots and other vegetables. It is served with meat, fish or poultry dishes and can also be used as a stuffing.

Feijoada completa The national dish of Brazil (see page 90).

Flamber To set alcohol alight. Usually to burn off the alcohol, but frequently simply for dramatic effect. (English: to flame.)

Flan Crème caramel of Spanish origins found in all Latin American countries. It is served plain or flavoured with coconut, cinnamon, almonds, cheese, chocolate, lemon, coffee or fruit (see page 216).

Fold To mix with a gentle lifting motion, rather than to stir vigorously. The aim is to avoid beating out air while mixing.

Frijoles Beans.

Glaze To cover with a thin layer of melted jam (for fruit flans) or syrup (for rum baba), butter or oil.

Granadilla A type of passion-fruit.

Gratiner To brown under a grill after the surface of the dish has been sprinkled with breadcrumbs and butter and, sometimes, cheese. Dishes finished like this are sometimes called *gratinée* or *au gratin*.

Guacamole Mexican sauce or dip made with mashed avocado mixed with tomato, chopped onions, coriander and chilli. It is served with almost any Mexican dish, especially tortillas and refried beans (see page 185).

Guarana The seed of a jungle plant used to make the most popular soft drink in Brazil. It has a tangy, fruity flavour. The seed has a small amount of caffeine and is used in the pharmaceutical industry to make herbal `pep' pills.

Guava Yellow to greenish, very fragrant tropical fruit, the size of a large plum. It has a soft skin covering reddish or white flesh, in the centre of which is a cavity containing pulp and small, hard seeds. Guavas are very delicate and should be eaten soon after purchase, either peeled or unpeeled. They are used to make compotes, fruit pastes and jams, and are very popular in tropical countries.

Guinea pig See Cuy.

Hearts of palm Also called palmito, these are the tender shoots of certain palm trees. They are about 8cm/3 inches long and 2.5cm/1 inch in diameter. Hearts of palm are to South Americans what asparagus is to Europeans. They have a delicate flavour and are served simply with vinaigrette or used in salads, cold soups and little turnovers. Even in tropical countries fresh palm hearts are difficult to find, so canned ones are acceptable. Those sent for export, however, tend to be smaller and have less flavour. In Brazil palm hearts are sold in glass jars so the quality can be checked before buying.

Humitas Sometimes wrongly called tamales, humitas are small pies made with fresh corn dough, wrapped in corn husks and steamed. The fillings vary from country to country, the most common ones being pork, chicken, sausage, cheese and peanuts. They are popular in Peru, central Brazil and Andean countries.

Infuse To steep or heat gently to extract flavour, as when infusing milk with onion slices.

Julienne Vegetables or citrus rind cut in thin matchstick shapes or very fine shreds.

Locro A thick soup, almost a stew, made of different vegetables, although potatoes are the most commonly used. Found traditionally in

Andean countries, such as Ecuador, Bolivia and Peru.

Macerate To soak food in a syrup or liquid to allow flavours to mix.

Maguey A large `century plant' from the arid areas of Mexico. It plays an important part in Mexican culture: its sap is used to make the popular alcoholic drink pulque, the leaves yield a strong, coarse fibre, which is used to make mats and ropes, and the roots can be eaten as a vegetable.

Maize Corn. There are many varieties of corn, with colours ranging from black to white and purple to yellow; the kernels also vary in hardness and size.

Manioc See Cassava.

Margarita A Mexican cocktail made with Tequila, lime juice, sugar and a dash of triple sec (see page 264).

Marinade The liquid used for marinating. Usually contains oil, onion, bay leaf and vinegar or wine.

Marinate To soak meat, fish or vegetables before or after cooking in acidulated liquid containing flavourings and herbs.

Masa harina Flour used to make tortillas and tamales. It is made by heating corn kernels with lime juice, which makes the skins come off easily. The kernels are then dried and ground. Masa harina can be white, yellow or other colours, according to the type of corn used, and can vary in coarseness, although it is usually made to the correct texture for tortillas.

Matambre An Argentinian beef dish, the name of which means `kill hunger'.

Mate or **Yerba mate** A tea made from the dried leaves of a shrub which grows wild in the southern countries of South America. Very popular in Argentina, Paraguay, Uruguay and

Chile, mate is drunk by gauchos (South American cowboys) in preference to coffee.

Mole **sauce** A traditional thick, savoury sauce from Mexico. Chillies, fresh, dried or smoked, are the fundamental ingredient. The most famous *mole* is *mole poblano*, which is made with three types of dried chillies and bitter chocolate (see page 75).

Moqueca A fish stew from Bahia, Brazil, frequently flavoured with chillies and dendea oil. It can also be made with prawns (see page 129).

Moule-à-manqué French cake tin with sloping sides. The resulting cake has a wider base than top, and is about 2.5cm/1 inch high.

Mulato chillies See chilli chart, page 199.

Nopales The young pads of the prickly pear cactus. These have their spines removed and are then used mainly in Mexican salads. Nopales canned in brine, vinegar or water are known as nopalitos and are available from shops specializing in Mexican food.

Okra Of African origin, this edible seed pod is found in the cuisines of the Caribbean and Brazil, where African slaves were brought to work on the sugar plantations. Buy bright green, firm pods which snap at the tip and do not bend. Wash and dry thoroughly, then top and tail the pods, or they will become slimy when cooked. They can be boiled, fried or cooked in hot oil, and the addition of a little lemon juice or vinegar will prevent them losing their bright colour.

Palm oil See Dendea oil.

Papas secas Dried potatoes (see Chunos).

Papaya A tropical fruit, also known as pawpaw. It has an elongated pear shape, is green and hard outside when unripe and yellow orange and soft when ripe. Cut in half when ripe, the fruit has a deep apricot-coloured flesh with lots of small, round black seeds which are scooped out and discarded. The flesh is sweet and aromatic, making it a favourite breakfast fruit in the tropics. It varies enormously in size, from 10kg/20lb giants to the small variety found in European supermarkets. Unripe papaya is used for a variety of dishes, including stews, sweets, chutneys and compotes; the ripe fruit is eaten fresh with lime juice or used to make fruit salads and drinks (see page 256).

Pasilla Dried chilli from Mexico (see chilli chart, page 199).

Passion-fruit Fruit native to South America, where there are many different varieties; purple, yellow, bell-apple, sweet calabash and granadilla are all used mainly for making juices, ice-creams and confectionery. The fruit's name comes from its flower, which is supposed to resemble all the elements of Christ's passion.

Peanuts Also known as groundnuts or monkey nuts, peanuts are peas rather than nuts and have a high protein and iron content. Native to Brazil, they grow in tropical and subtropical areas of the world and have many uses. In South America, peanut oil is extensively used, and peanuts appear in both savoury and sweet dishes.

Pibil Chicken steamed in a closed clay pot, a typical dish from the Yucatan region of Mexico.

Pibre A type of sea urchin, found on the Chilean coast.

Pimiento One of the mildest members of the pepper and chilli family and very similar in appearance to a sweet red pepper. Pimientos are usually canned in brine. They are very popular in Mediterranean cuisines.

Pipian Sauce used for slow-cooked stews and similar dishes. It is thickened with ground pumpkin seeds and can be flavoured with tomatillos and coriander for a green pipian, or with tomatoes and red chillies for a red version.

Pirao A porridge-type dish made with polenta or cassava meal mixed with enough juice from fish stews to give a soft consistency; served hot.

Pisco Peruvian brandy, which tastes a little like cognac, but is colourless. Very popular in Bolivia and Chile.

Plantain Belonging to the same family as the banana, plantains are larger than common bananas, with a firm and not very sweet flesh. As they ripen, they change from green to yellow and finally black. They can be used at any stage of ripeness, but must always be cooked. They are added to soups and stews as a thickening agent, fried in butter and oil and served as a vegetable or dessert, and steamed or barbecued in their skins. Widely used in Latin American cuisine, particularly in Ecuador, for savoury dishes as well as fruit pastes, jams, drinks, cakes, etc.

Praline Almonds cooked in sugar until the mixture caramelizes, then cooled and crushed to a powder. Used for flavouring desserts and ice-cream.

Prove To put dough or a yeasted mixture to rise before baking.

Pulque Fermented, beer-like drink from Mexico made from the sap of the maguey or century plant.

Purée Liquidized, sieved or finely mashed fruit or vegetables.

Quinoa A plant native to the Andes, which produces a small grain very high in protein and easily digested. Called `mother grain' by the Incas, it was regarded as holy and, together with potatoes, was a staple crop. It is used extensively in Peruvian cuisine, mainly as a thickening agent. It may be bought in healthfood shops and should be thoroughly rinsed before cooking. It can replace couscous or cracked wheat with great success.

Reduce To reduce the amount of liquid by rapid boiling, causing evaporation and a consequent strengthening of flavour in the remaining liquid.

Refresh To hold boiled vegetables under a cold tap, or to dunk them immediately in cold water to prevent their cooking further in their own steam, and to set the colour of green vegetables.

Relax or **Rest** Of pastry: to set aside in a cool place to allow the gluten (which will have expanded during rolling) to contract. This lessens the danger of shrinking in the oven. Of batters: to set aside to allow the starch cells to swell, giving a lighter result when cooked.

Render To melt solid fat (e.g. beef, pork) slowly in the oven.

Salsas Uncooked sauce of freshly chopped ingredients (see page 174).

Scald Of milk: to heat until on the point of boiling, when some movement can be seen at the edges of the pan but there is no overall bubbling.

Seal or **Seize** To brown meat rapidly, usually in fat, for flavour and colour.

Season To flavour food, generally with salt and pepper.

Soft ball The term used to describe sugar syrup reduced by boiling to sufficient thickness to form soft balls when dropped into cold water and rubbed between finger and thumb.

Sweat To cook gently, usually in butter or oil, but sometimes in the food's own juices, without frying or browning.

Sweet potatoes There are various types of sweet potatoes, all native to tropical America. The flesh can vary in colour from white to deep yellow. They are usually boiled in their skins to prevent the flesh from discolouring and are delicious roasted or baked; they can also be used in soups, candies and a pudding very much like sweetened chestnut purée.

Tabasco See chilli chart, page 197.

Taco A filled, rolled-up tortilla, the Mexican equivalent of a sandwich. Tacos can be eaten soft, or deep-fried with an enormous variety of stuffings (see page 163).

Tamales Mexican steamed pies made with masa harina dough. They may be eaten plain or stuffed with a savoury or sweet filling. The uncooked tamales are wrapped in corn husks or banana leaves and steamed (see page 170).

Tapioca See Cassava.

Tequila A popular Mexican drink made from the starchy root stock of a plant called *Agave azul tequilana*. Normally colourless, it can be pale yellow when aged (see page 259).

Timbale A dish cooked in a castle-shaped mould, or a dish served piled up high.

Tomatillos Also called husk tomatoes or Mexican green tomatoes, tomatillos are small tomatoes which are ripe, even when firm and green. They have a tart flavour, can be bought canned and are used extensively in Mexican cuisine. Green gooseberries make a reasonable substitute.

Tortilla Mexican flat bread made from corn or wheat dough (see page 162).

Tortilla chips Also known as tostaditas, these are wedges of maize tortilla fried until crisp. Black or blue corn can be used to make tortillas, which results in dark tortilla chips. Different flavourings, such as chillies, cheese and herbs, may also be used.

Tostadas Wheat tortillas which are deep-fried or baked into a basket shape, then filled with a variety of savoury fillings or fruits.

Tostaditas See Tortilla chips.

To the thread Of sugar boiling: term used to denote the degree of thickness achieved when reducing sugar, i.e. the syrup will form threads if tested between wet finger and thumb. Short thread: about 1cm/^{1}/2 inch; long thread: 5cm/ 2 inches or more.

Turrón Popular Mexican sweet paste made with ground almonds or peanuts mixed with sugar.

Vatapa Bahian fish stew containing peanuts, dried shrimps and chillies.

Well A hollow or dip made in a pile or bowlful of flour, exposing the tabletop or the bottom of the bowl, into which other ingredients are placed prior to mixing.

Yerba mate See Mate.

Zest The outer coloured skin of an orange or lemon, used to give flavour. It is very thinly pared without any of the bitter white pith.

SPECIALIST SHOPS

STREET MARKETS

Garcia and Sons
248 Portobello Road
London W11 1LL
Tel. 0171–221 6119
(cassava, beans, olive oils, sausages, dried chillies, masa harina)

Mexicolore
28 Warriner Gardens
London SW11 4EB
Tel. 0171–622 9577
(Mexican ingredients, tortillas, tomatillos, chillies, books, music, costumes etc.)

Wild Oats
210 Westbourne Grove
London W11 2RH
Tel. 0171–229 1063
(Sun-dried bananas, dried pineapples, coconut chips, quinoa, cornmeal, all types of beans)

Manila Supermarket
11–12 Hogarth Place
Earls Court
London SW5 0QT
Tel. 0171–373 8305
(Fresh chillies, all types of coconut milk, powder and cream, cassava, dried shrimp, ground anatto)

The Cool Chilli Company
P.O. Box 5702
London W10 6WE
Tel. 0171–229 9360
01973 311714
(Mail orders of all types of dried chillies, Mexican chocolate, masa harina, annatto, dried corn husks)

Brixton Market
Tel. 0171–926 2530
Monday to Saturday with half day on Wednesday
(Caribbean ingredients and large variety of fish)

Portobello Market
Tel. 0171–341 5277
Monday to Saturday
(Afro Caribbean ingredients with variety of foreign fruit and vegetables)

BIBLIOGRAPHY

BISSELL, Frances: *Sainsbury's Book of Food* (Websters International Publishers, London, 1989).

CUSICK, Heidi Haughy: *Soul and Spice* (Chronicle Books, San Francisco, 1995).

DeWITT, Dave and GERLACH, Nancy: *The Whole Chile Pepper Book* (Little Brown, Boston, 1990).

DeWITT, Dave, WILAN, Mary Jane and STOCK, Melissa T.: *Hot and Spicy Latin Dishes* (Prima Publishing, Rocklin, California, 1995).

DOWELL, Philip and BAILEY, Adrian: *The Book of Ingredients* (Mermaid Books, London, 1980).

HOBHOUSE, Henry: *Seeds of Change – Five Plants That Transformed Mankind* (Papermac, London, 1992).

LAROUSSE: *Treasures of Country Cooking Around the World* (Hamlyn Publishing Group, New York, 1979).

LEROUX, Guy: *La Cuisine Brasilienne* (Les Editions du Pacifique, Papeete, Tahiti, 1980).

MILLER, Mark: *The Great Chili Book* (Ten Speed Press, Berkeley, California, 1991).

ORTIZ, Elisabeth Lambert: *The Book of Latin American Cooking* (Penguin, London, 1991).

ORTIZ, Elisabeth Lambert: *The Encyclopedia of Herbs, Spices and Flavourings* (Dorling Kindersley, London, 1992).

PENDLE, George: *A History of Latin America* (Penguin Books, London, 1987).

RINZLER, Carol Ann: *Food Facts and What They Really Mean* (Bloomsbury, London, 1988).

RODEN, Claudia: *Coffee* (Penguin Books, London, 1981).

SCOTT, David and BLETCHER, Eve: *Latin American Vegetarian Cookery* (Rider Books, London, 1994).

STYLE, Sue: *The Mexican Cookbook* (Hamlyn, London, 1984).

TANNAHILL, Reay: *Food in History* (Penguin Books, London, 1988).

VERISSIMO, Gico: *Mexico* (Macdonald & Co., London, 1960).

INDEX